Reconstructing Russia

RECONSTRUCTING
RUSSIA

U.S. Policy
in Revolutionary
Russia,
1917–1922

Leo J. Bacino

The Kent State University Press • Kent, Ohio, and London

© 1999 by the Kent State University Press, Kent, Ohio 44242
All rights reserved
Library of Congress Catalog Card Number 99-21764
ISBN 0-87338-635-3
Manufactured in the United States of America

06 05 04 03 02 01 00 99   5 4 3 2 1

Library of Congress Cataloging-in-Publication Data
Bacino, Leo J., 1959–
Reconstructing Russia: U.S. policy in revolutionary Russia, 1917–1922 / Leo J. Bacino.
p.   cm.
Includes bibliographical references and index.
ISBN 0-87338-635-3 (cloth : alk. paper) ∞
1. Economic assistance, American—Russia (Federation)—Russian Far East—History—20th
century. 2. Russian Far East (Russia)—Relations—United States—History—20th century. 3.
United States—Relations—Russia (Federation)—Russian Far East—History—20th century.
I. Title.
HC340.12.Z7F2723   1999
338.91′73047—dc21   99-21764

British Library Cataloging-in-Publication data are available.

for my father

Contents

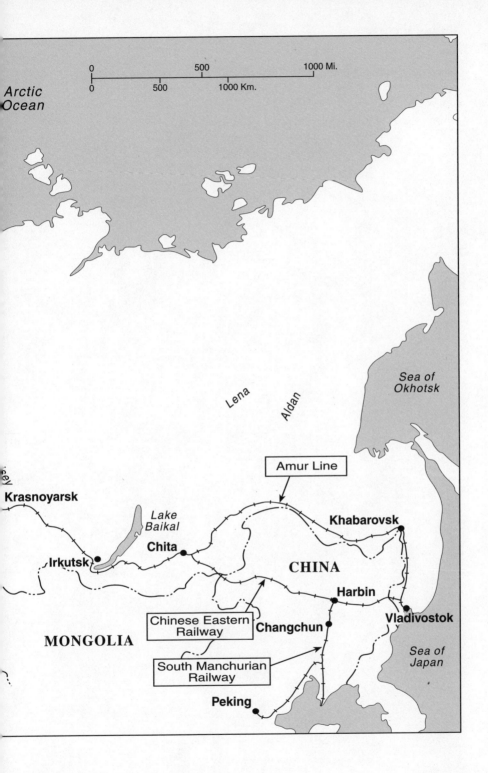

Acknowledgments

Over the years I have benefited enormously from the faculty and students of the Department of History at Northern Illinois University. I owe a tremendous debt to the NIU history faculty for a rich and diversified intellectual training; they are a credit to public education. Most importantly, I want to thank my director, Carl P. Parrini. He embodies the highest personal and intellectual qualities of a teacher-scholar. I also want to acknowledge my theoretical debt to Mary O. Furner and to thank her for her participation on my dissertation committee. From my earliest undergraduate courses, teachers like William Beik, C. H. and Margaret George, and Marvin Rosen provided direction and inspiration. Since this study is a revised version of my Ph.D. dissertation, I would also like to thank the other members of my committee, W. Bruce Lincoln and Anthony Scaperlanda, for their careful reading of my dissertation and the help they provided in the final stages of the dissertation process.

I have been very fortunate to have been associated with an exceptional group of students at NIU. I will always value the friendship and support I have received from this close-knit group. In particular, I want to acknowledge Bill Burr, Thomas Elkins, Brian Forberg, Linn Freiwald (who very generously took the time to edit the manuscript), Keith Haynes, Michael Hickey, Jean Kadel, Jim Livingston, Larry Lynn, Sandy Mazzola, Bruce Nelson, Sonia Nelson, Don Rodrick, Richard Schneirov, Paul Street, and Robert Tyree.

I have benefited greatly from my discussions with historians David Foglesong, Linda Killen, and Thomas Knock, whose research has enriched our understanding of Wilsonian foreign policy.

The editors and readers at The Kent State University Press have been exceptionally helpful and gracious throughout the process. I especially want to thank director John Hubbell and managing editor Joanna Hildebrand Craig for their assistance and assistant editor Erin Holman, who conscientiously guided the manuscript through the copyediting process at Kent State. Clarence Wunderlin and Mary Ann Heiss deserve special thanks for introducing me to this fine press.

For technical assistance I would like to thank Dennis Butzow, Ilga Janouskovec, and Joel Leer.

My research has been facilitated by the assistance of many generous archivists at the National Archives, the Library of Congress, Yale University, the International Harvester Archives, the Wisconsin State Historical Society, the Hoover Institute and Stanford University Libraries, and the manuscript department of the Regenstein Library at the University of Chicago. The staff at the Northern Illinois University library, particularly the interlibrary loan and government publications departments, have facilitated my research over many years.

Finally, I thank my mother, Elizabeth Bacino; my family, Dennis and Elizabeth Butzow; and Dr. William Cohen for all of their support.

Introduction

The American intervention in Siberia during the Russian Revolution and civil war left no lasting effects on the region, other than a legacy of bitterness and mistrust for future Soviet-American relations. But seventy years of Soviet-American rivalry has obscured the fact that, during the Russian Revolution and civil war, Siberia had been a focal point in the United States's struggle against the rival powers to recast the international economic and political order. This forgotten dimension of the American intervention in Russia represented a sophisticated foreign assistance program. It now deserves careful reevaluation in view of the important lessons it can provide for contemporary American policymakers who are struggling to devise effective policies for post-Soviet Russia.

In 1918, the decisive year of the calamitous world war, American statesmen were deeply concerned that the Russian Empire would be divided into German and Japanese spheres of influence. The origins of World War I itself lay in the rivalry over spheres of influence in semidependent developing regions, such as China, Eastern Europe, and the Middle East. The collapse of the Provisional Government in Russia at the end of 1917 intensified this rivalry among the remaining powers by transforming the Russian Empire itself into an arena in this global struggle between imperial systems. During the extraordinary years 1918 and 1919, when a political vacuum existed in the empire, Germany, Japan, Britain, and France all pursued policies in Russia that were aimed at establishing spheres of influence of one form or another. If these powers had been allowed to dismember the Russian Empire, this would have given added impetus to their ongoing struggle to divide the remaining developing regions. This possibility alone required the United States to become actively involved in Siberia as part of its larger effort to promote the Open Door.

In contrast to this framework of great-power rivalry, American statesmen viewed bolshevism as epiphenomenal, a symptom of the czarist regime's pervasive social and economic malaise that the war had unleashed. Indeed, during 1918 much of the Wilson administration's antagonism toward the Bolsheviks arose from the practical consideration that this revolutionary regime served as a pawn in the larger systemic conflict among the Great Powers.

At the threshold of a new historical epoch, American statesmen also perceived tremendous opportunities for Russian-American relations. The Wilson administration had greeted the March Revolution of 1917 in Russia as an event that could have a great impact on the postwar international order. With the establishment of the Provisional Government, the administration was encouraged that Russia would now begin to evolve a constitutional form of government. As a corollary to this social and political process, major American corporate groups believed a post-czarist Russia would welcome American investment as an alternative to the politically based pattern of European investment during the czarist years. In this event, Russia would be disposed to participate in the international economy on terms consistent with Open Door principles: a world system that operated under rules that guaranteed equality of opportunity for trade and investment—in direct contrast to the existing system of preferential spheres of influence.

Against this background, American statesmen attached great significance to Siberia. They believed that this vast developing region, with its relatively egalitarian social structure, would rapidly begin the transition toward a post-czarist civil society. As this social and economic transformation gathered momentum in Siberia, it would, in turn, provide a tremendous outlet for American investment and thereby help solidify an Open Door system. In order for the United States to unlock the full potential this unique region offered for economic expansion, the Wilson administration first had to overcome the challenges posed by the combined ambitions of the rival powers, as well as the new phenomenon of revolutionary socialism. Yet Siberia's unparalleled significance as an economic frontier and the distinct interest the United States exhibited toward it only made the interpower struggle for hegemony in the region more intense. In this crucible of war and revolution, American efforts to provide Siberia with economic assistance should accordingly be viewed as a distinctly Wilsonian experiment in foreign assistance policy. Unlike post–World War II foreign assistance programs, American policy in Siberia not only had to contend with anticapitalist revolutionary movements but also with the ambitions of formidable rival powers. Therefore, during the formative stages of Soviet-American relations, the counter-revolutionary tendencies inherent in Wilson's approach to Siberia were still subordinated to the progressive historical role American Open Door diplomacy played in its struggle against the more exploitative forms of imperialism practiced by the other powers.

This study examines the United States's effort to promote social and economic reconstruction in Siberia between 1917 and 1922. It will demonstrate that this endeavor constituted a major policy initiative at a pivotal juncture in the nation's evolution toward global preeminence in the twentieth century. This policy simultaneously represented the primary response of American statesmen to events in revolutionary Russia and an important new dimension in their larger struggle to achieve a structural transformation of the international political economy. The term "reconstruction" is used here to define the nature of American policy because it was consistently used by American statesmen themselves when expressing their purposes in Russia. More important, this term embodies the developmental impulses that motivated American policy. It conveys the American policymakers' recognition that Siberia's long-term development would ultimately hinge on fostering a stable civil society; efforts to gain immediate economic advantages in Russia would only hinder this goal. They clearly regarded their assistance policy in Siberia as a prelude to an ambitious developmental program that would reintegrate the former czarist empire and border regions like Manchuria into a global economy managed by the United States according to the rules of the Open Door.

Since American policymakers thought their initiatives in Siberia would have far-reaching implications for American prosperity and for the stability of the emerging international system, the failure of these efforts in no way diminishes their significance. The inability of the United States to incorporate the region on an Open Door basis and the eventual withdrawal of the Soviet Union from the world market undoubtedly contributed to the formation of closed economic blocs during the interwar period. The development of regional economic blocs in turn disrupted international trade and investment, which contributed to the depression and to the tensions between the powers that resulted in World War II.[1]

The Wilson administration's assistance policy focused on two complementary initiatives: the restoration of operations on the Trans-Siberian railway and the provision of commercial assistance to the Siberian population via the region's prominent peasant cooperative societies. These forms of assistance were geared toward reestablishing predictable and stable market relations along the continent-sized area traversed by the Trans-Siberian railway system. American policymakers were merely acting on the recognition that a more secure environment would provide an impetus for social and economic reconstruction in this region where czarist authority had been relatively weak and could be replaced by institutions more representative of the region's society.

In its initial stages, the American assistance policy attempted to commence the reconstruction process in Siberia by nurturing the recovery of Russian civil society, or by encouraging what Wilson called "self-government." Wilson's conception of self-government sheds valuable light on his approach to the whole Russian question because it denotes a level of socioeconomic development rather than a specific form of government.

In Wilson's view, self-government existed where there were political, institutional, or legal structures founded on the consent of the governed and that provided essential guarantees for personal and property rights. In other words, Wilson used the term "self-government" to characterize what amounted to a constitutional order: a civil society founded on voluntary associational activities and mediated by an institutional structure and a rule of law that accommodated individual liberty to public power.

Wilson attributed great significance to these self-governing social and political capacities because they were essential building blocks of the new international order he hoped to construct from the remains of the shattered system of European empires. As an alternative to the prewar system of international relations founded on a tenuous balance of power among rival empires, Wilson envisioned a rational system based on cooperation between powers, particularly with regard to their relations in developing regions. This type of system, which N. Gordon Levin has appropriately defined as liberal-internationalist, would operate within a framework of international law guaranteed by American economic and naval power.

While this study deliberately subordinates the anti-Bolshevik facets of the United States's Russian policy, it fully acknowledges that American policymakers were staunchly anti-Bolshevik. Since American policymakers considered bolshevism the product of pervasive instability, they believed that economic assistance would constitute the only effective antidote to the problem. In other words, the reconstruction program embodied the truly coherent, or class-conscious, response of American policymakers to revolutionary events in Russia. Furthermore, a successful American-sponsored assistance program in Siberia would also serve as the most effective means for influencing events in European Russia.

While the Bolshevik regime survived, contrary to the expectations of most American policymakers, this in no way lessens the efficacy of American expectations or of policies rooted in these assumptions. After all, the Bolsheviks themselves were doubtful of their future when it became clear that revolutions would not erupt in the advanced Western industrial countries.

Because the American policymaking establishment considered the Bolshevik Revolution a temporary phase in the revolutionary cycle, more attention must be paid to their concern that the Bolshevik regime would become a pawn in the broader systemic conflict among the powers. Indeed, Germany, Japan, and Britain all attempted to use revolutionary instability to further their designs in the Russian Empire. Therefore, although American reconstruction efforts in Siberia were implicitly aimed at combating bolshevism, a comprehensive assessment of these initiatives must take into account their role in the intense interimperialist struggle for control of the region. By viewing the American assistance policy as part of this broader imperial rivalry, this study provides a wider perspective on the debate over the American response to revolutionary events in the Russian Empire.

In the critical years of 1918 and 1919, the thorny issue of military intervention in Siberia limited Wilson's ability to undertake any substantial program of economic assistance in the region. Nevertheless, this study will demonstrate that Wilson's controversial decision to undertake a military intervention on behalf of the stranded Czecho-Slovak Corps in the summer of 1918 was essentially an attempt to reconcile Allied pressure for a military intervention with his primary goal of providing economic assistance to Siberia.

During the trying months between January and September 1918, Wilson repeatedly rejected Allied appeals for an effort to restore the eastern front. Wilson only accepted the efficacy of an intervention in Siberia when he learned that a consensus of anti-Bolshevik political representatives, especially the representatives of the peasant and worker cooperatives, would welcome an American-led intervention to bolster popular resistance against Germany. These sentiments convinced Wilson that the politically conscious segments of Russian society favored an Allied intervention in defense of Russian national sovereignty, if it did not threaten Russian territorial integrity. The attitude of the cooperative societies particularly influenced Wilson's decision to intervene, because these organizations were truly organic regional institutions that represented the material and social aspirations of a considerable segment of the Siberian population. After Wilson reached this decision, he steadfastly insisted that any Allied military operations in Siberia should be limited to providing logistical support for the Czecho-Slovaks, who, in turn, would provide security for the Trans-Siberian Railroad.

But the rival aspirations of Britain, France, and Japan in Siberia undermined American efforts to assist the reconstruction of civil society in the region during 1918 and 1919. By the end of 1919, Bolshevik forces triumphed over the conservative regime of Alexandr Kolchak. Kolchak had acceded to power in November 1918 with the support of British military officials. His regime was doomed by its exclusive reliance on military means to defeat bolshevism and by its unwillingness to develop support among the population. If the Kolchak regime's repressive practices were not sufficient hindrance to constructive policy in Siberia, Japan used its large military expedition to frustrate the work of the American railroad advisers and to impede the shipment of American goods west along the railroad. This study will demonstrate that the debate within the Wilson administration over recognition of the Kolchak regime was primarily motivated by its broader desire to finance economic assistance for Siberia.

The United States abandoned its assistance efforts in Siberia after the Bolshevik victory at the end of 1919. Even then, the Republican Harding administration persuaded the American railroad advisers to remain on the Chinese Eastern Railway, the Manchurian section of the Trans-Siberian system, for another three years until the end of 1922. The continued presence of American railway advisers on the fringe of the Trans-Siberian system demonstrates the importance American policymakers attributed to this transportation artery. While enormous obstacles stood in the path of these advisers' work from the time of their arrival on the Trans-Siberian railway in June 1917 until they left in October 1922, both the Wilson and Harding administrations never wavered in their belief that the stakes involved warranted a continued American presence on the system.

To fully appreciate the implications of the American commitment on the Trans-Siberian Railroad, it is necessary to view the venture in the broader context of American Open Door diplomacy in the Far East. Striking parallels existed between the direction of American policy on the Trans-Siberian system from 1917 to 1922 and major American initiatives in Manchuria a decade earlier. From 1905 until his death in 1909, E. H. Harriman, the American railroad magnate and financier, alternatively attempted to purchase partial control of the South Manchurian Railway from Japan or the Chinese Eastern Railway from Russia as part of his ambition to own a worldwide railroad network. To strengthen his bargaining position, Harriman even undertook negotiations with Chinese officials to build a line parallel to the South Manchurian Railway.

Harriman's proposals received strong diplomatic backing from the State Department during the Taft administration. In 1909, Secretary of State Philander Knox attempted to revive Harriman's plans when he proposed his "neutralization" scheme, whereby the powers would jointly finance China's redemption of all the Manchurian railroads. All of these initiatives failed because of Japanese opposition and because Britain and France ultimately refused to support these proposals over the objections of their respective Far Eastern allies, Japan and Russia. The continuity between the Harriman-Knox proposals and American policy toward the Trans-Siberian system between 1917 and 1922 became apparent in 1920 when the U.S. government officially supported inclusion of the Chinese Eastern Railway within the jurisdiction of the Second China Consortium Banking Group.

American assistance policy in Siberia also foreshadowed future foreign assistance programs. In early 1919, the Wilson administration negotiated an agreement with Britain, France, and Japan for supervision of the Trans-Siberian railway; this cooperative framework resembled, in basic respects, contemporary multilateral developmental agencies such as the International Monetary Fund and the World Bank. Subsequently, Wilson wanted to obtain a large congressional appropriation, similar to the Marshall Plan, for a large-scale program to assist Siberia's reconstruction. This plan, which was shelved during the treaty fight, demonstrates Wilson's recognition that the U.S. government must assume a major responsibility for promoting global stabilization and long-term economic expansion.

From one angle, the limited funding given the American assistance efforts in Siberia may seem to call into question the degree of commitment to the reconstruction of Siberia. But the American political system's lack of experience with large foreign assistance programs posed a formidable obstacle for American statesmen who recognized the potential significance of Siberia. In view of these political constraints, the Wilson administration stood no chance of justifying any large expenditures for the doubtful prospect of assisting a region suffering from widespread turmoil. Nevertheless, Wilson remained determined to obtain a large appropriation for Siberia from Congress in the summer of 1919, just as his political fortunes were waning.

Realist critics might respond that this study merely demonstrates the futility of American attempts to escape from the balance of power, which they view as the main source of international stability. But these writers overemphasize the causal role of the balance of power that has always served as a means of furthering other ends. Prior to World War II, American foreign policy challenged the balance of power because it was a serious impediment to tangible American interests. The existence of treaty arrangements, like the Anglo-Japanese alliance in the Far East, helped these powers preserve their spheres of influence from American encroachment. It was only when World War II brought about the complete collapse of the system based on spheres of influence that the United States could establish multilateral institutions to supervise international development. Therefore, in many respects the Wilson administration's Siberian policy represented a "test run" for the accomplishments of midcentury.

The first chapter in this volume provides a brief assessment of American views on the political and economic future of Russia and particularly of Siberia. This chapter demonstrates how Siberia's unique position within the Russian Empire made it a particularly attractive area for the prospective extension of American influence. American statesmen had a special affinity for Siberia because of its frontier characteristic, which lent itself to superficial analogies with the American frontier of the nineteenth century. The region's rich natural resources, its relatively egalitarian social structure and the weakness of czarist institutions appeared to make it fertile ground for rapid economic development after the Revolution of March 1917.

The American reconstruction program for Russia consisted of three phases. Chapter 2 examines the first phase of this process, which spanned the period of April through November 1917, when the United States furnished the Provisional Government with assistance to its railways. America's strategy to open the Russian "door" was based on establishing American managerial and technical influence on the Trans-Siberian and European Russian Railroads during World War I. The United States offered the Russian Provisional Government a body of prominent railroad engineers, the Advisory Commission of Railway Experts, in order to improve operations on the Trans-Siberian Railroad after April 1917. This commission was placed under the chairmanship of John F. Stevens, the most prestigious railroad engineer in the United States. Stevens would be the pivotal figure in the American reconstruction program until the end of 1922.

In the year between the Bolshevik Revolution and the Armistice in November 1918, the threat of German economic domination of Russia preoccupied American policymakers. American statesmen believed the Bolsheviks' seizure of power was merely a temporary phase in the revolutionary cycle; consequently, they feared this regime would merely pave the way for Germany's aims in Russia as the population sought liberation from revolutionary extremism. Chapters 3 through 6 cover the year 1918, during which the Wilson administration strove to defeat Germany's efforts to consolidate its economic position in the Russian Empire following the Brest-Litovsk Treaty of March 1918, which gave Germany extensive economic privileges. In this context, American economic assistance to Siberia during 1918 served two purposes: it played an immediate strategic role in the war effort against Germany and it attempted to provide the commercial assistance necessary to begin the reconstruction process. The inter-Allied

Goods Exchange Trading Company (Tovaro-Obmien), the Russian Bureau of the War Trade Board, and the plan for a temporary ruble currency in Siberia were all conceived to further these dual objectives. The Wilson administration even hoped the Czecho-Slovak Corps could play a role in this process as an Allied police force along the Trans-Siberian railway system. This force, which was originally slated for transportation to the western front, consisted of former Austro-Hungarian prisoners of war who were reorganized in Russia on behalf of the Allied cause.

Chapters 7 and 8 examine American efforts to restore effective operations along the Trans-Siberian railway and to strengthen its links to the international market. Any chance for promoting reconstruction in Siberia, and eventually in European Russia, now rested squarely on the fate of the Siberian railway system. Chapter 7 shows 1919 to be the critical year for Wilson's reconstruction program. After the conclusion of an inter-Allied railroad agreement in February 1919, the formulation of a comprehensive assistance program for Russia became a priority for the Wilson administration. By August, events in the Far East and political conditions at home undermined this nascent program. The defeat of anti-Bolshevik leader Admiral Kolchak, Japan's hostility to Stevens's efforts to stabilize the railroads, and domestic opposition to Wilson's Russian policy blocked any hope of implementing a government-financed reconstruction program for the region.

After the Allies withdrew from Siberia, the United States retained John Stevens in Manchuria to manage the Chinese Eastern Railway, the last major segment of the Trans-Siberian railway system. Chapter 8 surveys the intersection of the Siberian program with Chinese issues from 1920 through 1922. To prevent Japan from closing the eastern approach to Siberia, the United States sought inclusion of the Russian-controlled Chinese Eastern Railway within the jurisdiction of the new China Consortium. This chapter adds a new dimension to our understanding of America's Far Eastern policy by demonstrating the integral role Siberia once played in American calculations.

No existing study has recognized the scope or significance of the Wilson administration's policy initiatives in Russia. For decades, the political and intellectual climate created by the American-Soviet bipolar rivalry has led too many scholars to view Wilson's response to the Russian Revolution simply as a prelude to the Cold War. In his two-volume study *Soviet-American Relations, 1917–1920*, George F. Kennan, statesman, historian and a realist critic of Wilsonian foreign policy, eschewed any efforts at a broad appraisal of Wilson's Russian policy in favor of a narrative approach that emphasizes that the complexity of international relations militated against the efficacy of universalist worldviews such as bolshevism or Wilsonianism.

In his *American-Russian Relations, 1781–1947*, William A. Williams focused on the anti-Bolshevik motives of the Wilsonians. The single best source on the ideological basis of Wilsonian foreign policy is the work of N. Gordon Levin, who argued persuasively in his study *Woodrow Wilson and World Politics: America's Response to War and Revolution* that Wilson attempted to foster an environment favorable to the development of liberal constitutional institutions in the Russian Empire in opposition to both revolutionary socialism and militaristic imperialism.

The best introduction to the question of American involvement in Siberia is John A. White's study, *The Siberian Intervention*. Relying almost exclusively on published sources, this excellent study suggests several important points about the political economy of American policy in Siberia. White argues that it was the pressure exerted on Russia by Germany and Japan that gave purpose to the Allied and American intervention in Russia. Betty M. Unterberger's *America's Siberian Intervention, 1918–1920* provides a solid background on the subject of America's intervention in Siberia. She emphasizes that the Wilson administration undertook a limited intervention on behalf of the Czecho-Slovak Corps to maintain Russian sovereignty and to preserve the Open Door in Siberia and northern Manchuria against Japanese aggression. Her essay "Woodrow Wilson and the Russian Revolution," published in Arthur S. Link's *Woodrow Wilson and a Revolutionary World, 1913–1921*, provides a fine overview of Wilsonian policy.

Linda Killen's path-breaking study *The Russian Bureau: A Case Study in Wilsonian Diplomacy* is the first monograph to address the issue of American economic assistance to Siberia. This valuable study surveys American commercial assistance efforts in 1918 and 1919 and questions the consistency between Wilson's high-sounding rhetoric regarding his expectations for Russia's liberal-democratic potential and his reluctance to commit funds for a program of economic assistance.

Recent historiography on the American intervention in the Russian Revolution has polarized around exaggerated positions. David McFadden's *Alternative Paths: Soviets and Americans, 1917–1920* overstates the potential for a Soviet-American rapprochement and expanded trade with Soviet-controlled regions during this period; and Christine White's *British and American Commercial Relations with Soviet Russia, 1918–1924* also overestimates the significance of American trade expansion with the Soviet Union in the 1920s.[2] Alternately, David Foglesong's *America's Secret War Against Bolshevism: U.S. Intervention in the Russian Civil War, 1917–1920* emphasizes what he considers to be the counterrevolutionary nature of the Wilson administration's policy toward Russia. By ignoring the significance and complexity of the interpower rivalry in Russia and the sophistication of the

Wilson administration's assistance policy, Foglesong mistakes the distinctly progressive character of Wilson's policy for a series of covert operations against the Bolsheviks.

My use of primary sources demonstrates that American foreign policy is conceived and managed by a policymaking "establishment" composed of government officials and strategic representatives of the private sector. This "establishment" is fundamentally oriented toward promoting the stable expansion of the corporate political economy. This does not imply that U.S. foreign policy is a servant of specific interests, nor does it condemn foreign investment as necessarily harmful to developing countries. It merely recognizes the predominance of corporate capitalism and the leadership of both government officials and private individuals who assumed this system was the prime agent of progress.

The primary sources for this study are Record Group (RG) 59: The General Records of the Department of State; the manuscripts of the central figures in the Wilson administration; and RG 43: The Records of the Advisory Commission of Railway Experts to Russia, the Russian Railway Service Corps, and the Inter-Allied Railway Committee. RG 59 continues to be an indispensable resource for examining American foreign relations; this vast body of material can still yield new insights into the policymaking process. This study has also made extensive use of the papers of Woodrow Wilson, Robert Lansing, Frank Polk, Breckinridge Long, Edward M. House, Gordon Auchincloss, Roland S. Morris, Charles Evans Hughes, Vance McCormick, and British representative Sir William Wiseman. The records of the American Railway Experts in Russia have proved extremely valuable in revealing the connections between the engineers' technical and operational work on behalf of the Trans-Siberian railway and America's broader economic and political goals in the region. Samuel Harper's papers contain valuable correspondence with officials in the Russian division of the State Department. Finally, the papers of Cyrus McCormick Jr. have memoranda regarding American economic assistance efforts in 1918.

Records of Russian Bureau of the War Trade Board, RG 182; the country files of the Treasury Department, RG 39; the Bureau of Foreign and Domestic Commerce, RG 151; and the Commerce Department, RG 40; were all used in order to examine the complex range of problems American policymakers confronted and the sophisticated methods Wilsonian policy devised to solve those problems.

1

The Open Door, Wilsonianism, and the New Frontier in Siberia

The March Revolution of 1917 abruptly transformed the American view of the Russian Empire. In less than a fortnight, centuries of autocratic rule bolstered by a privileged bureaucracy collapsed and opened a space for progressive social forces to assert themselves. American statesmen believed the liberal character of this revolution would foster close political and economic ties between Russia and the United States in the future.

The interest American statesmen and businessmen took toward Russia after the outbreak of World War I was rooted in the fundamental secular trend in the development of American capitalism. Since the depression of the 1890s, American statesmen and business leaders recognized that America's industrial development had reached a crossroad. Foreign investment outlets were needed to absorb profitably the capital surpluses generated by industrial capitalism since the 1870s. This overinvestment of capital in the domestic economy caused the severe industrial cycles and the labor unrest that marked this thirty-year period. This crisis underlay the United States's staunch advocacy of the "Open Door" policy as its primary foreign policy objective by the late 1890s. Equal opportunity for trade and investment in developing regions would facilitate stable expansion of the capitalist system and reduce the sources of tension between the rival industrial powers.

Beginning in the 1890s, American statesmen believed the Chinese Empire offered the best prospects for American investment because of its huge population and rich natural resources. China was the only major developing region that had not yet been incorporated into the colonial empire of another power. Conditions in China, however, were not conducive to foreign investment. China's social and economic backwardness increased risk and discouraged investors. Much of the economy was based on subsistence or compartmentalized into regions that inhibited the penetration of market forces. The Chinese monarchy's rapid deterioration increasingly paralyzed its extensive governmental apparatus at the end of the nineteenth century, a process that encouraged the powers to erode China's territorial sovereignty through the establishment of spheres of influence after 1895. By the outbreak of World War I, China had still not become the viable investment outlet that American capitalists had hoped for.[1]

Prior to the March Revolution in Russia, a syndicate of investment banks led by the National City Bank had begun to exhibit confidence in Russia's future when they floated a series of loans to the czarist government worth $86 million. From Petrograd, Commerce Department attaché Henry D. Baker thought that these loans could become the opening wedge for the large-scale involvement of American capital in Russia's postwar development. At the time he reported that "it is anticipated that in connection with the great loan of $260,000,000 to the Russian Government now being negotiated by an American syndicate, headed by the National City Bank of New York, and also in connection with the Great International Corporation lately projected by National City Bank interests, there will be a great impetus created for American investment projects in Russia."

The American International Corporation was formed in late 1915 by a group of large American corporations, led by the National City Bank, to take advantage of the withdrawal of European capital from developing regions. Its purpose was to obtain concessions for developmental projects and to finance them in the United States. The emergence of American financial preeminence was not overlooked in Russia where Baker noted: "There seems an unusual tendency . . . to be favorable to the idea of American firms participating in the development of this country, as it is realized that owing to the great calls on other foreign countries engaged in the present war for capital and financing the war, that the only country now left in a position to give material assistance to Russia with the development of its internal resources is the United States."[2]

But it was the March Revolution in Russia that breathed new life into American conceptions of the Open Door. American businessmen and statesmen believed that Russia's adoption of liberal democracy after March 1917 had set Russia on a path of development that was complementary to that of the United States.

The American-Russian Chamber of Commerce, which had been recognized as an official organ by the czarist government, expressed the high expectations American capitalists attached to the development of outlets in postwar Russia. The chamber's vision of how relations between America and Russia would develop deserves close examination, since its members included numerous representatives of large corporations that hoped to participate in the development of Russia.

In September 1917 the chamber's president, Charles H. Boynton, compared Russia's position to that of the United States at the end of the Civil War. Like America during its era of Reconstruction, Russia would need large amounts of foreign capital to pay its foreign debt and to develop its manufacturing potential. Initially, the expansion of Russia's domestic manufacturing industry, through the help of protective tariffs and foreign capital, would stimulate exports and relieve the burden of Russia's large foreign debt.[3]

Boynton emphasized that the United States's historical experience placed it in a better position than any other nation to assist Russia's development. America had the necessary capital, the proper technology, and the organizing ability Russia needed to develop its industries. Yet beyond these complementary economic factors, Boynton stressed that many prominent Russians favored American capital because they considered it "untainted by political designs" unlike the "German exploitation of their economic life prior to the war." Before the war European powers like France and Germany had intensively exploited specific sectors of the Russian economy to advance their own political and economic objectives to the detriment of Russia's national development. In contrast Boynton believed the Russians would welcome American capital and expertise because "what she needs is the great extensive development such as we have had in this country because Russia is a great huge nation which requires a similar treatment to that of our own." Indeed, notwithstanding the various differences in cultures and climatic conditions between the two countries, Boynton did "not consider it too optimistic to assume that Russia's development during the next fifty years will be parallel to that of the United States during the last fifty years."[4]

Consistent with this assumption that Russia's development would resemble that of the United States, Boynton did not envision a neocolonial relationship between the two countries, even though Russia would furnish a large export market for American goods in the short run. Rather, American exports would hasten the process of reconstruction in Russia during the immediate postwar period. Because Russia's own manufacturing was in its infancy, Boynton suggested that American firms that were interested in that market should "have in mind that for a short time after the War, say two or three years, there will be a splendid opportunity for the sale of all kinds of American merchandise." He qualified this observation with the reminder that "the far-seeing business man will be laying his plans today for co-operating with Russian capital in the organization of factories in Russia for the production of standard American products which will meet the needs of the Russian market."[5] The recognition by the chamber in 1917 that Russia would require American exports to help reestablish domestic production helps explain why in the summer of 1918 the Wilson administration adopted a commercial assistance program to begin the process of reconstruction in Russia. At that time the chamber would help the administration to collect data from the private sector regarding the availability of goods for Siberia.

In the long run, American business had a greater stake in helping Russia develop its own manufacturing potential. Beyond the export of goods Boynton thought that in many cases, "it will be more advisable for American firms to interest themselves in the actual manufacture of their products in Russia through cooperation with Russian capital, the sale of their manufacturing rights, or the establishment of their own plants in the Russian field." Moreover, Russia's development was also expected to play an important role in maintaining American prosperity since "both from the standpoint of a market for American merchandise and for American equipment machinery, and as a field for the investment of American capital in manufacturing enterprises, Russia will undoubtedly present perhaps our most favorable foreign opportunity at the termination of the War."[6] This contention was supported by no less an authority on the American economy than Herbert Hoover, who attached great importance to the Russian market as an outlet for American capital and as a guarantor of continued American prosperity. As late as December 1921 Hoover still asserted to Secretary of State Charles Evans Hughes that "the hope of our commerce lies in the establishment of American firms abroad, distributing American goods under American direction and, above all, in the installation of American technology in Russian industries."[7]

Like most American observers in 1917, Boynton assumed that radicalism in Russia was an inevitable but transitory phase of the revolutionary process. It was important that American businessmen not be discouraged by these revolutionary vicissitudes because "the pendulum of political forces will continue to swing, sometimes violently, but it is certain to come to rest at a point of equilibrium where all Russia will join in a government of stability, of integrity and provide individual opportunity and freedom for its citizens."[8] For this reason Americans must not become involved in the "temporary political upheaval" because their attention should be fixed on the "Russia of the future." Thus, the public's attitude toward Russia would be best informed by America's diplomatic corps, consular service, and business representatives "whose judgments are best adapted to a clear conception and proper deductions from its passing events." This sound "American opinion of Russia" would always lead one to the overriding conclusion that even several years of social and political instability would not diminish Russia's tremendous economic potential.[9]

Woodrow Wilson was also dedicated to the objective of establishing the Open Door as a precondition for maintaining America's economic prosperity. Yet, in Wilson's system of values, an Open Door political economy served a higher moral purpose as well. Wilson believed capitalist social and economic relations and republican institutions were inseparably linked historically, together constituting the basis for political democracy, individual liberty, and economic development.[10] For this reason, Wilson understood that economic policy would always play a critical role in shaping a nation's civic qualities. This concern for a society's moral characteristics was the unifying theme in all of Wilson's political writings and speeches throughout his public career in academia and later in politics.[11] Wilson's commitment to encourage liberalism and democratic institutions abroad not only reflected American national interest, but also the moral principles embodied in his political economy. Through the instruments of the Open Door and the League of Nations he was endeavoring to construct a modern international commonwealth in which individual liberty, civic responsibility, and economic development were harmonized by constitutional-democratic institutions at both the national and international levels.

These ambitions inspired Wilson's enthusiasm for the March Revolution in Russia. Wilson regarded the March Revolution as an important step toward the construction of a new international political order based on liberal-democratic principles. In his request to Congress for a declaration of war against Germany on April 2, 1917, Wilson stressed that America would be joined by the new Russia as "a fit partner for a League of Honour," that now consisted solely of democratic nations. Wilson's optimism about the prospects for the March Revolution was based on the belief that the Russian people had always been essentially democratic in character. The population's democratic impulses had been shackled by the czarist autocracy, which Wilson thought had never truly been Russian "in origin, character or purpose." He asserted that "Russia was known by those who knew it best to have been always in fact democratic at heart, in all the vital habits of her thought, in all the intimate relationships of her people that spoke their natural instincts, their habitual attitude towards life."[12]

Wilson's overestimation of Russia's natural democratic qualities should be traced to the intellectual influence of his longtime friend and intellectual confidant Frederick Jackson Turner. In his influential essay, "The Significance of the Frontier in American History," Turner argued that American democracy had been revitalized throughout the nineteenth century by the influence of the western frontier. Frontier conditions fostered such liberal virtues as personal independence and industriousness among the settlers as they struggled to subdue nature in an environment unfettered by any preexisting social divisions. These virtues, in turn, were imparted into the democratic political institutions that emerged from this egalitarian social base. Once liberal-democratic political institutions were established, the liberal character of the society would persist through subsequent stages of economic development. Turner concluded his essay by speculating that America's inherent liberalism could serve as a guide for other peoples.[13]

Wilson's enthusiasm for the March Revolution appears less naive when the Siberian frontier is taken into account. Contemporary observers predicted that Siberia would play a role in promoting Russia's cultural development that was analogous to the American frontier in the nineteenth century. This new frontier would foster liberal-democratic qualities among the settlers and constitute the foundation for a long-term community of interests between Russia and the United States. The pervasive influence of Turner's thesis on the American policymaking establishment is exhibited by a confidential memorandum produced for the members of the United States's delegation to the Washington Naval Conference in late 1921. In this review of Siberia's settlement, the anonymous author credited "the natural movement of the Russian people eastward . . . led by the pioneer" as the motive force behind Siberia's integration with Russia. The author then portrayed Russian colonization of Siberia in terms that virtually restated Turner when he asserted: "After the explorer came the settler. Consolidation of Government followed. As a result the barren wild country, unoccupied save for a few scattered half savage Asiatic tribes, was transformed into a vigorous Russian commonwealth, adapted to the institutions and culture of the white man."[14]

The influence of John Locke's Natural Law is particularly apparent in the author's comment: "The advance was a natural movement of exploration and colonization by the Russian people themselves and was not a policy of annexation initiated or executed by the Government."[15] Slavic peasants were legitimately exercising their natural right to appropriate and exploit underdeveloped resources. Finally, the author presumed an historical parallel between America and Russia in declaring:

politically Russian, northern Asia must be considered as a country sharing in the institutions and social organization of Europe and America.

Notwithstanding the fact that, preceding the revolution, Russia was under a form of government denominated as autocratic, the genius of the people revealed in its culture and exemplified in local life was, like that of other western peoples, essentially democratic. In the case of Siberia this was even more marked by reason of a population largely drawn from the more independent and enterprising elements of the Russian people and further hardened in the struggle with primitive nature and the trials of frontier life.

Generally speaking the exploration and settlement of Siberia bears a striking resemblance to the opening of the American West and is in fact almost a duplicate of this romantic achievement.[16]

This fundamentally Turnerian outlook, together with prospects for close economic ties between the two continental empires in the postwar period, was the basis for Wilson's confidence in the future of liberal democracy in Russia.

In view of the absence of democratic institutions in Russia's history, Wilson's conception of self-government requires examination, lest his optimism for Russia's incipient democracy be dismissed as completely implausible. Wilson was essentially concerned about encouraging civic liberty in Russian society, rather than with promoting democracy as a specific form of government. As he explained in his essay of 1900, "Democracy and Efficiency," Americans cherished democracy "for the emphasis it puts on character; for its tendency to exalt the purposes of the average man to some high level of endeavor; for its just principle of common assent in matters in which all are concerned; for its ideals of duty and its sense of brotherhood." In other words, Wilson favored the democratic form of government because it was the most conducive environment for cultivating civic virtue in the whole population.[17]

But Wilson was quick to point out that "democracy is merely the most radical form of 'constitutional government,'" what he also called "representative government" or "self-government." He assumed that "constitutional government" could actually exist in a variety of forms. Constitutional government was distinguished by the existence of a covenant or fundamental law between government and the people, which was maintained by regular public consent; the covenant itself must guarantee individual liberty and delimit the authority and functions of government.[18] These fundamental principles could be preserved in different forms of constitutional government. In "Democracy and Efficiency," Wilson contended that it was an unfortunate irony that America's vigorous democratic character and principles had actually hindered the development of its governmental institutions. At the threshold of a new age,

Wilson regretted that America lacked the administrative ability necessary to assume the international responsibilities of a great power.

This evaluation of the American political culture suggests Wilson never supposed that American institutions could serve as a model of government for an infant democracy such as Russia.[19] Rather, the enthusiasm Wilson expressed for Russian democracy in his war address reflected his assumption that, with the collapse of the absolutist government, Russia would finally be free to evolve its own unique brand of constitutional government. In the context of his worldview, Wilson's assertion that Russia was "democratic at heart" should be interpreted to mean that he believed Russian society was endowed with considerable, if rudimentary, civic qualities. Wilson was confident these attributes would constitute the basis for a genuinely representative government whose actual form would be suited to Russia's specific historical and cultural conditions.

This analysis also provides the key to understanding Wilson's approach to the Russian question after the Bolshevik Revolution in November 1917. Both Wilson's policy of nonintervention in Russia's domestic politics and the United States's efforts to furnish commercial assistance to Siberia were consistent with his dictum from "Democracy and Efficiency" that what America had to offer the world was "the aid of our character . . . and not the premature aid of our institutions."[20]

❧

Recent developments in Russia lent credence to the historical comparisons American statesmen drew between Russia and the United States. Indeed, Donald Treadgold has devoted a whole study to the Siberian migration in which he argues that before World War I, the society that was developing in Siberia exhibited greater similarities with the nineteenth-century American frontier society than with its European Russian origins.[21] By 1913, over 5 million people had migrated to Siberia from European Russia—most of these after 1890. Yet, between the emancipation of the serfs in 1861 and the early 1890s, the czarist regime never formulated an effective migration policy to either forbid or to assist migration. Prior to the 1840s, the government tried to colonize Siberia with exiles and compulsory colonists. Illegal voluntary migration, however, outnumbered these officially sponsored initiatives as peasant colonists sought land and freedom from creditors, servitude, and government regulations.

During the 1820s, the governor-general of Siberia reported that it was senseless to prevent free migration to Siberia because it helped settle this underpopulated region and because it alleviated overpopulation in European Russia. In 1843, the government initiated a program whereby state peasants could leave overpopulated villages and be settled in Siberia with financial assistance from the state. Nevertheless, Treadgold emphasizes throughout his study that official sponsorship of migration failed to reduce the flow of illegal migration to Siberia, since peasants preferred to flee rather than subject themselves to the paternalism of the state.

After 1892, when the Trans-Siberian Railroad was begun, the government finally bowed to the inevitable and committed itself to a generously subsidized program of regulated resettlement. A large percentage of the migrants continued to avoid this official program. Between 1909 and 1913, from 31 to 47 percent of all migrants were still irregular. When Petr Stolypin became prime minister in 1906, he advocated a liberal approach to the question of migration. He reasoned that instead of attempting to regulate the migrants' destination, the government should let people choose their destination and then assist their endeavor.

Stolypin regarded the question of Siberian migration as especially important because he believed that the region's settlement would play a central role in the regeneration of the whole empire. The principal objective of his government was to dissolve the commune system and to replace it with individual peasant property. This process would stimulate Russia's economic development and enhance social stability, which was necessary if the monarchy was to survive in a constitutional form as Stolypin desired.

To facilitate the individualization of land tenure in European Russia, the surplus population had to be resettled in Siberia. Siberia was particularly suited to individualized land tenure. Virtually all of Siberia's land was legally owned by the state, rather than the commune, a factor that would expedite its transference into private holdings. Yet, independent of juridical issues, the sparsely settled Siberian frontier naturally tended to develop private landholding. Because of the region's abundance of land, the Siberian commune rarely evolved the authority to redistribute land. Instead, land tenure in Siberia was quickly evolving from some form of squatters' right at the consent of the commune to hereditary-household tenure without any redistribution occurring.[22]

Treadgold cites a good deal of evidence that shows that this natural migration to Siberia was producing a prosperous peasant class in that region. A survey commissioned by Stolypin and the Minister of Agriculture Aleksandr Krivoshein, published in 1911, revealed that, on average, a Siberian settler had more land, cattle, grain, and machinery than the average European Russian peasant. Furthermore, Stolypin also figured that yields and productivity were significantly higher than in European Russia and the income of a typical Siberian family was rising steadily.[23] Even the Soviet historian M. M. Stishov admitted that it was not unusual to find households with ten to twelve horses or cows in Siberian villages. Interestingly enough, he did not categorize these peasants as "Kulaks," but as a type of prosperous "middle peasant."[24]

Russian observers were taking note of Siberia's prosperity and of the unique social structure that was developing there. As Treadgold explained, by the turn of the century Russians frequently referred to Siberia as being "democratic" in character because of its high degree of social and economic equality, although political connotations were not implied prior to the March Revolution. Stolypin, who was the strongest proponent of individualized peasant proprietorship, was himself ambivalent about the democratic tendencies that were taking root in Siberia. He even confided to a familiar journalist a fear that "the Democracy of Siberia will crush us."[25] Treadgold did not interpret this concern as an indication that Stolypin expected the peasantry to demand universal suffrage in the near future, but rather, that Siberia's democratic culture would undermine the value system of Imperial Russia over time.

Following this theme, Treadgold demonstrates that Russian writers characterized the Siberian population in terms that were strikingly reminiscent of Turner. For instance, Treadgold quotes a statement by government demographer N. V. Turchaninov in which the latter described the Siberian migrant as:

> Representing, in the person of the settlers, the daring escapees from Russia proper, having moved here under harsh conditions sometimes even prior to the conquest of the region, and in the person of the recent settlers, the most energetic and enterprising representatives of their milieu—for only such migrants become firmly acclimatized and strike root in the new regions—the Siberian peasants indeed differ from the remaining mass of the Russian peasantry . . . in their greater steadfastness . . . in the struggle with [nature] . . . their greater mobility and readiness to accept every kind of innovation.[26]

Treadgold cites substantial evidence that the Siberian frontier also stimulated self-sufficiency and initiative among the settlers, as well as a high degree of equality. *Aziatskaia Rossiia*, a two-volume series of books on Siberia, observed that the Siberian peasantry was receptive to the use of modern agricultural machinery and to the technical advice of agronomists.

In *Asiatskaia Rossiia* the settlers' innovativeness was attributed to the network of cooperative societies that were developing rapidly in Siberia. This study emphasized that the Siberian settlers exhibited "an exceptional capacity for self-help by means of cooperatives, credit unions, and other types of unions and societies."[27] American policymakers viewed the rapid expansion of the cooperative movement in Siberia after 1914 as a phenomenon of great import, a development that would foster democratic civic values in Russian society and economic ties with the United States.

The cooperative movement in Russia received its original impetus from the penetration of market forces in the 1890s as peasant producers began to suffer from sharp increases in the cost of rye bread and meat. Cooperation made swift progress after a limited constitutional government was inaugurated in 1905, even though the cooperative movement did not enjoy the status of a legal personality under the czarist government.

The severe disruptions caused by war stimulated an unprecedented expansion of cooperative societies of all varieties, as they were the only institutions capable of organizing supply and distribution in this poorly integrated empire of small producers. The membership of all consumers' societies increased from less than 2 million in 1915 to 17 million in 1919. In Siberia alone the number of consumer societies grew from 519 in 1914 to 8,140 in 1918. By 1918 between one-fourth and one-third of the aggregate value of Siberia's entire retail trade was sold by local consumers' cooperatives.[28]

Russian cooperatives can be grouped into three general categories: consumer, credit, and agricultural, although functions increasingly overlapped as the societies multiplied rapidly during the war. The primary units of cooperation were the local societies that were formed voluntarily by their members. These local societies were combined into unions of cooperative societies at the district, provincial, and national levels to accumulate the financial resources and to derive the bargaining power to engage in efficient buying and selling. A few large cooperative unions, such as the Union of Siberian Creamery Associations, represented whole regions. Cooperative organizations were also established by labor organizations such as the prominent All Russian Railway Supply Union.

District and provincial cooperatives were centralized in two national organizations, the All-Russian Union of Consumers' Societies, and the Narodny (Peoples) Bank. The Central Union of Consumers' Societies was the leading organization of Russian cooperation after its reorganization from the Moscow Union of Consumers' Societies in 1917. This central union linked the network of consumers' societies into a national federation by coordinating wholesale supply and marketing activities. More than three thousand individual societies owned shares in the Central Union by 1917. After 1917, the Central Union evolved beyond its original cooperative trading endeavors into "a national institution with far flung interests, a state within a state."[29]

As private trade collapsed during the war, the major cooperative organizations, particularly the Central Union and the Union of Siberian Creamery Associations, increasingly assumed the status of quasi-state institutions because the government had become dependent on them for supplying the army and cities with provisions. The Central Union's prominence in the nation's economy was reflected in the numerous commodity departments or divisions that were established to manage day-to-day commercial activities. Separate departments existed for grains, fats and oils, fish and groceries, dairy, ironware, textiles, haberdashery, footwear, raw materials, finances, legal affairs, and transportation. An Economic and Organization Department handled supervision, policy formulation, and planned methods of organization. Finally, the Central Union's manufacturing operations were expanded to meet the severe shortages of many basic consumer goods.[30]

The Narodny (Peoples) Bank was founded in 1912 for the purpose of supplying funds to credit institutions and cooperative enterprises. Affiliated credit cooperatives, including the Central Union of Consumers' Societies, owned the bank's stock. The Narodny Bank maintained a paid up capital of 10 million rubles by 1918. During 1917 the bank had a turnover of 3 billion rubles. Like the Consumers' Societies, the Narodny Bank achieved the status of a quasi-governmental institution when the Provisional Government made the State Bank's credit available to it.

American observers believed cooperative institutions played an equally important cultural role in nurturing democracy and self-improvement among the rural population.[31] A wide range of educational activities were sponsored by cooperative institutions including schools, newspapers, lectures, conferences, children's playgrounds, social entertainments, amateur theatricals, concerts, choruses, and reading rooms. These nontrading activities were designed to encourage new social values such as self-reliance, thrift, cooperation, and the technical skills indispensable for economic progress. In fact, American observers viewed Russian cooperatives so favorably because their voluntary associational principles were seen as a necessary appendage to private enterprise at this stage of national development. Eugene Kayden, a War Trade Board specialist, emphasized that individuals joined cooperatives for their "material benefit" and "social welfare" and "to participate directly in an order of economic exchange which has been described as irredeemably private and capitalistic. Cooperation was therefore a socializing force within the framework of the present society, taking for its function the training and directing of the creative economic instincts toward a more harmonious and rational order."[32] William C. Huntington, an experienced Commerce Department attaché, recommended Russian cooperatives as worthy partners in America's effort to reconstruct Russia in a statement to a National City Bank official:

> Personally I look upon the cooperative movement with favor, and, while fully aware that it does not operate with the efficiency and initiative of a private business concern, believe it has accomplished much for the Russian people, and that it is a pretty good training school in constructive democracy. Last summer [1918] I sat in a directors' meeting of the Moscow Narodny Bank in Moscow, and, gazing at the men there, I got the impression that they were the nucleus of the future middle class of Russia.[33]

Both Huntington and Kayden were recognizing that the cooperatives represented organic social institutions that would play a critical role in fostering better integration between civil society and the state. War had given impetus to this process as cooperative officials were incorporated into the central state bureaucracy and war committees because of their ability to organize the supply of necessities for the army and urban areas.[34]

❧

American statesmen were confident that a progressive democratic government in Russia would naturally seek American technical expertise and capital resources after the war because they assumed an historical community of interests between the two continental empires. These historical impressions shaped the American response to Russian events between 1917 and 1922. American assistance to Russia after 1917 through agents such as the Stevens Railway Commission and the Russian Bureau of the War Trade Board represented the enlightened self-interest of the United States. Wilsonian impulses were intertwined with long-term American investment interests and the need to combat German economic domination of the Russian Empire. Thus, it would underestimate American policy to overlook the organic relationship between these constituent motives. Because American statesmen believed the United States and Russia shared complementary interests, they could sincerely disclaim selfish motives while fully expecting to derive the benefits from close economic ties with a kindred liberal empire.

2

❦

A Minister Plenipotentiary
for Russia's Railroads:
The Stevens Commission in Russia,
June–December 1917

American efforts to reconstruct Russia's political economy began in June 1917 where they would end in October 1922, on the Trans-Siberian railway system. Shortly after Russia's March Revolution, which brought to power a fragile coalition of moderate socialists and liberals, the Wilson administration offered military assistance to the Provisional Government in the shape of railroad experts to improve operations on the strategic Trans-Siberian Railroad. In early May 1917, the administration announced that renowned railroad expert John F. Stevens would head an advisory commission of railroad experts to Russia for the disinterested purpose of assisting its military effort against Imperial Germany. Yet for American policymakers, and especially Stevens himself, the defeat of German war aims in Russia had important implications for American postwar objectives. Indeed, Stevens's purely advisory role manifested the liberal principles Wilson hoped to infuse into postwar international relations generally. The United States hoped to open the Russian "door" by establishing the managerial and technical practices of the American corporate political economy on Russia's developing transportation infrastructure. An international Open Door environment would provide the widest vent for America's great financial resources and technical expertise.

Russia's liberal March Revolution was a key determinant in Wilson's decision to seek a declaration of war against Imperial Germany on April 2, 1917.

In his confidential letter to Wilson on March 19, the first justification Secretary of State Robert Lansing gave the president for declaring war against Germany at that time was that such a step would "encourage and strengthen" the new liberal-democratic government in Russia.[1] For this reason, after America's entry into the war, Wilson dispatched a special diplomatic mission headed by Elihu Root to Russia; the mission arrived in early June. Wilson hoped the Root mission would demonstrate America's goodwill toward the Russian Revolution and help Washington determine the most effective means by which the United States might assist Russia's war effort.

Meanwhile, the United States moved quickly to provide tangible assistance to the Provisional Government. On March 31, 1917, at a meeting of the Council of National Defense, Stanley Washburn, who had traveled extensively on the eastern front as a war correspondent, recommended that the United States send the fledgling government railroad experts to help improve the efficiency of the Trans-Siberian Railroad. Any improvement in Russia's war effort, and, ultimately, the very survival of the Provisional Government, depended on a major overhaul of the disorganized system of state-run railroads. Since early 1915, Russian industrialists had been criticizing government mismanagement of the railroads for the empire's constant fuel and transportation shortages. But the industrialists lacked the unity and political will necessary to pressure the czarist government into enacting fundamental changes in the management of the state railroad system.[2] Recognizing that timely American assistance might break this impasse, Daniel Willard, the chairman of the Railway Advisory Committee of the Council of National Defense (CND), immediately offered to organize a commission of railroad experts for Russia. Demonstrating both its rationalizing impulses and its global perspective on the war, the CND believed that "competent railroad men" could also extend the benefits of American expertise to the Russian railway system. Initially, the American experts would be expected to spend considerable time gathering data on the material and manpower needs of the chaotic Russian railway system.[3]

On April 2, 1917, the day Wilson requested a declaration of war against Imperial Germany, the State Department inquired of the Provisional Government whether it would welcome an inspection by six American railway experts.[4] A week later the Provisional Government's minister for Foreign Affairs, Pavel Miliukov, told Ambassador David R. Francis that he was authorized to accept the American offer. But shortly after this, Francis cabled Washington that he had not received formal consent. He had learned confidentially that the Russians had only reluctantly consented to the proposal, and he explained to the State Department that this hesitancy existed because the "Russian nature resents outside advice." Moreover, the Russians claimed it would take two months before the commission could complete a report, and by that time it would be late in the summer. Francis did not question the motives of the Russian railway officials whom he believed to be competent; he merely passed on the request of the government that the United States expedite completion of an existing order for 375 locomotives from American manufacturers. The State Department quickly obtained a pledge from the American manufacturers to give priority to Russia's orders.[5]

Washington anticipated that Russia would need extensive governmental credit to finance the purchase of locomotives and freight cars. Following a Russian request for an additional five hundred locomotives and ten thousand freight cars at the end of April, Treasury Secretary William Gibbs McAddo explained to Francis the terms under which the U.S. government could extend Russia credits under the congressional authorization that allowed the Treasury to finance cobelligerents. The Provisional Government was anxious to obtain loans directly from the United States and not through British intermediation, as in the case of previous private loans from American banks. When American loans were made through Britain the cost of credit was increased, and Britain maintained some control over the purchases made by Russia. Under the terms of this loan, all Russian purchases had to be approved by a U.S. Treasury Department representative. This stipulation would help guarantee that America's credit would be used for what the U.S. government believed to be the best purposes at a time when even its own financial resources were stretched. In other words, the United States would attach conditions to the loans it made to Kerensky's government in order to closely supervise the supplies Russia would purchase.[6]

On May 17 the United States announced its decision to establish a credit of $100 million for the Provisional Government of Russia. This credit bore an interest rate of 3 percent per year, the same terms upon which the United States furnished credit to the Western allies. Root's mission planned to discuss more fully with the Provisional Government Russia's financial needs for its war effort. Additional credits could be provided by the United States within the limits set by Congress as the situation might demand.[7]

Prior to this, on May 3, the State Department announced that John F. Stevens would head the railroad mission to Russia, which would leave for Vladivostok in one week.[8] A natural outdoorsman, Stevens built his reputation as a construction engineer in the American Northwest during his employment with James J. Hill's Great Northern Railway, from 1889 to 1903. In 1905 Secretary of War William H. Taft made him chief engineer of the Isthmian Canal Commission. During 1906 Stevens planned most of the construction work for the Panama Canal—many of his contemporaries believed he was largely responsible for the project's ultimate success.[9]

Temperamental and physically rugged, Stevens was a commanding figure who exuded confidence and authority. He would have little tolerance for the deceitful and pretentious qualities of the Russian officials with whom he was to work. In turn, Stevens's assertive management style would evoke resentment and much passive resistance from czarist officialdom. Nevertheless, his determination and his reputation as the leading civil railway engineer would help him to persevere during his trying service in Russia.

A controversy immediately developed between Root and Stevens over the commission's ranking. Since the railroad question was the most important issue confronting Russia, Root believed that his special diplomatic mission should be authorized to discuss the issue with the Russian government. He feared the credibility of his mission might be undermined if the Railroad Commission were not accountable to it. Root wanted the railroad experts to make preliminary reports to the diplomatic mission and for all of the experts' communications with the Russian government to pass through his hands.[10]

To head off a potential conflict over this issue Lansing drafted alternative instructions that defined the relationship between Root's mission and the Railroad Commission. Under the first scenario, Stevens's Commission would be directly subordinated to Root's mission. Stevens would be obligated to report to Root's mission and the railroad experts would function under Root's direction. Alternatively, Stevens would be instructed to restrict the activities of his commission to transportation questions. But, since Root would carry ambassadorial rank, Stevens would be instructed to confer with him and to negotiate transportation questions with the Russian government in accordance with Root's general recommendations.[11]

Wilson flatly rejected both of Lansing's definitions of the Railroad Commission's status on May 7, 1917; the president left no room for misunderstanding. Wilson intended the Railroad Commission to be entirely independent of Root's mission. Stevens and his experts were to be placed strictly at the service of the Russian government and were not to act as agents of the U.S. government. The commission would not report back to Washington, because it was accountable only to the Russians—to the extent the Russians desired its services. Perhaps because of his confidence in the technical ability of the American railroad engineers, Wilson believed the commission's recommendations would be favorably received by the Russians.[12]

Wilson's keen interest in this issue reflected the enlightened self-interest that characterized his Russian policy: he had a genuine desire to assist Russia's liberal Revolution and a mistrust of the Allies' traditional diplomacy. Wilson understood that American assistance to Russia must not only promote American interests; rather, an enduring and mutually beneficial relationship could only be developed if Russian national sovereignty was preserved. Wilson's policy demonstrated a recognition that it would be counterproductive for the United States to impose its agenda on the Provisional Government; not only would heavy-handed American intervention violate his pledge to support liberalism in Russia, it would further erode the legitimacy of this fragile liberal government. Indeed, following Lansing's offer to send the diplomatic mission to Russia in mid-April, Francis cautioned that the United States should work discreetly for the sole purpose of helping Russia to prosecute the war successfully. Francis counseled the State Department that great care should be exercised "in giving expression to views concerning internal affairs." He emphasized that America's prompt recognition of the Provisional Government, and President Wilson's enthusiasm for the Russian Revolution, had made a "deep impression and have greatly augmented republican sentiment." Francis consequently advised the State Department that the United States should "be careful to avoid anything likely to detract from a good record."[13]

❧

Wilson's desire to place the Stevens Commission at the service of the Provisional Government must also be viewed within the context of the rivalry that existed between the United States and the Western allies over Russia. Francis had informed the State Department that Russian officials had only consented grudgingly to allow the visit by the American railroad experts.[14] In view of this lukewarm reception, Wilson had all the more reason to demonstrate America's respect for Russian sovereignty when Britain immediately attempted to divert American policy for its own purposes. On April 21, Britain's ambassador, George Buchanan, told Francis that he was recommending to the Provisional Government that America be given control over Vladivostok and the whole Trans-Siberian railway system. As a quid pro quo, Britain had taken "control at Archangel."[15] This proposal was designed to erode Russia's sovereignty by drawing the United States into a system of spheres of influence in Russia. This plan would also enhance Britain's freedom of action by embroiling America with Japan in the Russian Far East. Francis reported that Britain's proposal had aroused resentment among the Russian officials who told him, "Russia does not need nurses."[16] This context of interpower rivalry explains why Wilson took a personal interest in the status of Stevens's Commission. Wilson's intervention in this obscure controversy would give the United States an important diplomatic advantage in the coming years. Mindful of the Provisional Government's tenuous position, Wilson shrewdly perceived the political advantage in having Stevens's

Commission formally appointed as an advisory body to this officially recognized regime. Following the Provisional Government's collapse in November 1917, Wilson's foresight placed the United States in a position to credibly assert that Stevens had been invested with the authority to assume trusteeship over the Trans-Siberian railway system.[17]

Wilson's insistence that Stevens's Commission act strictly as a body of technical experts, accountable only to the Russian government, certainly enhanced the credibility of the mission with important liberal-bourgeois elements in Russia, such as the Kadet party (Constitutional Democrats), a powerful force in the Provisional Government. While conservative on social questions, the Kadet party was eminently bourgeois in its view of itself as the steward of Russia's future national greatness. In his study on Russian liberals during the Revolution, William Rosenberg has shown that what unified the Kadet party was the notion that it stood above partisan politics as the party of national progress.[18]

Stevens's Commission arrived at Vladivostok on June 3. The commission's personnel consisted of Stevens, chairman; John G. Greiner, bridge expert; George Gibbs, a technical engineer; William C. Darling, a civil engineer; and Henry Miller, a transportation expert.[19] Stevens immediately fell ill and remained in a Petrograd hospital for the better part of June. Nevertheless, he quickly identified the problems that should be addressed first. From his sickbed, Stevens "diplomatically" advised his hosts that greater efficiency was required both in the operation of the railroads and in the utilization of repair facilities. Stevens estimated that the Trans-Siberian Railroad had more employees per mile and more motive power than any railroad in America, but the line was not being run efficiently. The Russian railroad officials, sensitive to Stevens's criticisms, quickly reacted because Francis informed Washington that they "apparently desire him to recommend large equipment purchases and [to] leave."[20]

Stevens believed that the inefficient operation of Russia's railroads was a result of overly centralized control by the Ministry of Ways of Communication at Petrograd. The officials who staffed this bureau generally had only a technical knowledge of railroad matters and were without practical operational experience. Many of the officials were college professors who did not even devote all of their time to the business of the ministry. Yet, the detailed operation of the government railway system was directly coordinated by this technical office. At the local level, a general manager supervised a simple track and station organization. There was no specialized middle management, such as division superintendents, superintendents of transportation, train masters, train dispatchers, traveling engineers, or traveling auditors. A general car dispatcher at Petrograd regulated car distribution. Station masters merely moved trains from station to station.[21]

On June 21, 1917, the commission made three preliminary recommendations to the Ministry of Communications, which it believed would bring about an increase in engine service on the Trans-Siberian railway. Locomotive mileage on Russian railways was limited by the practice of operating an engine with one crew along a short distance with a turnaround to complete the day's run. This method resulted in the loss of a great deal of time since the turnaround left the locomotive idle for more than half the time. To remedy this situation, the commission recommended first, that trains be run twice their current distance and second, that engines be provided with a double crew (pooling) to achieve these longer through-runs. Through this plan the number of engine terminals and relay points could be reduced from seventy to thirty-eight on the Trans-Siberian railway. Finally, the flexible American dispatcher system should be adopted to facilitate a more efficient movement of freight under widely varying traffic conditions. The commission believed these changes could increase tonnage service by 40 percent.[22]

To introduce these practices on the Trans-Siberian railway, Stevens arranged to have American operating personnel placed on the railroad commission. On July 30, 1917, Stevens cabled Willard that the Russian officials had requested a unit of 129 operating men to consist of division superintendents, dispatchers, train masters, traveling engineers, master mechanics, and a telephone expert to install telephone dispatching along the Trans-Siberian. Stevens informed Willard that "these men [were] merely to educate Russians in American operation."[23] This comment suggests the motive behind America's assistance to Russia's railroads. Stevens's Commission was transferring American technology and operational methods wholesale onto the Russian railroad network. This influence would not only help Russia's war effort, but it would also play a central role in fostering postwar economic reconstruction and a more productive use of national resources. After the Russians accepted the commission's recommendations in mid-August, Stevens again gave evidence of this motive when he declared, "There has been a great change recently in official spirit here, now apparently enthusiastic for American methods which we must make successful."[24]

The commission did recognize that Russia required a large number of new locomotives and freight cars. In late June Stevens anxiously inquired about an old order for 375 American decapod freight locomotives, which had been due in April. The commission estimated that an additional 1,500 freight locomotives and 30,000 to 40,000 boxcars per year would be necessary. On July 14 Second Assistant Secretary Frank Polk notified Francis that on recommendation of the Root mission 500 additional locomotives and 10,000 cars had been ordered in the United States. Another 1,500 locomotives and 30,000 freight cars were being considered. By February 1918 the United States planned to have 875 decapod locomotives shipped to Vladivostok.[25]

To facilitate the shipment of large numbers of American locomotives Stevens arranged to have locomotive assembly shops built at Vladivostok. When locomotives and boxcars were shipped overseas it was more efficient to transport them in pieces and then to complete their assembly at the point of destination. Stevens's Commission sketched a layout for those assembly facilities to be located just outside Vladivostok. The American locomotive builders would supply the necessary equipment, such as cranes, boilers, air compressors, hydraulic pumps, and the supervisory personnel to operate the plant. In the first week of August 1918, the Council on National Defense informed the commission that the length of the buildings had to be increased to provide for twice the capacity originally contemplated. For their part, the Russian purchasing agents in Washington used the matter of the assembly plants as a bargaining chip to pressure the United States for larger locomotive orders. George Lomonosov, representative of the Ministry of Communications on Ambassador Boris Bakhmetev's mission, advised American officials against building the plants at Vladivostok unless 1,500 additional locomotives were to be shipped there.[26]

The commission's recommendation that American locomotives and freight cars be introduced on the Trans-Siberian Railroad demonstrates the confluence of American economic interests with Wilson's desire to furnish Russia with objective technical assistance. The freight capacity of Russia's railroads was limited by Russia's use of light equipment. Russia's standard locomotives were not very powerful and the four-wheeled boxcar had a low carrying capacity. Consequently, large numbers of small trains limited freight movement and caused congestion on the lines.[27] Powerful American decapod locomotives and the eight-wheeled freight car equipped with state-of-the-art air brakes and automatic coupling would greatly increase the capacity of the Russian lines.

The recommendations of the American railroad experts were consistent with the Wilsonian worldview that a community of interests existed between the United States and Russia. The introduction of American equipment and operational principles on Russia's railroads would rationalize its transportation system and provide a tremendous stimulus for American trade and investment in postwar Russia.

On July 19, 1917, the commission submitted its final report to the Minister of Ways of Communication in regard to improvements that should be made on the Russian railways. This report was divided into two sections:

the first dealt with recommendations that could quickly be applied to all railroads, while the second dealt with permanent changes that should be implemented over time. Its format was thus in accord with the purpose of the commission to assist Russia's war effort, but it also pointed the way toward an extensive reorganization of Russia's railroads in line with American practices.

To immediately increase the daily work of the locomotives, the commission specified a number of simple mechanical expedients that would help refuel and water locomotives more quickly. It also stressed that the repair of locomotives and cars had to be expedited. The restoration of labor efficiency was the most critical factor in this regard. With the working day now limited to eight hours, the commission believed that the workers must be urged to increase their currently low productivity as a necessary sacrifice for the national defense. Since the eight-hour day would seriously reduce output, given the existing shop facilities, the commission strongly recommended that two, or preferably three, shifts be instituted at all main or division shops. Furthermore, all "limitations" that inhibited the fullest utilization of shop facilities should be abolished. Work should be apportioned between shops so that each one could do the work for which it was best suited. In general, the commission emphasized that all efforts should be concentrated on increasing the output of repair facilities while the construction of new locomotives and cars should be suspended in Russia.[28]

While permanent improvements would take considerably more time to complete, the commission recommended that they should nevertheless be systematically undertaken as soon as possible. These improvements should include mechanically operated facilities to coal and water the locomotives and a network of fully equipped roundhouses for all locomotives not in use. A systematic plan should be formulated for redistributing and rebuilding main locomotive and car repair shops. Finally, the old locomotives should be retired in favor of the more powerful American decapod locomotives and the eight-wheeled boxcar should replace the smaller Russian four-wheeled cars.[29]

The commission also made specific recommendations for the Moscow-Petrograd line and for the lines that ran from Moscow to the Donets Basin. These recommendations stressed the immediate establishment of division superintendents with their accompanying staffs, and a more efficient use of the heavy locomotives already in use on these lines.[30] With regard to the movement of coal from the Donets Basin to the industrial centers of Moscow and Petrograd, the commission's recommendations were designed to promote greater self-sufficiency for the Russian economy. It was estimated that 2 million tons of coal were ready for shipment from the basin. However, only 325 cars of coal per day were being moved northward.

With the existing equipment, basic operating changes could increase this amount to five hundred cars per day. If two hundred decapod locomotives were added to these lines with the suggested improvements in the facilities, one thousand cars per day could be moved. Moreover, the commission emphasized that coal output in this region could be doubled, which would alleviate Russia's prewar dependence on coal imports from Britain of four to five million tons, or 20 percent annually.[31]

Meanwhile, disaster had struck the Provisional Government in the weeks the commission prepared its recommendations. After its July military offensive collapsed amid widespread desertions, the Provisional Government lost the political middle ground that had enabled it to continue a defensive war for the limited goal of liberating Russian territory. This had been the only position upon which the moderate socialist-bourgeois coalition could maintain popular support for a continuation of Russia's participation in the war. Political conditions rapidly polarized following the summer military fiasco: on the extreme left, the Bolsheviks' call for an immediate peace attracted growing support from the war-weary peasantry and urban proletariat, while, on the extreme right, the army high command quickly lost patience with the government for its inability to maintain military discipline.

To further complicate matters for the American advisers, deepening governmental paralysis and frequent turnover in the Ministry of Communications led the Russians to delay approval of the commission's recommendations. Moreover, the Russian railway officials had been distinctly unenthusiastic about introducing American methods. George Gibbs revealed that Russian opposition to the American operational recommendations remained "emphatic" until early August. Most of the summer had passed with little accomplished when the American experts decided "to appeal to Kerensky personally." By that time, a "practical man," Kadet P. P. Yurenev, had been appointed minister of railways.[32] On August 10, 1917, the commission members met with Kerensky personally and summarized their activities. During this meeting, Kerensky promised to have the commission's recommendations implemented "in their entirety." Kerensky issued these instructions directly to the new minister of railways, whereupon the American experts "were able to obtain a clear-cut agreement upon the program especially in effecting operating changes."[33] In all likelihood the Americans insisted that they be given operational control over the Trans-Siberian Railroad to ensure the implementation of the reforms.[34]

It is even likely that the commission's assistance in expediting the equipment orders was made contingent on the Russians' acceptance of the experts' managerial control over the line. This is suggested in that it was only after the operational questions were finally resolved that the commission pressed its case for the equipment orders in Washington. With the operational questions now settled, Gibbs and John Greiner returned to the United States to work out the details related to the equipment orders.[35] On August 27 Willard informed Stevens that 275 decapods from the old order would finally be shipped by September and the remaining 100 would be sent by early October at the latest.[36]

From a broader perspective, this episode demonstrates the limits of Wilsonian "noninterventionism." The American experts undoubtedly felt justified in seeking Kerensky's intercession on behalf of their apolitical technical recommendations. Nevertheless, these technical and managerial issues had significant political implications since they were directly linked with America's global policy objectives.

Having finally overcome the resistance of the Russian officials, Stevens's experts were immediately dispatched to clear up the congestion on the Trans-Siberian Railroad.[37] By mid-September Stevens was able to report that a "decided improvement" in the operating efficiency of that line had already been achieved.[38] In early October, Henry Miller, who was directing the activities of the commission on the Trans-Siberian, reported that the accumulation of freight at Vladivostok had been reduced by 40 percent since May. Furthermore, the decapod locomotives had begun to arrive, and there were now fifty new ones at Harbin and Vladivostok. Since July eight hundred boxcars had been shipped from America and another three hundred were expected to depart for the Vladivostok assembly shops by October 1. One thousand gondola cars had been shipped since July 1, four hundred of which were being assembled at Vladivostok.

Even more encouraging for the Stevens mission was the imminent departure from the United States of the American operating personnel, and the expected completion of the locomotive assembly plants at Vladivostok by November 15. Ambassador Francis derived particular satisfaction from this progress since it finally enabled him "to successfully refute insinuations of [the] British and French that [the] American Railway Commission [was] effecting nothing."[39]

Unfortunately, the improvement of operating conditions along the Trans-Siberian Railroad during September was offset by the critical railroad conditions in European Russia. At the end of the month—during which the Provisional Government survived a coup attempt by Gen. L. G. Kornilov—the foreign minister, Mikhail Tereschenko, and the minister of Ways of Communication, A. V. Liverovskii, urgently requested to meet with Ambassador Francis about the transportation situation.[40]

Francis immediately instructed Stevens to return to Petrograd, leaving the supervision of the Trans-Siberian Railroad to Miller and William Darling.

And, given the magnitude of the transportation crisis in European Russia, Francis also requested the State Department to send another top railway expert with a competent subordinate staff. He added that this individual would not serve in a subordinate position but would work in cooperation with the minister of Ways of Communication. Thus, the American railway experts were now to be accorded plenipotentiary powers over the European Russian railroads as well as the Trans-Siberian Railroad.[41]

Because of the unprecedented mobilization of resources for the western front, Willard informed Francis that another high-ranking railroad official could not be spared for the European Russian railroads. He suggested that Stevens should take the position as adviser to the minister of railways. Meanwhile, Miller would be thoroughly capable of supervising the Trans-Siberian line, and he would be receiving welcome support soon. George Emerson, general manager of the Great Northern Railroad, would depart for Vladivostok in mid-November with a contingent of about three hundred skilled managerial personnel, mechanics, and interpreters to assist Miller in completing the introduction of American methods on the Trans-Siberian Railroad.[42]

Stevens met with Ambassador Francis and Minister of Foreign Affairs Tereschenko on October 23. He impressed Tereschenko with the urgency of the situation, and a conference was planned for October 25 for Francis, Stevens, Tereschenko, Minister of Ways of Communication Liverovskii, and the chairman of the Economic Committee, S. N. Tretiakov. The purpose of this meeting was to arrange Stevens's recommendations for all of the lines south of Moscow.[43] Once again, Stevens actually had to exert a great deal of pressure on Tereschenko. During his meeting with the foreign minister, Stevens harshly criticized the Russian officials for failing to implement any of the commission's recommendations on the European Russian lines. Over three months had passed since the general recommendations had been approved, but, with winter approaching, Stevens saw no improvement in European Russia. Stevens bluntly warned Tereschenko that, unless the Russian government immediately acted on the recommendations of the commission, it would be withdrawn from Russia. The withdrawal of the Railroad Commission would in turn signal a loss of confidence in the Russian government and thereby bring into question the advisability of extending further economic assistance to the Provisional Government. In view of the Provisional Government's weakness Stevens was skeptical whether any tangible action would result from the meeting on October 25.[44]

But Stevens's threats had their desired effect on the Russian officials. At the conference, which was delayed a day until October 26, they agreed to greatly augment Stevens's authority over the Russian railways. He would now be installed in the Ministry of Ways of Communication in an advisory capacity to the minister. Since the government immediately placed Stevens on assignment, his post was assumed by Henry Horn, who had been serving in Russia with the Red Cross. Ambassador Francis revealed that Stevens was to be much more than an adviser, as "the Council of Ministers will give [the] required orders for execution of his recommendations."[45] Stevens's role had been transformed from that of an adviser to that of a plenipotentiary with extensive authority over the Russian government. Ambassador Francis expressed the extent of influence the commission now wielded when he advised Washington that if "our recommendations [are] not executed promptly I shall seriously consider abandoning such position."[46] Later, Stevens would admit that he had become what amounted to a proconsul when he related that he "had been appointed to what virtually meant Director General of all the Russian Railways, and the Department of State had agreed to it, providing I was willing."[47]

It was out of desperation that the Provisional Government turned control of the whole Russian railway system over to Stevens. The Russians finally gave him this authority because he had become indispensable to the government. After his installation in the Ministry of Ways of Communication, the government dispatched Stevens on an assignment which it considered crucial to its survival. The government delegated to Stevens the urgent task of moving six million bushels of grain it had purchased in western Siberia at the end of the summer to European Russia before the onset of winter. This feat required the implementation of his recommendations across 2,500 miles of railroad that ran between Moscow and Omsk. The Russian officials were pleased with the rapid improvements Stevens had made on the Trans-Siberian railway system, and they were now pinning their hopes on his ability to accomplish similar results on the stretch of the line between Moscow and Omsk in a very short time.[48] Before leaving Petrograd, Stevens emphasized that "this line from Siberia must feed a great part of Russia, and Tereschenko tells me it is the most important problem in Russia."[49] Stevens also attempted to impress Willard with the gravity of the situation when he passed on the government's claim that the movement of grain was not only the most important problem facing Russia but that it was "absolutely vital to [its] existence." He then inquired whether the United States could furnish him with eight more railroad units for this duty.[50]

But by the end of October 1917, Stevens harbored no illusions about his ability to enhance Russia's fighting capacity. He emphasized to Willard that the United States would be making "a very great mistake if it places great dependence upon Russia as a favorable factor in the further prosecution of the war."[51] This comment is important because it indicates that broader policy objectives were at stake in Russia, which transcended the purely strategic question of maintaining an eastern front. It is likely that Stevens viewed the operational capacity of the Russian Army as a moot issue. Yet, it is under those circumstances that his central role in the American struggle against Germany's *Mitteleuropa* economic system becomes more apparent. In the Provisional Government's final days he concentrated his efforts on preventing a collapse that would facilitate Russia's absorption into a German *Mitteleuropa*. Stevens expressed this concern shortly after the Bolshevik Revolution when he wrote Willard that "there is no doubt now that the proper course for the United States and all the Allies is to stand by Russia as long as there is a shadow of hope left, and to throw up our hands now would simply hasten the throwing of Russia into Germany's hands."[52] Faced with this threat, Stevens believed it had become absolutely necessary to move western Siberian grain to European Russia in order to help maintain the army's cohesion and to diffuse social unrest in the cities.

Thus Stevens's final mission for the Provisional Government epitomized America's quest for a liberal international order. In working now merely for the government's survival, he was striving to head off social revolution and an inevitable separate peace with Germany. Stevens considered the Bolshevik movement, or as he caustically referred to it at the time, "the Bolchanks (the unruly element)," as little more than a disintegrative force.[53] He understood that Germany would attempt to use them as pawns.

On October 28 Stevens left Petrograd for Moscow to prepare the way for the Western Siberian grain shipments. There he found eight thousand freight cars loaded with food, ammunition, rifles, clothing, and medical supplies. Some of this freight had been there for as long as two years. Stevens spent nearly a week in Moscow attempting to unclog this bottleneck and to move some of this freight toward the front. He then traveled east along the southern branch of the Trans-Siberian railway as far as Chelyabinsk instructing the divisional officers on how to handle the wheat shipments. Shortly after he returned to Samara on the Volga River, the Bolshevik Revolution erupted. This marked the end of Stevens's efforts to prop up the Provisional Government.[54]

By the end of November, Stevens was so discouraged with the deterioration of conditions in Russia that he threatened to return to America. During this trying period Willard repeatedly urged Stevens to remain at Harbin in Manchuria until George Emerson's contingent of railroad personnel arrived. During December Willard repeatedly tried to encourage Stevens with the hope that the situation would "develop much better than you expect." Willard stressed that "there is great opportunity for most valuable work for you and Emerson in Russia, providing [a] stable government is established and [I] think it would be most unfortunate to abandon that plan as long as there is any hope."[55] This would continue to be the American attitude toward Russia for the next five years. While there was any prospect that stable conditions might be restored in Siberia, American policy favored the retention of American influence on the Trans-Siberian system.

Stevens's spirits improved when Emerson and his men arrived at Vladivostok on December 14. However, with America's Russian policy on indefinite hold, Stevens recommended that he and Emerson's Railway Service Corps await developments in Japan. Willard readily concurred with this advice, believing that stable conditions would be restored in Russia in the near future.[56] A note of confidence reappeared in Stevens's cables during mid-December even as he prepared to leave Vladivostok for Japan.

An important American representative in Russia, F. M. Titus of the American Locomotive Sales Corporation, forcefully argued the merits of retaining the Railway Service Corps in the Russian Far East. Titus was the engineer who was supervising construction of the assembly shops at Vladivostok where the American equipment was being completed. Therefore, his opinions represent quasi-official American sentiment, notwithstanding his particular interest in promoting his company's exports to Russia. His recommendations are also significant in that they reflect basic historical assumptions that informed the approach American businessmen and statesmen took toward the Russian question. Titus stressed that the United States was held in high regard by the "better element" in Russia primarily because "we have pledged our word to help Russia in the rehabilitation of her Railway system."[57] This assistance had engendered feelings of goodwill and friendship toward the United States, which would be of inestimable value after the war when America planned to expand its economic relations with Russia. However, Titus now likened Russia "to a great strong man who is ill." Thus, after promising assistance to Russia as a "friend," the United States could not abandon her to "hoodlums" (the Bolsheviks) without betraying her trust. He reiterated with particular emphasis:

> You realize that we will want Russia's friendship after the war is ended. We want her trade. We may want concessions for the development for her, of her vast deposits of coal and mineral wealth. In self defense we need to place her railways in a condition such as will enable her (and us) to handle efficiently the trade and commerce developed. If we abandon her now in her hour of need, can we hope to compete with another and gain that to which we have so long been looking forward, and for which we have been making preparation.[58]

Titus contended that the United States should assume a trusteeship over Russia, because centuries of autocratic rule had eroded the population's initiative. But he reasoned that "a comparably small force of Americans to form a nucleus would very quickly find itself surrounded by a vast number of the better class of Russians who, recognizing in them a strong 'leader with the initiative' to do things, would be glad to give their services, and their lives if need be, to again bring about order."[59] Emerson's railway personnel could play a strategic role in the reconstruction of Russian society if they were entrenched on the main communication artery.

Titus suggested that America's more recent experiments with trusteeship over its insular dependencies offered a precedent for a possible course of action in Russia. While he did not advocate armed intervention in Russia, Titus did think "that were the Allies to get together, and place in Petrograd today an 'International Control' based upon the principle of our 'Control' over Cuba and the Philippines, that it would accomplish quick and marvelous results."[60]

Ambassador Francis, Willard, and the State Department agreed that retention of the Railway Service Corps in Russia was of vital importance to future Russian-American relations. Francis articulated the enlightened self-interest that motivated American policy when he maintained that the corps served humanitarian purposes, such as famine relief, as well as the commercial interests of the United States. He believed the "moral effect" to be derived by the corps' humanitarian assistance would be "immense."[61] Thus, the American commitment to the Trans-Siberian railway system for the next five years was based on the objective of cultivating a community of interest between the United States and Russia, not merely assessments of short-term commercial gain.

Between March and November 1917, the Stevens Commission was at the service of the progressive political forces represented in the Provisional Government. After the Bolshevik Revolution, the efforts of Stevens and the Railway Service Corps to rehabilitate the Trans-Siberian railway system would continue to underpin America's Russian policy. Yet their trusteeship over the Trans-Siberian railway would now take on even more critical importance. This system became the artery through which the United States attempted to foster reconstruction of Russia's civil society. Economic assistance for progressive social groups, such as the cooperative societies and zemstvos, was necessary to contain social chaos, restore productive activity, and to forestall German economic designs in Russia.

3

❧

The Specter of a Divided World:
The Sources and Conduct
of American Economic
Warfare Against Germany,
January–August 1918

In the year between the Bolshevik Revolution and the Armistice in November 1918, the Wilson administration had to confront the threat of German economic domination of Russia. American statesmen believed the Bolsheviks' seizure of power was a high-water mark in the revolutionary cycle, a phase that would eventually be succeeded by the reestablishment of social stability, in a pattern similar to preceding European revolutions. Between the October Revolution and the Armistice, the Wilson administration feared the Bolsheviks would merely pave the way for Germany's aims in Russia as the population sought liberation from revolutionary extremism. Therefore, prior to 1920, American policymakers usually referred to the Bolshevik regime in terms that anticipated its eventual demise and the restoration of "order."

In the meantime, American statesmen were deeply concerned with the ramifications of Russia's withdrawal from the war and the Bolsheviks' peace negotiations with Imperial Germany. After its military collapse, Russia's immense material resources assumed a potentially decisive role for Germany's military effort and for its postwar ambition to create its own continental system. This eventuality would hold ominous implications for the Open Door. If Germany managed to harness Russian resources to its military effort on the western front, the scales could be tipped decisively in favor of Germany. A German victory on the continent would, in turn, fundamentally alter the pattern of global economic development. German domination of European

Russian and western Siberian resources would place the German Empire on an equal footing with continental America. In this event, a German-dominated *Mitteleuropa* would constitute an enormous bargaining chip in future trade negotiations with the United States.

During the spring of 1918, American policymakers feared that German domination of the Russian political economy might even act as a catalyst for the formation of new imperial blocs. For instance, they were deeply concerned over the possibility that Germany and Japan could reach an agreement over the division of the Russian Empire. This would effectively divide the world into British, German, and Japanese empires, restricting America to the Western Hemisphere.[1] Therefore, in the spring of 1918, with the outcome of the war still in doubt, Germany's economic initiatives in Russia became a serious cause for concern among American policymakers.

Reliable diplomatic and private sources enabled American policymakers to monitor German economic strategy in Russia during 1918. American businessmen with interests in Russia warned American officials about the scope of Germany's activities in Russia and neighboring countries. For instance, by mid-January 1918, William F. Sands, an officer of the American International Corporation, had alerted the State Department to the formidable diplomatic apparatus Germany had assembled in Stockholm, Sweden. This organization included financial, commercial, and political experts, together with press agents who channeled German influence into Russia.[2]

Germany's ambitions in Russia were the subject of a memo from Basil Miles, head of the State Department's recently created Russian section, to Lansing on January 4, 1918. Miles informed Lansing that Baron Wilhelm von Mirbach was heading a diplomatic mission to Russia. Mirbach's mission attracted Allied attention due to his success as an agent of German propaganda. However, Miles emphasized a concern that transcended immediate diplomatic and military aspects of the mission when he warned, "It is likely that he [Mirbach] will not only conduct a propaganda [campaign] but will also buy Russian Roubles which he will invest in Russian factories and other industrial enterprises and thus inaugurate the industrial penetration of Russia by Germany. His presence in Russia is thus a dangerous menace."[3] A telegram from acting Secretary of State Frank Polk to Ambassador Francis on January 12, 1918, which transmitted the substance of Miles's memo, indicated that Germany's threat to the Open Door in Russia underlay all policy questions associated with revolutionary Russia and its withdrawal from the war. Polk instructed Francis that "this situation requires the coordination of all American activities in Russia with which you are in touch. As made clear in the president's speech, the purpose of the United States is to see to it that the

Russian people secure freedom to work out their own political development, free from the domination of hostile interests."[4] Hence, Allied economic warfare against German purchasing activities during the summer was part of an effort to block Germany's long-range objectives in Russia.

Speculation in the ruble was the means by which Germany attempted to establish its permanent domination over the Russian economy. German interests were purchasing large sums of imperial ruble issues, which maintained their value, in contrast to currency printed after the March Revolution, which had depreciated precipitously because of over-printing. In the short term, Germany hoped to capitalize on Russian instability by inducing Russian investors to sell their property for stable monetary assets. However, Germany's manipulation of Russian currency had even more far-reaching implications. Germany expected that the Bolshevik regime would eventually collapse, putting German military power in a position to install a client regime as it had in the Ukraine. As a successor to the czarist legacy, this regime could be expected to honor its predecessor's financial obligations—a prerequisite being the reinstatement of imperial currency as the accepted monetary standard. These imperial rubles were redeemable in gold, or, alternatively, they could represent a lien upon all the natural resources of the Russian state.[5] Hypothetically, as the guarantor of a restored Russian bourgeois government, Germany would be in a position to assert such a claim on Russian resources.

German interests secretly engaged in large-scale purchases of imperial rubles through financial intermediaries in Switzerland, Sweden, and Denmark. These purchases were of such importance to the German clients that they directed their agents to buy rubles at rates that exceeded the market rate. In February 1918, a Swiss banker who was engaged in the purchase of rubles for German clients told an American consul at Bern that German purchasers intended "to use this currency in buying Russian factories and other business establishment[s] as soon as a degree of tranquillity has been restored to Russia, which the purchasers expect to occur through German permanent occupation of parts of that country."[6]

The pace of German economic penetration quickened after the Brest-Litovsk Treaty of March 3, 1918. Subsequent to the treaty and until the Armistice, the State Department received a steady flow of reliable information regarding German financial activities from experienced diplomatic personnel. Brest-Litovsk gave Germany economic privileges that aided its wartime effort and guaranteed its hold over crucial elements of the Russian economy. Consul General Maddin Summers at Moscow noted the momentum Brest-Litovsk afforded these activities when he reported on May 1 of "German agents taking advantage of depreciation of exchange, low prices, and guarantees [of the] peace treaty [to] purchase controlling interests, factories, banks, and other business enterprises also land and government securities."[7]

Events in Russia dismayed American statesmen during the spring of 1918 as Germany's victory in the East raised the specter of a decisive defeat for the Open Door on a global scale. Amid contradictory reports concerning Soviet resistance to Germany's onerous peace terms, the ramifications of Russia's collapse were not lost on American policymakers. A key architect of Russian and Far Eastern policy at the State Department, Third Assistant Secretary Breckinridge Long, exhibited Washington's pessimistic mood in an extensive diary entry on February 25, when he wrote: "This is blue Monday in the Allies' camp. . . . The consensus of Russian opinion seems to be resignation to domination by Germany instead of, and as preferable to, domination by Bolsheviki. This is the denouement of the Russo-German drama. It is the total collapse of Russia."[8] Long, a prominent Missouri Democrat, was also a staunch supporter of the Open Door. He now feared that Russia's defeat had triggered a new round in the redivision of the world into spheres of influence, this time under the auspices of Germany and Japan. Long anticipated a likely scenario, noting:

> It opens the way to Persia, to Afganistan, even to India, for German influence and trade. It makes Mesopotamia an unenviable spot to be in and probably untenable. . . . In the Far East it means the increased aggression of Japan and the probable annexation of Siberia—or Eastern Siberia—by her and, unless we can keep China in control of that part of the Trans-Siberian which crosses Chinese territory, the annexation of Northern China.[9]

Long's conclusion is a revealing glimpse at the crucial role American statesmen envisioned for Siberia in the postwar Open Door system and the crisis Germany's victory posed for America's system. He lamented: "The real danger lies in the possible coalition of Japan with Germany under an agreement for well-defined spheres and a sharp line of difference between the territories of each. The poor people of Siberia! They hate Germany and Japan equally but cannot even choose between them."[10] The difficulties associated with extending economic assistance to Siberia during 1918 reflected the alternative dangers of German economic penetration and Japanese intervention. After December 1917, Britain, France, Japan, and Italy vigorously lobbied for American approval of Japanese intervention in Siberia to reestablish an eastern front against Germany. Wilson and Lansing resisted strident Allied appeals for military intervention until July 1918, but were perplexed by the issue throughout the spring and summer. Long commented in his diary that Lansing considered the Siberian question the "most complicated problem he has ever had. Biggest problem and most complicated."[11]

Siberian intervention presented a dilemma for the Wilson administration because the fate of the Open Door hung in the balance. At the end of February, Wilson temporarily wavered on the question of intervention as a result of British and French pressure for a unilateral Japanese intervention that would occupy the Trans-Siberian railway as far west as the Urals. By March 1, Wilson directed the State Department to inform the British, French, and Italian embassies that the United States would not object if the Entente powers requested Japan to intervene in Siberia.

Meanwhile, having learned of this, the provisional Russian government embassy lobbied strenuously against this course with State Department officials. On March 2, John Sukin of the Provisional Government embassy told Long that a unilateral Japanese intervention in Siberia would be unfavorably received in Russia because of the population's antipathy to Japan. Such a move would only assist Germany's efforts to consolidate its economic and political hold over Russia. Sukin warned Long that Germany could derive a considerable political victory in Russia, and the Allied cause be dealt a severe blow if Germany were allowed to pose as Russia's liberator from Japanese aggression as well as from bolshevism. He argued that, while the Russian propertied classes still opposed Germany, they could be "seduced" into accepting German overlordship if stability were restored and economic development resumed.

In order to counteract this sophisticated "diplomatic endeavor to influence and control the social, economic, and industrial elements of the country," Sukin and Ambassador Boris Bakhmetev advocated a political-military expedition that would subordinate Japan's military activities to inter-Allied supervision. In conjunction with the military expedition, they also recommended a political base be established in western Siberia to combat Germany's extensive diplomatic and economic penetration of European Russia.[12] Following this conversation with Sukin, Long immediately drafted a memorandum advocating Allied intervention in Siberia under America's political and economic leadership, which he sent directly to President Wilson.[13]

On March 3, Edward House related to Wilson the view of Senator Elihu Root that "even if Japan should announce her purpose to retire when the war was over, or at the mandate of the peace conference, the racial dislike which the Russians have for the Japanese would throw Russia into the arms of Germany." House added that Russian ambassador Boris Bakhmetev held a similar opinion. If the president acquiesced in a Japanese intervention, House feared the United States "would likely lose that fine moral position you have given the Entente cause. The whole structure which you have built up so carefully may be destroyed overnight, and our position will be no better than that of the Germans." As a result of these protestations, Wilson reversed his position on March 5.[14]

The serious implications House warned of in his letter to Wilson were spelled out in an incisive memorandum by William Bullitt of the State Department, which Assistant Counselor Gordon Auchincloss passed on to the president. Bullitt persuasively argued that America would compromise its "moral position" in the war unless it publicly protested against a Japanese intervention in Siberia. Moreover, in challenging his superiors to reflect on their reasons for assenting to a Japanese intervention, Bullitt demonstrated the deep concern that existed within the American policymaking establishment over a redivision of the Eurasian continent between Germany and Japan. The administration was taking this step out of the widely shared belief that if the United States continued to oppose Japan, "she will switch to the side of Germany." American policymakers feared that Japan's desire to annex eastern Siberia was so strong that if the Allies did not consent to this ambition, it would arrive at a modus vivendi with Germany. In other words, American statesmen had to squarely face the fact that "our fear that Japan may join Germany is, therefore, admission that desire to annex eastern Siberia is at the bottom of Japan's proposed invasion." If the United States hoped to cultivate a "new world order," Japan would have to be kept out of Siberia, because it constituted "an autocratic imperialistic state in which the forces of liberalism and decency are far weaker than even in Germany."

Bullitt boldly asserted that, if the United States remained true to its moral principles, it would persevere under even the worst scenarios, because it could then harness progressive world opinion, which he conceived as a powerful trump card for Wilson. He predicted that, if the United States publicly opposed Japan, it would lack the support of the British and French governments but would gain the support of the Labor and Liberal parties in Britain, the Socialist party in France, and the mass popular base these political movements represented. If, on the one hand, Japan seized eastern Siberia in disregard of the president's wishes, it would have the support of the British and French governments, but these pro-interventionist governments would most likely fall and be replaced by progressive parties opposed to intervention. On the other hand, if Japan entered into an alliance with Germany, the conflict would then be clearly transformed into a battle between autocracy and democracy. In the case of such an unambiguous struggle for a "new world order," the emerging democratic forces in Germany and Austria-Hungary would be strengthened.

Alternatively, if Wilson did not adhere to his liberal principles, the United States's moral position would be reduced to that of Germany's, with attendant consequences. Similar to the essential point House emphasized in his note to Wilson on March 3, Bullitt astutely deduced that "If the United States assents to the Imperial Japanese army invading territory controlled by the Bolsheviki, for the ostensible purpose of restoring order, the United States cannot object to the Imperial German army invading territory controlled by the Bolsheviki for the ostensible purpose of restoring order."[15]

Two weeks later Robert Lansing summarized the administration's position on Japanese intervention in Siberia. First, he noted the unfavorable "moral" effect this course of action would have on Siberia. The various Siberian factions would likely unite against both Japan and its allies. Lansing then reiterated the danger of pushing the Russian population into Germany's arms "as the sole hope of resisting the 'Yellow Peril.'" Second, Lansing fundamentally questioned the merits of a military expedition. Japanese forces were not needed to prevent the movement of the accumulated military supplies at Vladivostok, because conditions along the Trans-Siberian limited freight movement. Finally, insurmountable logistical problems confronted any sizable movement of Japanese troops to western Siberia where, the Allies argued, they would attempt to interdict resources Germany was trying to purchase.

President Wilson thoroughly agreed with Lansing's view, while Long and Miles continued to favor military intervention under the auspices of American political leadership.[16] Wilson and Lansing were thus at odds with State Department officials like Long and Miles over the issue of Japanese intervention in Siberia. Nevertheless, the urgency of these debates illustrate the importance of Siberia to American statesmen. Both positions were essentially concerned with maintaining the Open Door in Siberia against both Germany and Japan.

Difficult decisions loomed on the horizon for the Wilson administration as spring approached. Although Wilson and Lansing continued to resist Allied pressure for military intervention, they recognized the likelihood of a unilateral Japanese intervention in the near future, particularly after Japan concluded a military agreement with China on May 16. Meanwhile, some type of assistance for the Russian people was needed to reverse German inroads. Wilson thus had to formulate a policy for combating Germany's determined effort to dominate Russia's economy without inadvertently sacrificing eastern Siberia and Manchuria to Japan's predatory designs.

The earliest American proposals to extend reconstruction assistance to Russia date from the beginning of 1918 and were originally conceived as a form of economic warfare against German commercial penetration. Between the spring and mid-summer of 1918, the Wilson administration expanded the consular service in Russia and developed ties with Russian cooperative societies through the inter-Allied purchasing company, Tovaro-Obmien (or Goods Exchange). Tovaro-Obmien extended credit to cooperative societies to reestablish normal commercial exchange in necessities and to deprive Germany of strategic commodities. This network laid the foundation for countering Germany's deep inroads in the Russian economy and for engaging in the process of reconstruction as domestic conditions permitted.

The Tovaro-Obmien purchasing company was established at a meeting of Allied military representatives on December 24, 1917. At this meeting, the military representatives agreed to turn operation of the Tovaro-Obmien over to Allied businessmen. This decision was made on grounds that private businessmen were the most familiar with commercial conditions, such as the location of goods and the means by which they could be obtained. Also, the Allied military representatives did not want to be placed in a position of responsibility for these activities if the German and Soviet governments concluded a peace treaty. The directors of the firm were prominent Allied businessmen in Russia: Pierre Darcy of France; Arthur G. Marshall of Great Britain; and R. R. Stevens of the United States, who was manager of the National City Bank's Petrograd branch.[17] Near the end of January 1918, Gen. William V. Judson, the American military attaché in Petrograd, requested $1 million as the U.S. contribution to the Tovaro-Obmien's purchase of strategic commodities in Russia.[18] These commodities consisted of copper, manganese ore, platinum, hides, oils, and fats—which were available on the open market—as well as military supplies and war matériels stockpiled in Vladivostok, Archangel, Petrograd, and at munition plants spread around the country. After gaining Wilson's approval, Lansing informed Ambassador Francis on February 14 that the U.S. government had granted the military attaché $1 million to collaborate with the British and French military missions in acquiring supplies in Russia.[19] This enterprise, however, did not become active until late April 1918, due to the confused situation in Russia during the winter and the threat of a German advance on Petrograd.

Meanwhile, Washington was beginning to show interest in the Russian cooperative societies as potential agents of a liberal reconstruction program. In late February 1918, a delegation representing Russia's cooperative societies visited the United States for the purpose of acquiring desperately needed agricultural machinery for future sowings. Basil Miles encouraged

International Harvester officials to contact these representatives and apparently suggested that the corporation furnish new credit to the cooperatives to finance purchases of agricultural machinery.[20]

At a City Club of Chicago luncheon on February 18, 1918, International Harvester officials met with George Lomonosov, a representative of the Kerensky government, Constantine Fabian, representing both the All-Russian Peasant Council and the Moscow District Supply Committee, and Leonidas Vtorov of the All-Russian Railway Employees Union. Speaking first, Lomonosov stressed Russia's desperate condition and tried to allay American reservations about extending further economic assistance to Russia. He impressed upon his American audience the danger of letting the Russian population turn to Germany for support if America failed to act. Lomonosov attempted to assuage American skepticism with regard to extending assistance by endorsing the cooperative societies as reliable beneficiaries of American aid. He emphasized that cooperative societies were institutions established voluntarily by peasants and workers and were not affiliated with any political party. Moreover, he continued, the provision of economic assistance by America would fulfill Wilson's repeated pledge to assist the Russian people without legitimizing Bolshevik rule. Addressing the possibility of American goods falling into German hands, Lomonosov merely forewarned his audience that a commitment by America to Russia at that time would avert huge expenditures in the future if Russia were integrated into a German continental system.[21]

Fabian and Vtorov spoke of the prominent role their organizations played in providing necessities to their members. Fabian explained that the Moscow District Supply Committee facilitated the exchange of agricultural and manufactured goods for roughly 50 million people in central Russia. The committee held about 500 million rubles in deposits from its local branches and operated factories, workshops, and grain mills. Its agents traveled throughout the region to determine the needs of the people and reported their requirements to Moscow. Fabian underscored the fact that grain could be obtained from the peasantry only in exchange for manufactured goods—not rubles. American manufactures distributed through his committee would restore normal commercial relations between rural and urban areas and alleviate hunger in the cities.[22]

Vtorov, from the Railway Employees Union, followed the same approach with the Harvester officials as his colleagues by working on the Americans' fear of losing the Ukrainian market to German manufacturers. Vtorov called attention to his organization's capital of 200 million rubles and its extensive distributive machinery to demonstrate its reliability as a supplier for its membership. This organization had the ability to control Russia's railroad system, and Vtorov offered its cooperation to America as a competitive advantage against rival German exporters.[23]

In a discussion after the meeting, the Russian representatives were questioned further about the relationship of their organization to the Bolshevik regime. All three Russians contended that these societies were strictly economic organizations that eschewed politics. Because of the cooperatives' importance, these representatives did not believe the Bolsheviks would interfere with their activities.

Cyrus McCormick held an interview with Fabian and Vtorov the next morning in his office at which Harvester officials A. E. McKinstry, George W. Koenig, and G. A. Ranney were present. Fabian and Vtorov requested credit for the purchase of shoes, clothing, and agricultural machinery for their members and locomotives for the railroads. The Russians were willing to help secure additional railroad transportation and material for International Harvester's manufacturing plant at Lubertzy, east of Moscow, but they were primarily interested in gaining extensive new credits to purchase more agricultural machinery in the United States. Fabian, however, admitted that the Moscow Committee could pay only in rubles for these imports. Harvester officials then patiently explained that their company already held liquid assets of about 100 million rubles in Russia, which were effectively frozen under the circumstances. International Harvester would not increase its investment in Russia but would only export machinery for dollars paid in the United States. In further discussion, the Russians spoke of the Germans accepting rubles in payment for manufactured goods with the prospect of using this currency to buy interests in Russian companies.[24]

The Harvester officials promised to continue supplying Russia's needs through the company's branch manufacturing plant at Lubertzy. The company had just concluded an agreement with the Narodny Bank to handle Lubertzy's entire output for the coming year, which would be sold in Russia for rubles to the extent that conditions permitted. Under their contract of February 21, 1918, International Harvester agreed to manufacture 7,682 mowers, 1,530 binders, 3,077 *lobogreikas,* and 11,902 reapers for the 1918 harvest season on the basis of cost plus 10 percent.[25]

Because of the difficulties involved in procuring the necessary production materials, railroad transportation, and the cash to pay wages and salaries at the plant, the company depended heavily on the Narodny Bank's extensive marketing and credit connections in order to continue production. By late August 1918, Harvester officials who had just left Lubertzy reported that this arrangement with the Narodny Bank had worked well up to that point, the company having collected over 22 million rubles for completed orders. Through the help of the bank, the Lubertzy plant had achieved considerable success in obtaining materials and in receiving payment from the bank, via its constituent credit societies.[26]

While the risks in Russia limited private initiatives, Washington was very interested in the proposals of the cooperative societies. On February 23, Basil Miles informed Frank Polk that he was preparing a memo regarding the financing of supplies for the railway unions and cooperative societies, adding that President Wilson wanted to hear their "proposition."[27]

The poised and urbane Miles had served as the secretary of the Root mission in the summer of 1917. A descendant of early New England settlers, Miles had characteristic energy and application that would be much in evidence during the discussions concerning economic assistance for Russia, which proceeded throughout 1918. He drafted a steady volume of memoranda which urged the administration to provide an extensive amount of financial assistance to Russia for the purpose of hindering the spread of German influence and to help begin the reconstruction process. In his memo of March 4, Miles addressed the serious danger posed by German domination over the Ukraine. Germany was threatening not only to tap the resources of the Ukraine for her "immediate needs," but also, "if she is left undisturbed in her present program, then complete domination is the natural result."[28] Miles thus perceived a continuity between Germany's wartime purchasing activities and its long-term quest for economic hegemony in Russia. German purchasing commissions were ubiquitous agents of this process as they attempted to forge links with all sectors of Russia's economy.

In view of this threat, Miles believed America could not await the reestablishment of a central government in Russia, since there was little prospect of a viable regime emerging in the near future. To check German ambitions, he proposed that America funnel assistance to Russia's approximately thirty thousand credit societies—comprising roughly twenty million members whose activities were coordinated by the Narodny Bank. Miles presumably conferred State Department approval on the cooperatives when he acknowledged their claims of political autonomy. Moreover, the cooperatives' wide range of productive and marketing activities enhanced their value as agents of reconstruction. Since the railroads were a strategic factor in this program, the cooperation of the Railway Employees Union had to be ensured by providing assistance to its members.

Miles recommended that a Russian commission be formed to coordinate operations between the credit societies and the railway union. An American government agency operating in Washington would coordinate supply operations with the Russian commission and function as a clearinghouse for Russia's requirements by evaluating its need for necessities such as clothing, medical supplies, shoes, and hardware, as well as agricultural machinery, railroad equipment and supplies, and electrical equipment and appliances. The program was designed to supply badly needed manufactured products to the extent that transportation conditions permitted. It would also facilitate the exportation of Russian products, if possible, to accumulate credits in favor of Russian exporters.

Miles contended that a program of this scope could not be financed by the private sector but could succeed only with "the liberal support of our government." The results of a successfully executed program "should not only set up strong competition to Germany in Southern Russia, but should build a relation with Entire Russia which would not only free her from German commercial domination but also maintain a field for future relations as well." In conclusion, he warned that, although America could do the most to assist Russia, if it failed to do so, "Russia will turn to Germany for what she can get parceled [sic] out to her."[29] Miles's plan was ultimately designed to prevent Germany from gaining control of Russia's economy, and he hoped to achieve this goal indirectly by enhancing American credibility with the Russian population through the provision of commercial assistance, thereby contrasting American motives with Germany's exploitative practices. His plan for coordinating commercial assistance through the Russian cooperative societies clearly foreshadowed the War Trade Board's Russian Bureau of the fall of 1918.

At a meeting in Elihu Root's apartment in New York City on March 9, Basil Miles briefed the members of the Root mission to Russia on the status of America's policy toward Russia. Cyrus McCormick's rough notes indicate that Miles's proposal had been adopted as the basis for policy discussions in Washington. Root's visitors were also told that Alonzo E. Taylor had begun to work on the Russian situation. Taylor had assisted Herbert Hoover on the Belgium Relief Commission and was now called on by the War Trade Board to devise a plan for undertaking economic warfare against Germany in Russia.

However, the danger of Japanese military aggression in Siberia stood in the way of any relief initiatives. McCormick recorded that, "Jap[anese] sit[uation] has temp[orarily] upset this. Our Gov't sitting still. Jap[an] going in and will lead to complications."[30] Therefore, until the perils associated with Japanese intervention were mitigated, American assistance would be restricted to supporting purchasing operations by the cooperative societies within Russia that the Tovaro-Obmien had been organized to conduct. Thus, when McCormick noted a comment by Frank Polk that the "State Dep't wants to sit quiet temporarily feeling that G[ermany] may begin ruthless actions," it was perhaps trying to make a virtue of a necessity.[31] Polk's comment also implies the State Department may have been biding its time, anticipating heightened social discontent against German requisitioning practices in the Ukraine. The critical shortage of manufactured goods in the Ukraine, now exacerbated by German exploitation, would tend to prepare an even more favorable reception for American commercial influence in the region.

Despite the restraints placed on American policy because of the ominous presence of Japan, in late March the first steps were taken for waging economic warfare against Germany in Russia. At this time, a State Department group—which included Miles, the trade adviser Julius Lay, Assistant Secretary E. T. Williams, and Consular Service Chief Wilbur J. Carr—was evaluating a report by Dr. Alonzo E. Taylor of the War Trade Board.[32] Taylor suggested two different strategies for obstructing German purchases in Russia. First, the United States could alter its trade agreements with the neutral countries of northern Europe and encourage them to shift their food purchases from America to Russia. In exchange for food, these neutral countries would supply Russia with badly needed manufactured goods and give added competition to German producers in the Russian market. Second, America could also endeavor to trade manufactured goods for Russian supplies from the east through Siberia in cooperation with the Allies. In either case, the objective was to compete with Germany over the exchange of manufactured goods for Russian food and primary products in order "to force the mark upon the open exchange mart of the world, which cannot have any other effect than to lower its value." Miles also emphasized that it would be important to "bring the mark into foreign exchange especially in Russia."[33] By forcing Germany to spend marks for its purchases in Russia, the rate of exchange would worsen for Germany and thus reduce its ability to obtain precious commodities.

In commenting on this plan, Miles particularly recommended that certain commodities essential to Germany's war effort be engrossed, such as western Siberia's surplus grain and dairy products, together with free supplies of copper, platinum, and manganese. He also suggested that these goods could simply be stored or moved to safe places if their exportation was impossible.

Miles also devoted much attention to the necessity of establishing an infrastructure for rendering assistance to Siberia at a later period. First, the United States would endeavor to restore normal transportation along the Trans-Siberian Railroad by increasing John Stevens's managerial authority and by distributing the recently arrived Russian Railway Service Corps across the line's vast distances to the borders of European Russia. Second, more consular representatives would be required to assist the ambassador's staff "in political, economic, industrial, and financial matters" associated with the emerging American program.[34] From the end of January, Miles had been discussing the need for expanding America's consular network with Consular Chief Wilbur Carr.[35] By late March, vice consuls were established at Chita, Krasnoyarsk, Tomsk, Novonikolaevsk, Omsk, Ekaterinburg, and Samara, and there was another consul general at Irkutsk.[36] Consul General Summers was also authorized to employ six more National City Bank employees and as many International Harvester employees as possible.

These representatives were instructed to contact leaders from the various political factions such as the former Provisional Government, the Constituent Assembly, and the Siberian Conference, together with the cooperative societies, railway unions, zemstvos, and municipalities.[37] The American military mission was responsible for establishing liaisons with the different military contingents—particularly the Czech Army Corps, but also Generals Alexiev, Kornilov, and even the Cossack leader G. M. Semenov. The State Department did not intend to compromise American neutrality toward the rival political factions but to "provide the skeleton of an organization which could be rapidly expanded and which would be of definite value in the meanwhile."[38] Implicit in this comment is the American assumption that Bolshevik fortunes would eventually wane. Implicit also is a desire to strategically position the United States to assist the reconstruction phase. At that time, America's presence in Siberia could also play a role in nurturing a constitutional political order by encouraging cooperation between anti-Bolshevik forces.

In late March Miles anticipated that it would take some time for the United States to furnish Russia with commercial assistance. During this period the State Department could devote its attention to building an infrastructure for supplying commercial assistance in the future when reconstruction measures could proceed. Meanwhile, as the supplementary consular officers gradually took up their positions at commercial centers along the Trans-Siberian Railroad, the Tovaro-Obmien purchasing organization was prepared to begin operations in European Russia.

Miles's deliberations also shed light on the delay involved in commencing commercial assistance as well as the apparent paralysis that afflicted the Wilson administration's Russian policy throughout the summer of 1918. He assumed little or no shipping would be available until the fall because of America's commitment to the critical military effort on the western front. Furthermore, none of the initiatives proposed in Taylor's report or in the State Department's discussions would be threatened by a unilateral Japanese intervention.[39]

Another factor prevented America from providing commercial assistance in the spring of 1918. While the State Department was discussing Taylor's recommendations, it was becoming clear that the Russian cooperative societies would be unable to guarantee against American shipments falling into German hands. As early as February 25, Lansing had indicated the State Department wanted to continue shipping "non-warlike stores including railway material, agricultural machinery, binder twine, army and civilian shoes, and leather, together with Red Cross supplies" to dispel the Russian people's "impression that they are being abandoned by the Allies or by the United States."[40] Nevertheless, Lansing cautioned that Germany must not be allowed to acquire the goods. A month later when the Moscow Supply Committee was trying to buy a million pairs of shoes, Lansing directed Consul General Summers to cooperate with the committee to ensure the distribution of American goods to the cooperative societies' members in exchange for grain deliveries to the cities.[41]

Summers, however, was very uncertain the Moscow Committee could safely distribute their large order for shoes and consequently recommended that any goods shipped to Russian ports be held indefinitely upon their arrival pending "future developments." He also requested to be consulted before any goods were transported inland.[42] Summers's reservations were heeded at the State Department, which notified Francis on April 22 that none of the five hundred locomotives or ten thousand cars ordered before the collapse of the Provisional Government would be shipped until the department was sure they would not benefit Germany.[43] Four days later, on April 26, Summers was informed that, until he advised the State Department on a procedure for safeguarding the shipment of shoes and other goods to Russia, all export licenses were being suspended.[44]

Two hours after Summers was notified that export licenses to Russia were being halted, Lansing issued another instruction to Ambassador Francis. The State Department now wanted a complete report regarding supplies "especially desired" by Germany, including their quantity, price, location, and the amount that could be exported or relocated beyond German reach.[45] On May 11, Francis reported that available Russian supplies useful to Germany consisted of fats, copper, tin, lead, ferro-alloys, textiles, and rubber. Sunflower seed oil was the most prevalent commodity and was available throughout European Russia. Petrograd and Moscow held large quantities of copper, tin, and raw rubber, together with cotton and wool cloth. Germany wanted a large amount of ferro-alloys, but little was available. Finally, raw cotton could be purchased in Turkestan.

Francis did not know which supplies could be moved to ports or relocated within the country due to the extent of commercial dislocation. Yet, if American goods were bartered for these supplies, he suggested that it would be necessary to guarantee that the imports would not come under German control if they were shipped to Vladivostok or Archangel. Murmansk was not secure, given the possibility of a Finnish attack. As an alternative, the Allies could purchase goods to be resold in Russia.[46]

Miles, in a summary of this report by Francis, suggested the specific form of economic warfare toward which the State Department was leaning. He acknowledged the desirability of bartering American goods for Russian supplies that could not be purchased with cash and the distribution of American imports through the cooperatives to the Russian population. Two American exporters, the R. Martens Company and George C. Sherman, had applied to the State Department for export licenses to barter shoes and clothing to the railway unions in return for calf skins, hides, copper, and platinum, which were commodities sought by the War Industries Board. However, after the suspension of export licenses to Russia in the previous month, these contracts were not going to be consummated in the foreseeable future.

Nevertheless, Miles expressed interest in the ambassador's suggestion that the Allies could purchase Russian supplies and distribute them in areas beyond German influence which "would do much to revive trade in Russia."[47] Consequently, although America would be unable to supply needed manufactured goods in the short term, it could assist the cooperatives' efforts to hasten reconstruction from within Russia and thus strengthen the resistance of the population to German enticements. This conclusion was substantiated by Miles's assertion that "at the beginning no additional tonnage will be essential." The necessary tonnage would be made available by the U.S. Shipping Board "if the plan develops and it is desirable to ship goods to or from Russia."[48]

During mid-May, the Allied Military Missions began to evacuate military supplies from Petrograd under the auspices of the Tovaro-Obmien. Around May 15, the American military attaché Naval Lt. Peter I. Bukowski joined British and French officers at Petrograd to assist the Bolsheviks' evacuation of the vast stores of military supplies concentrated there. Bukowski reported that the Bolsheviks now considered Germany a much greater threat to their existence than the Allies because of Brest-Litovsk's harsh terms and because of the initial successes of Germany's long-awaited spring offensive on the western front. He believed the "interests of the Bolsheviks and the Allies coincided at the time" since the military stores at Petrograd had now become particularly valuable booty.[49] Indeed, German designs on Petrograd's supplies became evident immediately after the Brest-Litovsk Treaty was ratified in mid-March, as "enemy commercial and financial representatives commenced arriving in large numbers. They began at once their intensive activities by purchasing materials and endeavoring to ship them to Germany."[50]

Col. James A. Ruggles, chief of the American military mission, thought Allied assistance with the evacuation was necessary if only to encourage Bolshevik resistance to German pressure. This motive explains Raymond Robins's assignment as liaison with the Bolsheviks during the spring and early summer. Robins's personal rapport with the Bolsheviks notwithstanding, the Wilson administration had no intention of extending any form of recognition to the Soviet government. Rather, Washington purposely used Robins to dangle faint prospects of assistance before the Bolsheviks to avert a possible Soviet capitulation to German demands. Accordingly, Bukowski expressed the purely mercenary nature of his relationship with the Bolsheviks when he revealed that the Allied military missions were only "working with the Soviets where [their] aims were coincident with ours, and working against them when our aims differed."[51]

By the end of May, Francis reported from Vologda that good progress had been made in evacuating supplies from Petrograd.[52] When the operation was abandoned in August because of the deterioration in relations between the Allies and Bolsheviks, 170,000 tons of supplies had been evacuated, which represented from 85 to 90 percent of the valuable supplies in Petrograd and neighboring industrial centers. The evacuated material consisted of the following: copper, lead, nickel, and alloys, high-speed instrument steel, ferroalloys, machinery such as telephones and lathes, rubber products, and war matériels including cartridges, naval guns, field guns, and shells.

The shipments evacuated by water arrived at cities along the Volga. Most of the important shipments arrived at their destinations before the Czech Army Corps' uprising of late May, and consequently fell into their hands. The rail shipments, which constituted two-thirds of the tonnage transported, were widely dispersed throughout the eastern part of European Russia, which prohibited Germany from re-collecting them. Bukowski spent just over thirty thousand dollars of the million-dollar appropriation to the Tovaro-Obmien. Nevertheless, the successful evacuation of Petrograd's military supplies spurred the Tovaro-Obmien on to further efforts.[53]

By late May, the Tovaro-Obmien was sufficiently organized to begin work, and Francis accordingly requested additional funds for its operations. On June 13, Lansing authorized Francis to draw an additional $5 million to purchase Russian supplies while stipulating that the organization should cooperate with the consular service and the Allies to prevent these supplies from coming under German or Bolshevik control.[54] From the end of June until August, the Tovaro-Obmien was principally engaged in the purchase of the following commodities: the sunflower seed oil supplies in the northern Caucasus, the large stock of textiles around Moscow, and flax near the German lines in the South.

Consul General Dewitt C. Poole disclosed the organization's strategy for disposing of supplies on July 16. At that time the transportation of goods to Archangel for export was impossible. He informed the State Department that "our plan was rather to break up concentrated stocks and distribute them beyond the power of the Germans to recollect."[55] The Tovaro-Obmien used the prominent Central Union of Consumers' Societies as the purchasing agent since it was "the only element in Russian commercial and credit apparatus which has survived complete destruction." The Allied company extended credit to the financially strapped Central Union which, in turn, undertook the purchase of textiles and sunflower seed oil and supervised their distribution among the population. Poole revealed the motivation behind this strategy when he commented that "such economic warfare is effective, humanitarian and associates us with a powerful permanent democratic force in Russia." Hence, this program contributed to a number of American objectives in Russia, especially to the development of ties with progressive social and economic forces such as the Central Union.[56]

Between June 29 and August 5, disbursements totaling just over $1,775,000 were made from American funds to the Central Union for purchases of sunflower seed oil in the Kuban. Sunflower seed oil was an important commodity, since it was a prime ingredient in the production of soap for the population. The Central Union organized and financed the transportation of the oil to factories in the interior where it was converted into soap for distribution. Darcy, the French representative on the Tovaro-Obmien, reported on June 27 that "the buying of oil is now progressing. The Centrosoyouz appears to be remarkably active."[57] At that time, one contract had already been negotiated to supply the Central Union with 24 million rubles (over $2 million). Now, in view of the apparent success of the program, Darcy recommended that a total of 100 million rubles should be furnished to the Central Union. This request resulted in the conclusion of a second contract for 24 million rubles, which reflected the limits placed on British and American credit. The Tovaro-Obmien was unable to fulfill this second contract because of the difficulty it encountered in obtaining rubles.

Repeated setbacks plagued efforts by the Tovaro-Obmien to finance the Central Union's textile purchases. Despite the nationalization of commerce inaugurated under Soviet rule, the Central Union received a monopoly for distributing textile stocks among the peasantry; the state monopoly could not administer the task. In July, the Tovaro-Obmien was negotiating with the Central Union to help it finance a sale of textiles worth approximately one billion rubles. The plan called for France, Britain, and the United States each to advance 100 million rubles. However, because rubles were difficult to procure, America's share was to be deposited as $10 million in the United States and used as credit for purchasing rice and tea in China, together with American goods. This credit would be repaid in installments of rubles at the rate of ten per one dollar as the Central Union sold its stocks of textiles.[58] In any event, a single credit of $10 million was well in excess of the $6 million appropriation the Wilson administration was able to provide the Tovaro-Obmien.

On July 31, the Tovaro-Obmien agreed to open credit to the Central Union for 50 million rubles. Once again, due to the scarcity of rubles, on August 14 the Central Union agreed to accept the equivalent of two 25-million–ruble advances in the form of deposits at New York City and London totaling $2.5 million and 600,000 pounds respectively.[59] A confused situation arose after Poole drew the $2.5 million draft payable at the National City Bank of New York, because the draft was lost in transit to the United States. It was not until June 1919, when the various legal technicalities involved in duplicating the original draft were resolved, that the credit was finally placed in the account of the Central Union at the National City Bank of New York.[60]

French and American merchants handled flax purchases as agents of the Tovaro-Obmien owing to their experience in the trade. These firms were financed by the Tovaro-Obmien to buy what flax they could with the option of repurchasing any stocks that were exported. French merchants were advanced $106,704, and the American firm of Slav and Joffe received $43,866 for flax purchases.[61]

Drafts for a total of $4,797,500 were drawn by the Tovaro-Obmien against the $6 million appropriation when its operations were discontinued after mid-August. Although this represented a modest sum, all credits that were actually advanced were apparently spent successfully—in spite of the difficult conditions under which the organization worked. Moreover, Consul Frank C. Lee suggested that any assessment of the program had to take into account its psychological effect on German purchasing activities. The organization's purchases were concentrated in areas adjacent to the German-occupied Ukraine, which were being infiltrated by German purchasing commissions. Thus, as Lee pointed out, "The moral effect on German purchasers was also important. The fact that the Allied Governments were back of the Tovaro-Obmien could not long be concealed and finally the business was openly advertised. The Germans, knowing the former strength of the cooperatives, believed that they, backed by enormous Allied loans, were purchasing all available stocks of materials, and consequently their activities were lessened."[62] At the very least then, the Tovaro-Obmien attempted to discourage German purchasing agents, and it may have bid up prices of commodities that Germany was anxious to obtain.

While the scope of American economic warfare against Germany in Russia was restricted to the Tovaro-Obmien during the spring and summer of 1918, the stakes were considered very high. State Department experts viewed Germany's purchasing activities as merely the cutting edge of a concerted effort to gain a preeminent position in Russia's economy. The Wilson administration's limited response to the German threat was a consequence of circumstances that were beyond its control, such as the dangers associated with an intervention by Japan, the lack of available shipping, and the risk that American goods might fall into German or Bolshevik hands. Nevertheless, the State Department had already begun to conceive a program for rendering commercial assistance to Russia, and it had already begun to station the necessary consular personnel in Siberia as part of the infrastructure that would be required to undertake the task. The Wilson administration's effort to cultivate ties with the prominent cooperative societies was a crucial facet of this process. It represented a calculated moral investment in the future of Russo-American relations in that it attempted to develop American prestige among the progressive sectors of Russian society.

4

❦

Between Germany and Japan: Wilson, the Czecho-Slovaks, and the Decision to Intervene, May–July 1918

Between the spring and mid-summer of 1918, the Wilson administration struggled to devise a policy toward Siberia that would reconcile a military intervention with the primary goal of furnishing economic assistance to the region. It was the threat of an expanded German influence in the Russian Empire that ultimately forced Wilson to undertake a limited intervention in support of the Czecho-Slovak legion and to temporarily postpone economic assistance. This interpretation does not discount the genuine humanitarian concern Wilson felt for the welfare of the Czecho-Slovak Corps. More important, this view is entirely consistent with the arguments that have emphasized Wilson's desire to preempt Allied pressure for a large-scale Japanese intervention. However, this analysis goes further to present a comprehensive picture of the dangers that preoccupied the Wilson administration in the summer of 1918.

At this critical phase of the war on the western front, Wilson opposed a Japanese intervention precisely because this step might force crucial segments of the Russian population to accept even closer ties with Germany out of their legitimate concern over Japan's ambitions in the Russian Far East. In other words, the Wilson administration's Siberian policy was essentially motivated by the underlying clash of competing German and American world systems, which had been the catalyst for America's entry into the war. In supporting an intervention on behalf of the Czecho-Slovaks, Wilson believed he had found a strategy that would facilitate the process of reconstruction in Siberia amid the complex challenges America faced in the region: the instability resulting from war and revolution, the menace of bolshevism, the urgent threat posed by German economic influence, and the rival aspirations of Japan, Britain, and France.

American assumptions concerning Siberia's unique social structure hold the key to understanding Wilsonian policy toward Siberia after the Bolshevik Revolution. During this period the views of Paul Reinsch, the American minister to China, were a particularly important influence on the administration's policy, since, as a progressive internationalist and student of Frederick Jackson Turner, his recommendations received special attention at the White House.

In a cable dated May 10, Reinsch proposed the formation of an American-led Allied commission to furnish Siberia with commercial assistance. In his view, American aid would be particularly beneficial since "conditions in Siberia [are] not unlike America therefore we can be most helpful."[1] However, Reinsch emphasized that Allied support should come in the form of economic assistance rather than through a military intervention, and that, "should intervention come first there is danger that it will be understood to be in favor of reaction and capitalism and will alienate the people permanently."[2]

By May, Wilson had decided the only practical means for providing economic assistance to Russia was through a program of barter trade, featuring the exchange of American manufactured goods for Russian raw materials. The consensus of opinion Wilson received advocated some form of barter trade because of the dislocation of normal commercial activity and the consequent collapse of the ruble. During a conversation about the Russian situation at the White House on May 13, Wilson agreed with Cyrus McCormick's view that barter was the only means through which America could "negotiate with the Russian people." Wilson suggested that he would request Secretary of Commerce William C. Redfield to convene a conference of businessmen with experience in Russian affairs to solicit "practical suggestions as to what barter . . . could be undertaken."[3]

While Russia's social and economic instability necessitated an elementary program of barter with Siberia, this context only reinforced Wilson's belief that commerce was an important agent for promoting international harmony. Once, in a speech before the Chicago Commercial Club in 1902 Wilson declared that commerce was the "most statesmanlike occupation" since the trader had to have even a better grasp of social and political conditions on the international level than the statesman. Wilson continued: "Tradesmen have been inside the life of nations the outside of whose policy statesmen have observed, and traders have been able to tell statesmen the things necessary to control a policy, and to dictate it, make it intelligent. It is the trader's business, in short, to know the world. Instinctively, therefore, men who are engaged in commerce feel the pulse of affairs."[4]

Hence, the merchant fostered mutual understanding among societies through intimate contact with, and sympathy for, foreign cultures. This faith in the virtue of commerce explains Wilson's resolve to "negotiate" with the Russian people through the instrumentality of barter. American traders could be counted on to reliably assess the prevailing mood and aspirations of the enigmatic Russian population, as well as their material requirements.

A system of barter between the United States and Russia was therefore uniquely suited to advance Wilson's vigorously liberal moral objectives. First, barter served profoundly humanitarian ends by providing basic manufactured goods to a desperate population. Concurrently, the resumption of simple commercial transactions would begin the process of reconstruction by encouraging self-help initiatives among the population at the local level. Finally, a barter program would demonstrate America's friendly intentions toward Russia and distinguish its motives from the other powers' ambitious financial schemes—difficult to implement under highly unstable conditions, but likely to further erode Russian sovereignty. Barter thus appealed to Wilson as an expedient application of economic policy to the higher purpose of moral statesmanship.

By the end of June 1918, after soliciting advice from organized business groups such as the American-Russian Chamber of Commerce, Wilson decided that commercial assistance would have to be undertaken by the private sector, without government financing. The president evidently rejected a recommendation by Commerce Secretary Redfield for a $100 million government-financed program of commercial assistance for Siberia, because he did not think Congress would appropriate the funds. While he believed that commercial operations could be effectively handled by private interests, he nevertheless thought their activities would have to be supervised by a coordinating commission to prevent exploitation of the Siberian population.[5]

Near the end of May 1918, Reinsch stressed a dimension of the Siberian question that was rapidly becoming a critical factor in American calculations about commercial assistance to the region. He argued that the Allies must take immediate action in Siberia to deny Germany the rich resources of western Siberia. On May 30, he warned that "all sources indicate extreme need for Allied action [in] Siberia. German influence extending eastward while armed prisoners, though strategically unimportant, facilitate pro-German organization. West Siberia[n] source of supplies, is at stake. Positive action is required also in order to prevent Russian moderate elements in despair accepting German influence."[6] This cable stressed two important points that would soon influence Wilson's decision to support a limited intervention. First, Reinsch emphasized that the German prisoners posed a potential danger because they could mediate the extension of German purchasing activities in Siberia. Second, as Germany expanded its economic links with European Russia and Siberia, the propertied classes and moderate political elements would accept German help in their desperate search for an alternative to Bolshevik rule. Eventually, a German-sponsored "Thermidor" would inevitably draw these groups into a close association with the German continental system.

Wilson's views toward the questions of intervention and economic assistance were being shaped by these considerations. On May 16, Reinsch concluded a cable on the Siberian situation with the recommendation that the "situation in Siberia seems more favorable than ever for effective joint action of Allies and American initiative. A commission authorized to command moderate financial support would be able to reconstruct at least Siberia as an Allied factor. Should America remain inactive longer friendly feeling is likely to fail."[7] Wilson thought this suggestion important enough to request Lansing's "comments and judgment" on the matter.

Later, on May 30, in a conversation with the British agent William Wiseman over the question of intervention, Wilson vigorously expressed his objections to Britain's proposals for a Japanese intervention on the grounds that it would push Russia into Germany's hands. Wilson told Wiseman that he thought an advance along the Trans-Siberian Railroad by "a large British-American force" might "have rallied the Russian people to assist in defense of their country." But if the Western allies relied mainly on Japanese military assistance, he believed "we should rally the Russians against us," with the exception of a "small reactionary body who would join anybody to destroy the Bolsheviki." Wiseman off-handedly remarked that in any case the situation could not possibly get worse than it was already. But Wilson "entirely disagreed" with this attitude. On the contrary, he was convinced "We would make it much worse by putting the Germans in a position where they could organize Russia in a national movement against Japan. If that was done he would not be surprised to see Russian soldiers fighting with the Germans on the Western Front." When Wiseman retorted in frustration with the query whether the Allies should simply do nothing, Wilson responded firmly, "No, we must watch the situation carefully and sympathetically, and be ready to move whenever the right time arrived."

Wilson proceeded to explain that he was inclined to send to Siberia and Murmansk a "Civil Commission" consisting of British, French, and American personnel, which would help organize the railroads, food supplies, and a system of barter. While he was aware "it would take a long time before any results could be expected from such a movement," Wilson did leave open the possibility that "if in the meantime we were invited to intervene by any responsible and representative body, we ought to do so."[8]

Wilson's desire to pursue a constructive policy of economic assistance would be hindered throughout the summer by the Allies' persistent efforts to draw him into a large-scale intervention through Siberia. But when the Czecho-Slovak Corps became embroiled in the Russian civil war, Wilson perceived an opportunity to solve his dilemmas in Siberia. Wilson gambled that the popular Czecho-Slovak Corps could at once be used to diffuse Allied pressure for a large-scale intervention, to neutralize German influence in Siberia, and to provide the security for an American-led reconstruction program.

Evidence of German attempts to infiltrate the Siberian economy were filtering through to the State Department by the spring and early summer of 1918. Menacing reports from American foreign service personnel confirmed the presence of German purchasing agents in western Siberia during the spring of 1918. Upon his arrival at the International Harvester Company offices in Omsk on March 9, Commercial Attaché William C. Huntington was alarmed to learn that German influence had penetrated deep into Siberia's interior when he recorded that the "International Harvester officials gave us authentic reports of German agents actively at work taking orders for mowers and insisting not on cash but raw materials in payment!"[9] Huntington was also informed that there were large quantities of grain and dairy products in the area.

In early April, J. Butler Wright, who had been serving as counselor to the American embassy in Petrograd, substantiated the existence of large stores of wheat in western Siberia's Altai district, as he traveled across the Trans-Siberian Railroad during his return to Washington. While noting that the peasants were only willing to barter their wheat for needed supplies he added, "German commercial agents are coverning [sic] the country promising early delivery of such supplies. This region is perilously near the Urals." Finally, Wright warned that "every effort is being made by German agents to secure metals of the Urals principally gold, platinum, regarding the latter of which mine is owned" (presumably by German interests).[10] Near the end of April the American consul in Omsk reported that a German purchasing commission was in the city and buying wheat, potatoes, cotton, wool, flax, and smoked meat for delivery to Germany.[11]

Many American and Allied statesmen believed western Siberia's grain surplus might decide the outcome of the economic warfare against Germany in Russia. In July Consul General Poole explained the potentially decisive role western Siberia's grain could play in guaranteeing Germany's continental conquest. Favorable weather conditions were offsetting reduced sowings in European Russia, presenting the possibility that European Russia would be self-supporting after the 1918 harvest. However, large amounts of European Russian grain were required to feed Germany's population, making this crop insufficient to the combined need of both Germany and Russia. Therefore, the "key to the situation which is in turn the key to German success or failure in Russia, is the stored grain of [the] western section [of] Siberia."[12] Without western Siberia's grain, German requisitioning policies would create food shortages in European Russia and threaten to ignite social unrest against Germany. Civil disorder would then disrupt production needed by Germany to sustain its war effort.

Poole urged an immediate intervention in support of the Czech Army Corps (which had by this time taken control over most of the Trans-Siberian Railroad since their uprising against Bolshevik forces in late May) to reestablish a front running from the Murmansk peninsula south along the Kama and Volga Rivers to the Kuban.[13] Therefore, although the Wilson administration would remain adamant in its rejection of Anglo-French appeals for a Japanese military expedition to interdict supplies around the Urals, Washington was aware of German designs on the region.

But Germany's efforts to extend its influence in the Russian economy were only the first stages of a process through which it hoped to attract the Russian Empire into its continental system. In building its influence in the Russian economy, Germany hoped to attract support from the Russian bourgeoisie, who sought an end to Bolshevik rule. As resentment toward bolshevism intensified, Germany awaited the moment when nationalist and bourgeois elements would favor a German intervention against Lenin's regime. Subsequently, in its role as ultimate guarantor of social stability and of bourgeois rule in Russia, Germany would assume a position of great influence within the empire.

Indeed, by late June 1918, the German minister plenipotentiary Wilhelm Von Mirbach discussed this scenario in a report to German State Secretary Richard von Kuhlmann. Mirbach was confident the Bolsheviks would soon fall and that "we should seek to ensure that we are in a position to fill the vacuum which will result from its disappearance with a regime which would be favorable to OUR designs and interests." But Mirbach did not recommend that Germany support purely monarchist elements, who he considered "too confused and lazy," and who were "fundamentally only interested in winning back their former secure and comfortable living conditions with our help." Instead, in a statement that revealed the sophistication and breadth of Germany's continental ambitions, Mirbach explained that

> The nucleus of which we are thinking should be composed of moderates from the right wing, Octobrists and Kadets (these reaching as far to the left as possible), especially as such a combination would ensure that we had a large percentage of the influential men of the industrial and banking worlds serving our essential economic interests.
>
> This bloc, which is already quite powerful as it stands, could be further strengthened and hardened if we could draw the Siberians into it—though this would indeed be our hardest problem. Then, even further vistas, based on the mineral resources of Siberia, would appear, and, in this connexion, I will just touch on a few wider, almost unlimited possibilities of development which point us to the far and farthest East.[14]

The Wilson administration was closely monitoring Mirbach's activities in Russia. In early June, William Bullitt passed on to Wilson a memorandum from the French Embassy that exhibited the approach Mirbach was taking with certain conservative bourgeois groups in Moscow. The French consul general at Moscow reported, from a source he considered to be reliable, that Mirbach had been attempting to cultivate support from conservative Kadet party elements by asserting that "although Germany had made it a principle not to meddle with Russian domestic affairs, all her sympathies went to the parties of order and industry. If those parties should succeed in setting up a government, he was authorized by Emperor William to announce that if appealed to he could have German troops at Moscow in forty-eight hours.[15]

Mirbach also endeavored to appease the nationalist sentiments of these conservative bourgeois groups by alleging that "Germany would be disposed to revise the Brest Litovsk treaty as she never intended to make that instrument the true foundation of her future economic relations with Russia which she desires, in accordance with her interests and sympathies, to see restored to a normal and prosperous life."[16]

Similar reports reached the State Department from American military intelligence officers stationed in Scandinavia. At Christiania, Norway, U.S. military intelligence learned from a Kadet source that in early May Mirbach had proposed to the Kadet Central Committee in Moscow that Germany would finance its efforts to overthrow the Bolsheviks. On this occasion he even promised that Germany would assist the reunification of the Ukraine with Russia and that it would effect a fair settlement of the disputes between Finland and Russia. The Kadet Central Committee rejected these German offers to reconcile relations between their nations.[17]

Throughout the critical period between May and August 1918, the Kadet party Central Committee staunchly resisted German overtures as it continued to declare its allegiance to the Allied cause. However, some prominent Kadets did waver in their loyalty to the Allies. None other than Pavel Miliukov, perhaps the most prominent Kadet leader, seriously explored the possibility of accepting German help to overthrow the Bolsheviks. Miliukov suddenly shifted his position with regard to Germany after he witnessed the occupation of Rostov by German troops in mid-May 1918. He had remained in the city when the White forces of Kaledin and Kornilov were driven south by Bolshevik forces in March. Miliukov was so impressed with the Germans' ability to maintain order in the areas under their control that he actually entered into negotiations at Kiev between early June and mid-July with German ambassador Baron Philip Mumm and with officers from the general staff, over the possibility that Germany could assist Kadet efforts to overthrow the Bolshevik regime in Russia proper. These negotiations were cut short by the assassination of Mirbach in early July and by the Allies' decision to support the Czecho-Slovak Corps, events that reinforced German resolve to hold the Ukraine and to continue its relationship with the Bolsheviks, who constituted a buffer against the Allied-backed Czecho-Slovaks.[18]

By the beginning of the summer of 1918, the threat of German economic penetration in Siberia gave urgency to the administration's debates over American policy in the region. In particular, memoranda by J. Butler Wright and the War Trade Board demonstrate that the immediate objective of any assistance program would be to counter German efforts to draw Siberia into its economic orbit. Wright's memo carefully outlined the situation and recommended a detailed program for assisting Siberia and Russia that was very similar to what Wilson was contemplating.

The views of the highly respected Wright, who now joined Basil Miles in the State Department's Russian section, undoubtedly received careful attention within the administration in light of his firsthand knowledge of the current conditions in Siberia. From his personal observation of conditions along the Trans-Siberian Railroad during March and April and his extensive contact with reliable official and private sources, Wright believed Siberia was not as "saturated" with German military and economic influence as European Russia. He believed Bolshevik authority was "waning" and the "Red Guards" were "feared and detested throughout the country." Nevertheless, a predominantly military intervention, especially one with "preponderant Japanese participation," would arouse resentment and opposition among the Siberian population and lend credibility to German propaganda. Conversely, a program principally designed to rehabilitate the Trans-Siberian Railroad and to furnish agricultural and economic assistance would be welcomed by the "better peasant classes," the railway workers, the "great Russian Co-operative Societies," and the "better elements."[19]

Wright also pointed out why some form of intervention would necessarily have to accompany a program of economic assistance. He emphasized "that the maintenance, operation and control of the Trans-Siberian Railroad be made the initial and preeminently important step in a program of immediate assistance to Siberia and neutralization of German economic and political endeavor in that region." The Russian Railway Service Corps, which was still awaiting duty at Harbin, should now be utilized to reorganize the whole railroad system and to prepare the way for commercial and humanitarian assistance.[20] However, during their meeting at Harbin in April, John Stevens had insisted to Wright that he "absolutely refused to allow his men to extend their work along the Trans-Siberian without adequate protection."[21] Therefore, Wright estimated that an "Allied Military Police Force" of twenty-five thousand men divided equally into five-thousand-man contingents from the United States, Britain, Japan, France, and China should be organized for the sole purpose of protecting the Railway Service Corps and its auxiliary units.[22]

In Wright's view educational work and reconstructive assistance should follow the extension of the Railway Service Corps' activities. Experts from the Department of Agriculture would disseminate technical knowledge adapted to Siberia's particular conditions. Furthermore, "information and advice regarding our solution of the problem of the disposition of the National Domain—which is the basic consideration in the all important Agrarian Question should also be provided." As in the case of Reinsch, the pervasive frontier "mentalite" figured prominently in Wright's recommendations for Siberia. Educational work and humanitarian efforts by the YMCA and Red Cross would undertake the formidable task of rebuilding Siberia's social infrastructure, including its inadequate educational system, medical, and sanitary facilities.

Wright believed the United States and Russia should develop mutually profitable trade relations either through an American purchase of Russian supplies or through barter. In particular he noted that commercial operations should further the "distribution of agricultural implements, which are sorely needed throughout Russia and small quantities of which the Germans already are endeavoring to tempt the peasants to relinquish their stores of grain." An "Allied Commission or Council" composed of representatives from the five Allied powers would administer these activities, supplemented by a military staff from the Allied Police Force. This commission would operate either by majority vote or delegate its authority to a "Commissioner-in-Chief." Wright thought the Czecho-Slovak troops spread across Siberia could play an integral role in the Allied policing operations.[23]

At the end of May, War Trade Board chairman Vance C. McCormick established a committee within the agency to examine methods for encouraging the exchange of goods between Russia and America and for maintaining the economic blockade against Germany in Russia.[24] The committee, composed of Thomas L. Chadbourne, Clarence M. Woolley, and John Foster Dulles, based their report of June 5 on discussions with individuals who had recently returned from Russia, including J. Butler Wright.

These sources all agreed certain general conditions had to be taken into account in planning a program of economic assistance. First, the complete breakdown of transportation had made it impossible to distribute food and materials in many areas. Second, the collapse of the ruble meant the population, and particularly the peasantry, was no longer willing to exchange commodities for currency. Therefore, since the population lacked basic manufactured goods such as boots, shoes, socks, cotton goods, nails, corrugated iron, railway materials, agricultural machinery, and seed grain, these types of products could be offered to the Russians in exchange for their primary commodities. Yet, in contrast with the State Department's recommendations, this committee urged that America should only exchange goods on a nonremunerative basis to gain the Russian peoples' trust and to disassociate its motives from Britain, France, and Japan. Since President Wilson had always expressed America's goodwill toward Russia, the committee believed any offer of economic assistance would be received with favor by the Soviet government. Although the Wilson administration clearly was not inclined to render assistance to the embattled Soviet regime, the committee's essential point concerning the Russians' mistrust of Allied motives would not be lost on the administration.

Prompt steps were also necessary to counter Germany's strategy of supporting conservative client governments, such as the Ukraine and Finland, as alternatives to Bolshevik rule. Germany was presently courting the conservative bourgeois elements in Soviet-controlled Great Russia with the hope these groups would eventually prefer German hegemony to Bolshevik rule. Therefore, while the War Trade Board was immediately concerned with the humanitarian and strategic angles of the Russian question, it was because these factors were at the forefront in the struggle "to prevent the enemy from securing permanent hold upon Russian economic resources and commercial opportunities," and "to prevent Russian acceptance of German political leadership."[25]

To accomplish these objectives the War Trade Board committee recommended sending an industrial mission to Russia under the direction of a Russian commissioner who would be responsible for coordinating its activities from Washington. The mission's work was to be performed by specialized departments dealing with commercial transactions, financial matters, and transportation. After arriving at Vladivostok, the mission would begin to advance westward with a local chairman selected from among the body of experts. As the mission advanced along the Trans-Siberian Railroad it would establish contact with the cooperative societies and thereby help facilitate the exchange of necessities in Siberia. On June 14, in a note to Second Assistant Secretary William Phillips, Miles indicated he essentially concurred with this plan when he commented, "The plan outlined is to my mind a good one and could be adopted to anything now under consideration."[26] While the War Trade Board's proposal bore a strong resemblance to Wright's recommendation of June 3, it was distinguished markedly by its provision that America act independently of the Allies in Siberia. The administration's mistrust of the Allies and its subsequent decision to pursue an independent program of commercial assistance would encounter the obstructions posed by the Allies' unilateral initiatives.

Throughout this period when American policy toward intervention and economic assistance was being debated, Basil Miles, head of the State Department's Russian section, advocated an even more ambitious range of economic measures and a substantial amount of governmental support in order to block German influence in Russia. He went so far as to suggest that the government should support efforts to purchase the stocks of Russian companies in order to forestall Germany's attempts to monopolize these assets. Moreover, the administration should finance barter exchanges with Russia, while endeavors to safeguard Russian supplies from German control "should be supported as far as called for."[27]

While Miles, Wright, and the War Trade Board experts may have overestimated the threat of German activity in Siberia, their concern, and the breadth of their recommendations, was necessarily influenced by the military crisis that had arisen on the western front from the early successes of Germany's massive spring offensive, which made even the potential access to Russian raw materials vital strategically. Taking this analysis of the State

Department's political economy a step further, they correctly perceived that German commercial policy was not merely a wartime exigency, but part of a persistent effort to acquire financial dominion over Russian resources.

By early June, the State Department was exploring the possibility of encouraging the Russian population to resist German influence. On June 5, at Lansing's request, Consul General Poole was instructed to determine the views of the Union of Siberian Cooperative Unions and the Central Union in regard to the organization of resistance against Germany in Russia.[28] One week later Poole cabled a lengthy statement from Alexander Berkenheim of the board of the All-Russian Union of Cooperative Societies, which included the Union of Siberian Cooperative Unions and had relations with the prominent Siberian Creamery Associations.

American sources regarded Berkenheim as a thoroughly reliable representative of the Siberian cooperative associations because he had proven himself as an able manager of their purely business activities. In his statement Berkenheim asserted that the cooperative societies were prepared to help save the people of European Russia from starvation during this period of economic crisis, but foreign assistance would nevertheless be needed. While the European Russian population generally opposed Germany, they were now willing to accept military intervention by "either the Allies or even the Central Powers" out of their desire for an end to Bolshevik rule and the restoration of stability. Berkenheim stressed that the cooperatives' political sympathies were with the Allies, and "in Siberia where the Cooperative Societies represent the people here in the fullest measure there is a special feeling of friendliness fixed and unshaken toward America." A military intervention by the Allies was the only means of resisting Germany, but the Western allies had to participate in any expedition because Japan was not trusted among the Siberian population. Consequently, if America guaranteed Russia's sovereignty, the Siberian population and the cooperative societies would welcome an Allied intervention.[29] Prior to this, during a secret conference in April the Siberian Creamery Associations had already decided to call for an intervention by the Western allies.[30]

Lansing brought Berkenheim's statement to Wilson's attention on June 19. Without delay Wilson enthusiastically replied, "this dispatch has interested me very much. These associations may be of very great service as instruments for what we are now planning to do in Siberia." Wilson added that Thomas Masaryk, president of the Czech National Council, also approved of the plan.[31]

This communication held particular importance for American policy as the odyssey of the Czecho-Slovak Corps rapidly unfolded. Events in Siberia would now revolve around the Czecho-Slovaks' effective occupation of the

Trans-Siberian Railroad, which offered Wilson an opportunity to solve his dilemma over the issue of military intervention. During March 1918 approximately forty thousand Czecho-Slovak troops, formerly Austrian prisoners of war, began a journey to Vladivostok for trans-shipment to the western front. The Wilson administration held these troops and their political leadership in the highest regard, believing they represented the democratic aspirations of the eastern European peoples, were loyal to the Allied cause, and enjoyed friendly relations with the Russian population. The determination of the Czechs' political leadership to contribute their troops to the western front was part of their campaign to further justify Czechoslovakia's claim to national independence. These factors made the Czechs a particularly attractive agent for promoting Wilsonian objectives in central Europe.

The Bolshevik authorities and the Czechs had signed an agreement on March 26 that allowed the Czechs passage on the Trans-Siberian Railroad to Vladivostok. This agreement required the Czechs to surrender their arms at Penza and travel as civilians, not military detachments. Mutual distrust between the Bolsheviks and Czechs was evident from the beginning and resulted in numerous delays. At the end of May, while the first contingent of fifteen thousand Czechs had already arrived at Vladivostok, fighting broke out between Bolshevik forces and the remaining Czechs in central and western Siberia. In late June the Czechs at Vladivostok took control of the city and appealed to the Allies for a military force to assist the rescue of their comrades stranded deep in the Siberian interior.[32]

The Czech uprising finally gave Wilson the moral grounds upon which he could agree to U.S. participation in a military expedition with the Allies while strictly limiting its objectives to a supporting role. More importantly from the American standpoint, however, was the Czechs' occupation of the Trans-Siberian Railroad itself. With the support of the Czech forces the United States could begin to restore railroad operations across Siberia and finally commence a program of commercial assistance. This fortuitous development gave the Wilson administration hope that it was now in a position to reconcile the problematic relationship between military intervention and economic assistance.

Differences of opinion had existed between the Allies from the beginning over the disposition of the Czech troops. As early as April 1, the British War Office suggested maintaining the Czechs in Siberia as a nucleus around which the eastern front could be reopened. Both the French and Czechs strongly opposed this idea at the time, insisting these forces must be transported to the western front. At the Supreme Allied War Council meeting in early June, Britain only reluctantly agreed to the transportation of the Czechs to western Europe and to request Japan to supply the tonnage. Britain was particularly dissatisfied with the diversion of Japanese shipping for this task, since it would prevent Japan from mounting an expedition into Siberia. In fact, much evidence indicates Allied officials encouraged the Czech revolt in the Bolsheviks' rear to threaten Germany with the possibility of restoring the eastern front.[33] Since May, many State Department officials such as William Phillips, Basil Miles, and Joseph E. Grew, acting chief of the west European division, also believed the Czechs should be kept in Siberia.[34]

Therefore, a good deal of sentiment already existed within the State Department that viewed the Czechs as essential to a reconstruction program, when a telegram from Minister Reinsch in Peking arrived at Washington on June 13. Reinsch stressed the opinion of the Allied representatives in Peking, with which he fully concurred "that it would be a serious mistake to remove the Czecho-Slovak troops from Siberia." The Czechs needed only a small amount of assistance from the Allies in order to "control all of Siberia against the Germans," since "they are sympathetic to the Russian population, eager to be accessories to the Allied cause, the most serious menace to [the] extension of German influence in Russia. Their removal would greatly benefit Germany and further discourage Russia. If they were not in Siberia it would be worthwhile to bring them there from a distance."[35]

Wilson reacted favorably to this recommendation on June 17 when he commented to Lansing, "There seems to me to emerge from this suggestion the shadow of a plan that might be worked, with Japanese and other assistance. These people are the cousins of the Russians."[36] Since Reinsch had specifically been emphasizing the danger of German economic penetration in Siberia, Wilson's response suggests he eagerly endorsed the view that the Czecho-Slovaks' presence there would assuage Russian sensibilities over an unavoidable Japanese presence in Siberia. In other words, Wilson appears to have been deeply impressed with the prospect that a Czecho-Slovak occupation of the Trans-Siberian Railroad would demonstrate to the Siberian population the Allies' commitment to restore regional stability under the auspices of a military force sympathetic to the Russian population.

The State Department was also elated with information from Adm. Austin M. Knight of the flagship *Brooklyn* that the Czechs at Vladivostok had "completely modified" their attitude about retiring from Siberia. On June 21, Knight reported that the Czechs were now willing to cooperate with the Allies against German activity in Siberia and to participate in the reestablishment of the eastern front. The Czech presence would also allay the Siberian population's misgivings of an Allied military intervention by subordinating Japan's role.[37] J. Butler Wright seized on this news with alacrity, urging Miles that "This is a 'Godsend'. It's just the news we want. Masaryk is in town! Let's concentrate on this with all our power at once!"[38]

For the Russian division the Czech uprising was the catalyst they had been looking for to hasten the organization of an economic program for Siberia. In a letter to Wilson on June 23, Lansing revealed the true thrust behind America's sudden interest in maintaining the Czechs in Siberia when he suggested, "Is it not possible that in this body of capable and loyal troops may be found a nucleus for military occupation of the Siberian Railway?"[39]

At the beginning of July 1918, the Wilson administration was prepared to undertake a limited military intervention in Siberia to support a program of commercial assistance, but events rapidly overtook Wilson's deliberate approach to the problem. On July 2, the Supreme War Council forced Wilson's hand with an urgent appeal for his immediate consent to a military intervention in Siberia. While Wilson would not accept the Allies' recommendations, their message raised dangers that were consistent with the warnings he had been receiving from Reinsch and from the American ambassadors in Europe. In this message the Allies presented the issue of intervention in terms that placed Wilson's moral leadership on the spot. First, the Allies argued it was a moral obligation to assist the large Czech forces who were in danger of being cut off in central and western Siberia. An expedition in support of the Czechs would also enable the Allies to establish stability in Siberia. Second, Allied intervention was necessary to prevent Germany from gaining control over western Siberia's resources. Finally, the reestablishment of an eastern front was crucial for the whole war effort since Germany would then be prevented from transferring divisions to the western front. To further assuage Wilson's reservations, Japan was willing to guarantee Russian sovereignty and promised not to interfere in Russia's domestic politics.[40]

The State Department used the Allied message as a means of prodding Wilson to take the initiative on the question of intervention in Siberia. On July 4, Lansing initialed a memorandum to the president that stressed that the remarkable success of the Czecho-Slovak forces across Siberia had introduced "a sentimental element" into American calculations. He asserted that America had a responsibility for protecting the Czecho-Slovaks because they were supposedly in danger from German and Austrian prisoners who the Bolsheviks were arming to attack them. Lansing suggested that the fifteen thousand Czech troops at Vladivostok be furnished with enough arms to relieve the twenty-five thousand west of Irkutsk. Some Allied troops should be sent to help police the railroad and provide logistical support for the Czechs. Lansing emphasized that this expedition would not attempt to restore order or interfere in the civil war. Nevertheless, he believed the Japanese would have to provide most of the troops although he thought it "wise" and "probably necessary" that American and Allied troops also participate. He also believed the policy should be publicly announced immediately and it should include a declaration promising noninterference in Russia's internal affairs and the withdrawal of all military forces once the danger of German and Austrian aggression was over.

Finally, he recommended that a peaceful commission headed by a political high commissioner should immediately proceed to Vladivostok. Its members should include representatives from industry, commerce, finance, and agriculture together with spokesmen on moral issues. Their purpose would be to assist the "Russian people by restoring normal conditions of trade, industry and social order." This commission would closely follow the Czechs westward "with due regard to safety," and "the final destination [of the Commission] should depend in large measure upon their reception by the Russians and the resistance made to the military forces."[41]

Two days later on July 6, Wilson decided to embark upon a policy of intervention in Siberia during a conference at the White House that was attended by Lansing, Secretary of War Newton D. Baker, Secretary of the Navy Josephus Daniels, Gen. Peyton C. March, and Adm. William Benson. Wilson remained adamant that the United States should reject the Allied appeals to reestablish an eastern front, because the task was "physically impossible." Under the present circumstances Wilson insisted that no advance beyond Irkutsk should be considered. America's consent to military action would be based strictly on its obligation to help the Vladivostok Czechs reestablish contact with their compatriots in western Siberia. Although the United States could not furnish any considerable forces on short notice to assist the Czechs, Wilson decided that a joint military force of seven thousand American and seven thousand Japanese troops should be used to guard the Czech communication lines. Japan should supply the Vladivostok Czechs with the necessary arms and the U.S. government would share the expense. Wilson stated that further steps should await developments. Lansing informed Japan's ambassador, Viscount Kikujirō Ishii, of America's proposal on July 8, yet Wilson did not wish to consult Britain and France until after Japan had agreed to a joint and equal military expedition.[42]

While Wilson had decided to proceed first with an intervention on behalf of the Czecho-Slovaks, he was essentially struggling to reconcile the necessity of some form of intervention with a program of economic assistance for Siberia. He revealed to House on July 8 that he was preoccupied with this dilemma when he confided: "I have not written recently because I have been sweating blood over the question what is right and feasible (possible) to do in Russia. It goes to pieces like quicksilver under my touch, but I hope I see and can report some progress presently, along the double line of economic assistance and aid to the Czecho-Slovaks."[43]

Indeed, Wilson's thought on this question had evolved rapidly in early July, as his conversations with British ambassador the Marquis of Reading clearly demonstrate. On July 3, Wilson told Reading that he was still primarily interested in sending an economic commission to Siberia. Reading reported to the foreign office Wilson's belief that:

> although we could not consider an Eastern Front at the moment we should consider intermediate courses and he informed me that he [Wilson] had been still considering and examining the plans for an Economic Commission on a great scale and that he recognized that it would be necessary to protect this Commission. His idea was that the Commission should be of first importance, that the policy of economic assistance to Russia should be kept to the front and that the military force should play a secondary part.[44]

In his summary of this interview with Wilson, Reading emphasized "that it shows that the President's mind is crystallizing (if he has not already decided) in the direction of the Economic Commission and the armed protective force." Wilson particularly recognized "the necessity for armed protection of the Commission so that as it advances it may be protected from attack in the rear or from being cut off, and that it is incumbent upon U.S. and Allies to assist and protect the Czecho-Slovaks and that immediate action must be taken."[45]

Three days after this interview, Wilson shifted his stance when he gave priority to support for the Czecho-Slovaks. On July 9, Lansing explained to the Allied ambassadors that because of the urgent need to assist the Czechs the United States would "not wait for the formation of the Economic Commission but will in the first instance send troops and will send the Commission later thus reversing the order of the original proposal."[46] However, Wilson had not altered his views on the question of intervention or in the importance he attributed to an economic assistance program. Rather, he had come to the conclusion that he must immediately extend support to the Czecho-Slovaks, because they must necessarily initiate any Allied-sponsored reconstruction efforts.

The sequence of events that took place between mid-June and early July 1918 indicate that Wilson's decision to support an intervention on behalf of the Czecho-Slovak forces was part of an astute maneuver on his part that aimed to achieve a number of related American objectives in Siberia. First, this course of action was certainly an attempt to forestall Allied appeals for a large-scale military intervention. More important, since the cable from Ambassador Reinsch on June 13, Wilson had been considering the possibility of retaining the Czecho-Slovaks on the Trans-Siberian Railroad, both as an anti-German force and as a vanguard for the distribution of economic assistance through the cooperative societies. In the weeks prior to his July 6 decision, the consensus of opinion Wilson received from Allied and American diplomatic sources indicated the Bolsheviks were on the verge of collapse.[47] By July, the accumulated weight of these reports must have presented a compelling case to Wilson that speedy Allied military action might be required to prevent Germany from filling the political vacuum in European Russia, and possibly western Siberia, that would result from a Bolshevik collapse. At this point, the Supreme War Council's urgent appeal of July 2 finally forced Wilson's hand on the question of intervention by impressing him with the desirability of helping the Czecho-Slovaks to consolidate their forces, an operation that would necessarily solidify Allied control over the Trans-Siberian Railroad. Yet, the decision to intervene created a new dilemma, because the sudden introduction of Japanese forces would have been the wrong signal to send to liberal segments of the Russian population, for it would have increased the risk of legitimizing a German protectorate as a curb against Japanese incursions. This danger may explain why Lansing's July 4 memo advised that an Allied intervention be represented strictly as a humanitarian mission on behalf of the Czecho-Slovaks. As William Bullitt had warned in early March, if the Allies intervened in Russia for the explicit purpose of restoring order, what could morally prevent Germany or Japan from doing likewise? But if the Western powers intervened for the purpose of saving the stranded Czecho-Slovak forces, this would deter Germany or Japan from launching a large-scale intervention under the pretext of a "police action." Lansing hinted at this political motive when he suggested that "furnishing protection and assistance to the Czecho-Slovaks, who are so loyal to our cause, is a very different thing from sending an army into Siberia to restore order or to save the Russians from themselves. There is a moral obligation to save these men from our common enemies, if we are able to do so."[48]

Wilson's decision to undertake a limited intervention also demonstrates that he was able to discriminate between the Allies' alarmist appeals regarding the necessity for a large-scale intervention to restore a second front and the longer-term threat of German economic hegemony in Russia. Nor did Wilson overestimate the extent of Germany's current hold over Russia, for he recognized that it would take Germany a year and a half to tap significant quantities of Russian resources.[49]

In favoring a westward advance by the Czecho-Slovaks, Wilson believed he would be furnishing support to a force that enjoyed particularly friendly relations with the Russian population. From his standpoint, their presence in Siberia appeared to offer a particularly favorable opportunity for an Allied effort to reestablish a degree of social stability along the Trans-Siberian railway, an initiative that would undercut German commercial influence or the potential appeal of Germany as a bulwark against bolshevism or Japan.

To illustrate this point, an immediate task of an Allied force would be to ensure control over the German and Austro-Hungarian prisoners who were concentrated at different locations in Siberia, such as Omsk. In early 1920, shortly after the Bolshevik defeat of Admiral Kolchak, the American Red Cross commissioner to Siberia, Robert B. Teusler, thought the presence of these prisoners in Siberia was a "serious menace" because "so many of them are officers with university training and highly qualified professional men." Besides these actual military prisoners, Teusler had discovered from his experiences that "there are also a large number of so-called civilian German prisoners in Siberia who are not imprisoned. These men have lived in Siberia for many years, were interned at the beginning of the war, and now remain to form very definite contacts with the Russian people themselves."[50] For these reasons it is conceivable that these German prisoners in Siberia, both military and civilian, could have helped facilitate the extension of German economic influence in Siberia after Brest-Litovsk, had there been no Allied countermeasures.

In their role as an Allied gendarmerie for Siberia, the Czecho-Slovaks would help establish the preconditions for any assistance program that was subsequently undertaken. Initially, they would provide security for the Railway Service Corps along the whole of the Trans-Siberian railway system, a guarantee that John Stevens had insisted upon in his conversation with J. B. Wright. This protection would be essential for the reconstruction of Siberia, since commercial assistance could only be effectively furnished to the region after the American engineers restored operations across this transportation artery. The Czecho-Slovak forces would also directly assist the work of the American railroad engineers because they had several locomotive shop work battalions in their contingent. These units were assigned to work in various shops and roundhouses on the Trans-Siberian Railroad.[51]

Wilson understood that his consent to a military expedition was a calculated gamble. He admitted as much to General March at the July 6 conference when March dissented from the policy on grounds that Japan could not be trusted to comply with the terms of the United States.[52] By mid-July Japan had still not replied to the proposal of the United States for a limited military intervention on behalf of the Czecho-Slovaks, while Britain had unilaterally begun to prepare its own expeditionary force. But Japan would not cooperate with Wilson's proposal because it was fully aware of America's strategy. During a meeting of Japan's Advisory Council on

Foreign Relations, Foreign Minister Shimpei Gotō bluntly asserted that "America looks on the Czech forces as its own army."[53]

Wilson accordingly resorted to moral suasion with the Allies when he delineated America's purposes in Siberia through an aide-mémoire that was given to the Great Powers on July 17. In this statement Wilson categorically refused to participate in any military intervention through Siberia that had as its aim the restoration of an eastern front, because it would only worsen "the present sad confusion in Russia rather than cure it, injure her rather than help her." He declared that military intervention would "be merely a method of making use of Russia, not a method of serving her" and the Russian population would "be used to maintain foreign armies, not to reconstitute their own." The United States would consent only to a military action "to help the Czecho-Slovaks consolidate their forces and get into successful cooperation with their Slavic kinsmen and steady any efforts at self-government or self-defense in which the Russians themselves may be willing to accept assistance." Wilson called on the Allies to publicly assure the Russian people they would not interfere with Russia's political sovereignty or infringe on Russia's territorial integrity at the present time or in the future. In conclusion, Wilson indicated that the United States intended to provide economic assistance for the Siberian population. He modestly explained that the U.S. government would:

> take advantage of the earliest opportunity to send to Siberia a commission of merchants, agricultural experts, labor advisers, Red Cross representatives, and agents of the Young Men's Christian Association accustomed to organizing the best methods of spreading useful information and rendering educational help of a modest sort, in order in some systematic manner to relieve the immediate economic necessities of the people there in every way for which opportunity may open. The execution of this plan will follow and will not be permitted to embarrass the military assistance rendered in the rear of the westward-moving forces of the Czecho-Slovaks.[54]

Wilson's memorandum was consistent with the strategy he had been considering since mid-June of using the Czecho-Slovaks to block the spread of German economic influence in Siberia. Moreover, Wilson's view that the Czechs could encourage efforts at "self-government or self-defense" among their "Slavic kinsmen" is crucial to understanding his conception of the reconstruction process. The reinvigoration of these basic civic capacities in the Siberian population would engender the confidence necessary to revive normal commercial activity and to reestablish governmental functions. In other words, implicit in Wilson's emphasis on "self-government or self-defense" was the fundamental liberal precept that security for person and property was an essential basis for economic development.

American enthusiasm for the Czecho-Slovak Corps stood in sharp contrast to the reserved attitude the Wilson administration took toward the rival anticommunist political factions who were vying for Allied support in the late summer 1918. Instead of supporting any of the fragile Siberian governments—a move that would only embroil the United States in the Russian civil war—Wilson placed American support behind the Czecho-Slovaks' occupation of the Trans-Siberian railway in an effort to help restore civil order. Wilson justified this limited intervention on the recognition that none of the Siberian governments were viable or sufficiently representative of the popular will. Near the end of July, Roland Morris, the American Ambassador to Japan and a longtime progressive Democrat, conveyed this position to representatives of the various anti-Bolshevik political movements who were attempting to form a unified government. For instance, Morris told P. V. Vologodskii of the provisional Siberian government that while the United States would not recognize his government, this did not mean that America "would treat such governments in an unfriendly way or withhold its sympathy and assistance." In other words, the United States might be willing to enter into practical relationships with existing governments under certain circumstances. This statement foreshadowed the pragmatic approach Wilson would subsequently take toward the Kolchak government in 1919. Morris then made Wilson's essential conditions for recognition more explicit in a meeting with representatives of Dmitri Khorvat's ultraconservative Far Eastern Committee for the Defense of the Homeland. In a pointed comment that expressed Wilson's disapproval of any reactionary political settlement, Morris told them that the United States would delay recognition of any government because "the convictions of the American people inclined them toward Government that arose from the bottom up, rather than in favor of the authority imposed from above."[55] Events would soon justify American caution. The disparate Siberian political groups were completely out of touch with the region's population and incapable of transcending their factional rivalries—even for the purpose of forming a united front against the Bolsheviks. Unity would only be achieved by force in November 1918, at the hand of Adm. Aleksandr Kolchak's military dictatorship—a regime that rapidly imploded because of its callous disregard for the public's welfare.

Perhaps further light can be shed on Wilson's intervention policy by examining the memoranda of Julius Lay, the State Department's trade adviser. Following Wilson's aide-mémoire of July 17, Lay produced memoranda that were consistent with the policy enunciated in the president's declaration and that were apparently drafted to offer recommendations on how the policy should be carried out. In the three memos that spanned the period from July 19 to 23, Lay advanced his views on how the specific military and economic aspects of the intervention should be implemented to achieve American objectives.

On July 22, Lay argued that the principal objective behind an intervention in Siberia was to defeat Germany. To achieve this goal, not only would it be necessary to divert German troops from the western front for strategic ends in the present war, but it would also be necessary to prevent Germany from dominating Russia after the war. Otherwise, regardless of the outcome of the war in the West, Germany would be left in control of enormous resources, which would radically alter the global relations of power.

In accordance with the president's basic position, Lay did not advocate a large military intervention that would attempt to reopen an eastern front. Like Wilson, Lay believed hostilities against Germany could only be resumed in the east if the expeditionary forces boosted the population's morale and became a nucleus around which Russian forces could rally and begin to organize an efficient army. Also consistent with the president's decision to undertake a limited intervention, Lay recommended that a moderate-sized expedition should be sent to Siberia, in which American troops played a prominent role. These expeditionary forces should be composed largely of logistical troops who would support the Czecho-Slovaks, who, of course, would constitute the predominant military force.[56]

Lay's memoranda are particularly interesting for the emphasis he placed on using a limited military intervention by Allied forces as a means to counteract German economic influence in Siberia. Indeed, he was certain this step should actually precede economic measures. Lay shared the prevailing State Department view that the immediate objective of America's Siberian policy should be to deny Germany the use of Russian resources for its war effort. He hoped the intervention would deprive Germany of the resources of western Siberia and of Russia east of the Volga, which would largely reestablish an effective blockade against Germany. However, while acknowledging the essentially economic nature of the German threat in Siberia, he nevertheless emphasized that it would be a mistake for the United States to initially undertake a strictly economic program to counter German influence, because "all classes and all parties have implored our aid against the Germans and interpret our promise to stand by them as a promise of military assistance."[57] He warned that ever since the Brest-Litovsk Treaty the "gravest danger that had threatened the Allies in Russia" was the possibility that the bourgeois elements, "despairing of Allied aid," would accept German intervention against bolshevism. Neither was Lay given to exaggerate the extent of German influence over Russian liberals and conservatives for, with the exception of a few monarchists, he believed they were "consistently pro-Ally." Nevertheless, he had to take into account that "it is reliably reported that they have already through their leaders entertained German proposals." On the basis of these assessments, Lay concluded his July 19 memorandum with a scenario that echoed the sentiments Wilson had just expressed in his aide-mémoire, when he stated that "Should a small Allied army entering Siberia meet with a sympathetic reception and Russian soldiers join the colors under their leadership to fight Germany, the pro-Ally elements in Russia might be encouraged to hold out against German overtures."[58]

In a memorandum from July 23, Lay also provides a possible explanation why Wilson, in his aide-mémoire, had subtly shifted his ground from advocating an economic commission that would operate on a "great scale" to a modest endeavor that would assist the people's efforts to help themselves. Lay cautioned that

> there is danger lest a purely economic mission should be regarded simply as a scheme by America to achieve economic penetration and commercial advantages. Such a view will be industriously circulated by German agents and much will be made of the popular idea that America thinks only of financial gain. It may be added that numerous articles are appearing in the Japanese press setting forth the same point of view.[59]

Paul Reinsch related that this issue had been a very important consideration for Wilson throughout the summer of 1918 when many in the administration recommended that a prominent businessman, such as Herbert Hoover, head an economic commission for Russia. In discussing possible candidates for this position, Wilson told Reinsch that "he feared to place a representative of 'big business' in such a position; men would suspect selfish national motives. I felt he [Wilson] wished America to lead in giving the Russian people such aid in reorganizing their economic life as would permanently benefit them and preserve them for our common cause."[60]

If, then, Lay's memoranda constitute a record of discussions from within the policymaking apparatus over how to proceed with the policy Wilson laid out in his July 17 aide-mémoire, then it also indicated the extent to which the president's intervention policy was influenced by the potential threat of expanded German influence over the Russian political economy.

In retrospect, it may seem implausible that the threat of expanded German economic penetration in Siberia played such a prominent role in influencing the policymaking decisions of the Wilson administration from the spring to the end of the summer of 1918. Nevertheless, it cannot be disputed that the specter of German economic penetration into Siberia, whether actual, prospective, or merely hypothetical, attracted a great deal of attention at the State Department and the White House.

American officials may then seem vulnerable to the charge that they were fighting a phantom in believing Germany could derive any significant material benefits from Russia proper, or Siberia, at this stage of the war. Yet, in view of the highly unstable and rapidly changing conditions that existed throughout the vast Russian Empire, and considering the ongoing difficulties the administration encountered in obtaining accurate information, American policymakers had to take this danger seriously. At that time, with the outcome of the war on the western front still hanging in the balance and with Allied policy toward Russia paralyzed by deep divisions among the coalition powers, it would not be hard to envision a scenario in which important segments of the Russian population could reconcile themselves to a strong German political and economic position in the empire; this as an acceptable alternative to continued Bolshevik rule, or to Japanese encroachments upon the Russian Far East.

The case of Pavel Miliukov demonstrated how even a staunch Russian nationalist could entertain the possibility of a German protectorate. In this context, the decision to support the Czecho-Slovaks constituted a timely strategic initiative that demonstrated Allied resolve to counter German influence. Indeed, the Czecho-Slovaks quickly fulfilled this purpose, as a party of American officials reported upon their arrival at Harbin, Manchuria, in early September 1918 (they had been traveling with George Emerson of the American Railway Service Corps from locations in western and central Siberia). At that time Consul Douglas Jenkins learned from one of his colleagues that during June the Czecho-Slovaks' occupation of the Tobolsk grain-producing area west of Omsk had blocked the activity of German purchasing agents.[61] Although subsequent events undermined Wilson's strategy, in mid-summer 1918 the Czecho-Slovaks' hold over the Trans-Siberian railway system appeared to offer the United States the best possible circumstances for undertaking a program of economic assistance in this hotly contested region.

5

❧

The Genesis of the Russian Bureau:
The Sources and Conduct of the
American Economic Assistance Program,
July–September 1918

Wilson decided to support a limited military intervention on behalf of the Czecho-Slovaks because he hoped their presence in Siberia would block German influence, strengthen Russian efforts at "self-government," and constitute an advance force for the economic commission he was then contemplating. But, Wilson's strategy was quickly subverted by the Western allies and Japan, who immediately seized the opportunity to launch a large-scale military intervention that would further their own interests in the Russian Empire. Wilson's problems were compounded at home by a bureaucratic rivalry that stemmed from the Commerce Department's efforts to organize its own commercial contacts with the Siberian cooperative societies. In its attempt to circumvent the State Department's coordination of American assistance efforts, the Commerce Department created further complications for the administration during the difficult period when it was endeavoring to craft the various facets of Wilson's Siberian policy into an effective program that would foster reconstruction.

The administration's plans for the economic mission were put on hold pending Japan's response to the American proposal for sending American and Japanese contingents of seven thousand troops.[1] This question is crucial to understanding the troubled course American assistance policy would follow in August and September 1918. The Allies would not accept the limits Wilson wanted to place on the intervention, nor would they cooperate on questions of economic assistance. Japan never agreed to limit its expeditionary force to the seven thousand men the United States believed was sufficient for the limited task of supporting the Czechs. Japan's intervention would take on particularly menacing implications near the end of July when it announced it would be sending divisions to patrol both the Amur section of the Trans-Siberian Railroad and the Chinese Eastern Railway in northern Manchuria.

By the beginning of September, Japan took steps that would directly threaten John Stevens's authority when it placed all Siberian railroads under military control. At the end of October, it would have approximately twelve thousand troops stationed on the mainline itself, with another twenty thousand preparing to winter at Chita, the juncture of the mainline and the Amur line. These forces would obstruct the westward movement of all freight traffic in order to discriminate in favor of Japanese commerce. Wilson's policy had in fact become distorted; the presence of the Czecho-Slovaks in Siberia gave Japan a rationale to maintain its troops in the Russian Far East and in northern Manchuria.

Britain encouraged Japan to disregard America's resolve to limit the number of troops that were introduced into Siberia. On July 20, British foreign secretary Arthur Balfour instructed his ambassador in Tokyo to inform the Japanese that Britain believed the American proposal was inadequate. On August 12 the British Embassy in Washington urged the State Department to request Japan to send as many troops as it thought necessary, while in private discussions a week later Foreign Secretary Balfour impressed upon Japan's ambassador that "the amount of forces required to achieve our objects in Siberia was entirely a military question and His Majesty's Government would approve anything which the High Command in Tokyo thought necessary."[2] British collusion with Japan explains why Wilson did not want to inform the Western allies of America's consultations with Japan over a limited military expedition until after Japan had agreed to his terms. While Wilson has been faulted for his attempt to exclude Britain and France from these discussions, his desire to avoid their participation in the intervention was well-founded. Britain and France would have considered an American request for their participation in the military expedition as an opening wedge for the eventual restoration of an eastern front.[3] Indeed, the unwillingness of Britain and Japan to cooperate in a limited military intervention doomed Wilson's hopes of utilizing the Czechs as a stabilizing force along the Trans-Siberian railway. At the time of the Armistice on November 11, Japan had sent nearly seventy thousand troops to Siberia.

Britain also complicated the efforts of the United States to formulate a commercial assistance program. On July 25 Britain moved to preempt American plans when it informed the United States it was taking steps to begin its own program of commercial assistance for Siberia. Although it was inevitable that America and Japan would provide most of the supplies needed by Siberia, Britain nevertheless maintained it was desirable to give assistance efforts as much of an inter-Allied character as possible. Consequently, Britain planned to supply goods from British stocks at Vladivostok and Khabarovsk. An interdepartmental committee had already been established in London to coordinate British efforts and a high commissioner was being appointed at Vladivostok to supervise all local arrangements and to serve as the British representative on a proposed inter-Allied commission. The British government intended to enlist private British trading firms in the Far East both to serve as its agents and to operate for a fixed commission—not for profit. Goods were to be sold at cost to avoid profit-making and to allay the population's suspicions of Allied motives. Private firms could nevertheless lend their knowledge of local conditions to promote a more efficient rehabilitation.

The Hong Kong and Shanghai Banking Corporation was also considering the possibility of opening a branch bank at Vladivostok to improve monetary conditions, which the British government encouraged. To avoid controversy between the governments over the terms by which goods were supplied to the population, Britain believed the Allied governments should agree to pursue the same policy. Britain suggested these questions be referred to the proposed inter-Allied commission, which would determine the Allies' commercial policy on the basis of local conditions.[4]

Britain's economic and political objectives in Siberia during the summer of 1918 were designed to further its overall spheres of influence policy toward the Russian Empire.[5] Its nonprofit commercial program sought to place British commerce in good standing with the large Siberian cooperative societies and thus establish an advantageous position for British commerce in Siberia's postwar trade. Basil Miles called Vance McCormick's attention to the likelihood that the Narodny Bank would become an agent for promoting postwar trade between Russia and Britain through its contact with British cooperative societies.[6]

Britain also took steps to enhance its political influence in Siberia. In July it named Sir Charles Eliot as its high commissioner to supervise the government-run Siberian Supply Company, and Gen. Alfred W. F. Knox was made head of Britain's military mission in Siberia to counsel pro-Ally Russians. After the Czech's rapid military successes of mid-September, Britain was even more encouraged by the prospects that the limited intervention could be transformed into a full-fledged effort to restore the eastern front. British military and diplomatic officials concluded that the various political factions in Siberia had to be united under a provisional military government.

A candidate had already been groomed by the British to assume absolute political control in Siberia, the conservative Russian admiral Aleksandr Kolchak. Both Eliot and Knox enjoyed friendly personal relations with Kolchak, and British officials had been in close contact with him for well over a year. Knox had strong ties with czarist elements and by the fall of 1918 he had begun to rebuild the Russian Army in Siberia from remnants of the reactionary officer corps. Strong circumstantial evidence suggests Knox and his staff were instrumental in organizing the coup of November 1918, which overthrew the Coalition Directorate government and installed Kolchak as "Supreme Leader" of the Omsk Siberian government.[7]

Kolchak's reactionary government was a vehicle through which Britain could advance its spheres of influence policy in Eurasia. For instance, Britain never recognized Kolchak's Omsk government as anything but a "Siberian government," not an "All-Russian government." Likewise, in their efforts to build lasting economic ties with Siberia, British businessmen preferred to work through the Council of Ministers, who favored a constitutional Siberian Federation.[8]

For these reasons and cognizant of Britain's desire to feel out America's intentions, the Wilson administration responded to Britain's commercial proposal with reserve. On July 25 State Department counselor Frank Polk spoke with British chargé Barclay concerning the United States's position on economic assistance. Polk endeavored to emphasize that commercial activity played a subordinate role in America's prospective plan, an assertion that was quite misleading. After expressing the United States's appreciation of Britain's desire to cooperate in a program of assistance, he stated: "It is apparent, however, that the British Government has in mind a purely economic mission rather than a mission which would have for its main object the study of the situation and would endeavor to ascertain in what way the Russian could be assisted to help himself. In other words, the Red Cross and educational side of the mission would be very much more to the fore than the economic side."[9]

Polk then evaded the question of what America did intend to do when he claimed no definite policy would be pursued until the exploratory mission had reported on conditions in Siberia. Therefore, the U.S. government was not in a position to discuss questions that involved "the class of goods which ought to be sent, the advisability of establishing branch banks, or the terms on which goods are to be sold to the Russian Government."[10] Polk revealed the wish of the administration to conceal its program when he told Wilson, "I have been very guarded in what I have said to the Allied representatives concerning our plans for an Economic Mission."[11]

On August 22, Assistant Secretary of State William Phillips informed Lansing that the Allies had designated high civilian officials to oversee the political questions that would arise from the introduction of Allied military forces. Britain's high commissioner, Sir Eliot, had already arrived; France also intended to send a high commissioner, and Japan was sending an economic commission that would have diplomatic assistance. Moreover, France now proposed that an inter-Allied board be organized to coordinate civilian work in Siberia, with an American representative at its head. Phillips favored the idea, and the British were willing to support whomever the United States chose to head the Board.[12]

Lansing and Wilson were extremely wary of these developments. Lansing recognized this overture was a thinly veiled effort to gain American acquiescence for a more extensive intervention. He advised Wilson "that this is another move to impress our action in Siberia with the character of intervention rather than relief of the Czechs. The suggestion that our High Commissioner be the head of an international commission seems to be a bait to draw us into this policy which has been so insistently urged by Great Britain for the past six months."[13]

To discourage these Allied machinations once and for all, Lansing suggested he be authorized to inform the Allied ambassadors bluntly that the United States would not appoint a high commissioner. Without American participation the commission would then be effectively undermined. Wilson concurred wholeheartedly with this assessment and instructed Lansing that "I hope you will do just what you here suggest. The other governments are going much further than we and much faster,—are, indeed, acting upon a plan which is altogether foreign from ours and inconsistent with it."[14] The French ambassador should be told the United States did "not think political action necessary or desirable in eastern Siberia because we contemplate no political action of any kind there, but only the action of friends who stand at hand and wait to see how they can help."[15] Yet, by rejecting the Allied scheme for a commission, Wilson also foreclosed this type of organization as an option for America's commercial plans. Allied policy had further complicated Wilson's dilemma over the operational details of a commercial assistance program.

In early September, Gordon Auchincloss, Miles, and Long emerged as the decisive figures in the American policy debate when they urged a solution on the president that was compatible with his principles. On September 8 these officials reviewed the questions of relief for the Czechs and of economic assistance for the Russian population. Their objective was to have the president appoint Vance C. McCormick of the War Trade Board as coordinator of all Russian economic work in Washington, or in Long's words to "centralize it and direct it."[16] Auchincloss was then designated to draft a letter to Wilson "which should embody the president's plans, some of his ideas as we interpreted them and our ideas of what should be done to get supplies to the Czechs and Siberians and Russians."[17]

Auchincloss's letter was approved by Miles and Long and sent to Wilson with Lansing's signature on September 9. It addressed the problems associated with furnishing assistance to the Czech military forces and the civilian populations of northern Russia and Siberia. Preliminary steps had been taken in regard to the Czechs, as Wilson was ready to furnish money from his war fund and Bernard Baruch of the War Industries Board had been consulted about their requirements for clothing, shoes, arms, and ammunition. Siberia's population did not need food from the United States, but clothing, shoes, and other specific commodities were in very short supply. Russian ships that had been chartered by the U.S. Shipping Board should now be returned to Russia's service to transport these goods. The population of the Murmansk Coast and Archangel, however, would need food and these shipments had to go forward by October 1 to ensure their delivery before their ports were closed by ice. A revolving fund of $5 million would be adequate since the food should be sold and not given away except to prevent starvation.

Complex operational problems involving methods of barter and exchange still had to be resolved. War Trade Board chairman Vance McCormick was recommended to direct this work because he agreed with Wilson's policies and because he was in close contact with the other departmental heads. Since the War Trade Board was composed of experts from the Treasury, Commerce, and Agricultural Departments, the Food Administration and the Shipping Board, it was particularly well suited to study the various problems that confronted the program.[18]

On September 11, Wilson met with his War Board heads, Baruch, McCormick, and Edward Hurley of the shipping board, and made them collectively responsible for administering commercial assistance for Siberia. This arrangement was not satisfactory to the State Department, who had McCormick discuss the matter with Wilson again on September 13. At this meeting Wilson voiced objections to placing a "separate organization" in control of the program.[19] Apparently, Wilson was still not certain a single board would provide the necessary coordination between departments, because McCormick had to argue him "into agreement to close cooperation between the three named" (i.e., McCormick, Baruch, and Hurley), and representatives of each would have to meet daily at a designated location.[20]

Long considered this compromise an adequate basis on which a definite plan for economic aid could be formulated and executed. He was confident that "McCormick will eventually be supreme in it—at least that is the plan, because we feel he has the confidence of the President to a remarkable degree and the facility of getting him to agree to things."[21] Indeed, McCormick was initially given the "whip hand" because Wilson authorized him to call a meeting with Baruch and Hurley at the War Trade Building on Monday, September 16. In his diary Long explained this maneuvering on grounds that, "We felt it [commercial assistance] was not properly the function of the State Department, was the proper field for activity of 'war' board or boards, and that Vance would be closer to and cooperate with us better than either of the others."[22]

Undoubtedly the State Department lacked the personnel to administer the program, but there is also the implication that State Department control would endow the program with political overtones, which were better avoided considering the relations with the Allies. Yet, it is clear the State Department favored McCormick precisely because he would cooperate with it on political questions and because the War Trade Board was a less conspicuous agent of American policy.

The State Department was especially determined to get the commercial assistance program into the hands of the War Trade Board in order to head off an independent Commerce Department initiative with certain Siberian cooperative associations. After the meeting between Vance McCormick and Wilson on September 13, Gordon Auchincloss, possibly the chief State Department strategist on this issue, revealed in his diary that the State Department was trying to play the War Board chiefs against Redfield. On September 14 he explained to Lansing "that we should play with McCormick, Baruch and Hurley as against Redfield and that we should let Redfield fight with McCormick and Baruch, rather than with ourselves. This he agreed to do."[23]

Since late June a rivalry had been brewing between the State and Commerce Departments for control of the economic commission. On June 29 Lansing protested to Wilson about information he had gathered concerning efforts by Commerce Department officials to organize the Russian Commission themselves and their intention to entirely exclude the State Department from the operation. Lansing was particularly incensed by an article, which appeared that same day in the *Washington Post*, that stated a commercial commission was being organized. This article created "considerable embarrassment" for Lansing as he had been declining to comment on the issue publicly for fear of compromising American policy. Lansing blamed the Commerce Department's uncooperative attitude on subordinate officials and tactfully avoided direct criticism of Redfield. He reiterated that whatever agency was chosen to work in Siberia "must be guided by the political effect" and therefore a "subsidiary council" based in Washington must coordinate and regulate the commission's work. After repeating his concern about the Commerce Department's ambitions, Lansing revealed something of Wilson's attitude on the subject when he reminded the president that on the previous day, June 28, he had also expressed opposition to Commerce Department control of the program.[24]

A comment Auchincloss made to Polk on June 29 suggests that Redfield had overstepped his bounds in attempting to organize the commercial assistance program through the Commerce Department. Speaking with great contempt for the commerce secretary, Auchincloss informed Polk that

> Redfield is giving everyone the impression that he is running the Russian situation and has been commissioned by the President to set up a separate Bureau to handle the matter. . . . I think that all the President has asked him to do is to investigate the commercial situation and to give him a report on it, like your old favorite pup he is all blown up with his own importance, and I suppose sooner or later he will give out some newspaper statement which will cause his down fall.[25]

Lansing's letter to Wilson on that same day was undoubtedly aimed at hastening Redfield's "downfall." Auchincloss's assessment of Wilson's intentions appears to be consistent with the president's own statements on the issue. When Wilson began to consider seriously the question of commercial assistance in mid-May, he only directed Redfield to solicit practical recommendations from the private sector. There is no evidence Wilson ever authorized Redfield to organize a program through the Commerce Department.

In September this conflict resurfaced because the Commerce Department representative at Vladivostok completed a tentative commercial agreement with Siberian cooperative associations that bypassed the State Department. On September 14, the American consul at Vladivostok, John K. Caldwell, informed the State Department that the Commerce Department trade commissioner, Charles L. Preston, had negotiated a tentative agreement at Vladivostok to purchase five hundred thousand dollars worth of squirrel pelts from the Union of Siberian Cooperative Unions *(Zakupsbyt)*. Some of these furs had already arrived at Vancouver, Canada, in early August. The National City Bank was apparently ready to advance 50 percent of the appraised value of the furs charging bank rates. The Commerce Department then planned to sell these goods for a 2-percent commission fee. With the proceeds from these goods the union wanted to buy agricultural machinery and implements, spare parts, dry goods, and shoes.[26]

The Zakupsbyt had made an initial shipment of about 250 tons to North America in June on its own initiative. The Narodny Bank encouraged the endeavor as a means of accumulating dollar exchange for the cooperatives to finance Siberian imports from America. In late July, while this first shipment was en route to North America, Preston requested authorization from the Commerce Department to ship large additional quantities of the Zakupsbyt's wool, bristles, and pelts from Vladivostok. Adm. Austin Knight, a strong advocate of American trade with Siberia, told August Heid, International Harvester's marketing representative in Siberia, that Preston was urging his superiors in Washington to conclude a large barter arrangement with the Siberian cooperatives. Heid learned Preston's recommendations specified that a large percentage of the American exports to Siberia should consist of agricultural machinery and binding twine. These negotiations received a great deal of attention around Vladivostok.[27] For instance, this initiative was backed by the Russo-American Committee of the Far East, an organization of Russian businessmen and officials that was attempting to attract American capital with the lure of vast concessions.[28]

This Commerce Department initiative immediately created complications for the administration. When the Zakupsbyt's first shipment of furs arrived at Vancouver, Canada, in early August, it was denied entry into the United States because War Trade Board regulations classified them as luxuries. Isaac J. Sherman, representative of the Narodny Bank in New York, advocated the Zakupsbyt's cause with the War Trade Board and the Bureau of Foreign and Domestic Commerce in early September. First, he denied that squirrel pelts were a luxury. In view of their cheapness, they should more accurately be considered a necessity. Unfortunately, there was not much of a market for squirrel pelts in the United States and the product was certainly a low priority in the American war effort. In light of these facts Sherman even argued that the pelts were of strategic significance for the economic embargo against Germany. Earlier in the war, the czarist government prohibited the exportation of squirrel pelts to Sweden fearing Germany might buy them for its military needs.

Sherman's most effective argument was that important political considerations were at stake for the United States. A rigorous application of the War Trade Board's regulations would discourage the resumption of commercial relations between Russia and America, the principal objective of the Wilson administration. Such an apparent indifference to the needs of the Russian population would jeopardize America's reputation with the vast

Siberian cooperative movement. The permission to import these furs would enhance American prestige with the cooperative movement and provide an incentive for Siberian producers. Sherman suggested that in the future the cooperatives could be persuaded to send mixed shipments, containing raw materials and agricultural products that were needed in the United States.[29] From Vladivostok State Department consul Caldwell voiced his support for this arrangement, which he referred to as "the Department of Commerce plan."[30]

Sherman's arguments had an immediate effect on the State Department. On September 16, the State Department asked the War Trade Board to make an exception in its regulations for the Zakupsbyt's shipment "on the ground of policy."[31] But this solution did not resolve the bitter jurisdictional dispute between the State and Commerce Departments. Moreover, as a question of policy these negotiations were problematic because they were creating the impression among prominent Russians, cooperative officials, and the suspicious Allies that the United States was preparing to finance the shipment of large quantities of agricultural machinery. This misrepresentation of the administration's intentions threatened to compromise Wilson's policy among the Siberian population.

In September, the Commerce Department continued to obstruct the administration's policy by stubbornly resisting the State Department's efforts to wrest from it jurisdiction over the commercial negotiations with the Zakupsbyt. Lansing's diary entries from September 19 and 24 indicate Redfield was reluctant to surrender his department's work to the War Trade Board.[32] At this point the president interceded, settling the conflict once and for all. On September 24 an irritated Wilson told House that he would no longer tolerate Redfield's meddling with commercial assistance and that he had definitively placed the program under War Trade Board jurisdiction. In frustration Wilson declared to House that Redfield had so "messed the matter up" that up until then it had been impossible to proceed with the assistance program. Wilson related to House that he had taken the "economic and relief policy" away from Redfield and placed it under the War Trade Board's authority with the hope that "something would come of it." After this conversation House candidly revealed in his diary that Wilson "did not know that Gordon [Auchincloss] had worked this out and arranged it."[33]

Gordon Auchincloss devised the arguments the State Department used with Wilson to obtain this arrangement. He recommended that the State Department exploit Wilson's opposition to the creation of a new organization to coordinate America's supply efforts. Auchincloss agreed that the establishment of a new agency at this time was both "unnecessary and inadvisable." Nevertheless, he pointed out that ten different governmental agencies were involved in some aspect of the Russian policy and these efforts needed coordination. On these grounds Auchincloss was able to persuasively argue that the War Trade Board was the logical agency to undertake the task. Along the same lines as his letter to the president on September 9, he stressed that the War Trade Board was "peculiarly adapted to take on such work, because it is composed of representatives of all the Departments interested." But above all, McCormick was the ideal individual to direct this work because "he is devoted to the President and he shares his ideals." At the same time he "can work harmoniously with practically every man who now heads the War Organizations in Washington."[34]

Before his appointment as chairman of the War Trade Board in late 1917, McCormick had built an impressive record as a progressive reformer and administrator in his hometown of Harrisburg, Pennsylvania, during the early years of the century. By 1912, McCormick's influence in the Pennsylvania Democratic party enabled him to play a prominent role in bringing about Woodrow Wilson's nomination for president. McCormick's reputation as a progressive gained national attention during his unsuccessful bid for the Pennsylvania governorship in 1914, when Theodore Roosevelt personally campaigned in the state on his behalf.[35]

By late September Auchincloss's arguments ultimately persuaded Wilson because it had become imperative that some agency must coordinate and set priorities among the various supply efforts to which administration policy was committed in Siberia. As late as September 23 no such authority existed. On this date Henry B. Van Sinderen of the War Trade Board succinctly addressed this problem in a memorandum that stressed that America would soon be involved in five separate supply operations in Siberia. In the first place, the administration would have to furnish John Stevens additional railroad equipment and supplies for his personnel if it wanted him to maintain operational control over the Siberian railway system. Next, the forty-thousand-man Czecho-Slovak Corps needed both military and nonmilitary supplies. A central organization in the United States would have to determine priorities between these two categories of supplies. Funds would be needed to supply all three of these supply operations.

These prior commitments to Stevens and to the Czecho-Slovaks dictated that similar provision be made for the civilian population of Siberia. Van Sinderen emphasized that if America intended to transport supplies for the Czecho-Slovaks across 4,800 miles of the Trans-Siberian Railroad, it must also make scarce supplies available to the civilian population or else risk stirring resentment among the Siberians. Van Sinderen implied that since almost $4 million in nonmilitary supplies was being furnished to the Czecho-Slovaks, the U.S. government itself should be prepared to finance the shipment of a comparable sum of supplies to the Siberian population. It appears that up until this time War Trade Board planners had assumed these emergency shipments would have to be supplied by private trade even though this would complicate these critical transactions. Finally, to successfully revive trade in Siberia, it would be necessary to have a central organization "backed by the Government," in order to expedite the shipment of supplies and to control their distribution in Siberia, "in view of the large number of people and large territory to be reached." Van Sinderen also suggested that this coordinating organization might establish a stable currency, a question that would be integral to the United States's assistance program.

In conclusion, Van Sinderen raised additional points that demonstrated the need for coordination. It would be important to develop a distributing organization in Siberia that could "make recommendations to Washington regarding the urgency of the requirements of the five groups mentioned above." In Washington there should be an organization to arrange for the procurement and appropriate allocation of freight space, to centralize the purchase of supplies to avoid market disturbances at home, and to handle details connected with the provision of credits.[36]

The implications of Van Sinderen's assessment were twofold. First, unless these five functions were centrally coordinated, the United States's supply efforts would likely work at cross-purposes, or become disorganized, leaving American policy in chaos and discredited among the Siberians and Czecho-Slovaks. Second, to ensure the equitable distribution of American supplies and to facilitate the restoration of normal market conditions in Siberia, the government would have to furnish some emergency supplies itself.

Following the resolution of the organizational question in late September, the War Trade Board began to plan its supply operation in detail. These preparations reveal a great deal about the liberal worldview that motivated American policy. In the early stages of its operations the War Trade Board tried to evaluate specific types of potential exports in terms of the moral effect they would produce among the recipients. These considerations figured prominently in discussions between the liberal officials from the Russian embassy and the War Trade Board. Russian ambassador Boris Bakhmetev and the embassy's financial expert, Serge Ughet, urged that economic assistance must be adapted to Russian conditions, particularly that it should foster independence and self-sufficiency among its recipients. In a memorandum on the subject written in September, Bakhmetev emphasized that economic assistance should promote "national reconstruction." Economic assistance had to be directed toward reestablishing a "material basis" upon which social stability could be sustained. This process of restoring social stability necessarily "has to be performed by the population itself" with the Allies providing essential supplies. Like his counterparts in the Wilson administration, Bakhmetev believed the American program had to facilitate an organic process of reconstruction. Accordingly, the American program had to have the flexibility to "conform itself . . . to the development of events changing and assuming new forms with the progress of national consolidation."[37]

In a conversation with Henry Van Sinderen of the War Trade Board, Ughet listed the goods that should be sent to Siberia by their order of importance. He believed that priority should be given to categories of supplies in the following order: foodstuffs and railway material, clothing, shoes, crosscut saws, seeds, and agricultural implements. Ughet placed "especial stress on the necessity of distributing products in such a way as to avoid attitude of relief." It was his "desire to have the Russian people understand that they can procure the necessities of life if they work for them."[38] Thus, from the standpoint of the Russian embassy officials, the reconstruction of Russian society would be contingent on cultivating the basic liberal qualities of independence and self-sufficiency in the population.

The War Trade Board followed these guidelines as it prepared its estimates of the goods the Siberian population would need through December 1918. In early October its research bureau produced a detailed preliminary report on the supplies that should be immediately sent to Siberia. Eugene Kayden, the research bureau's chief economist, stated that "only the ordinary, fundamental needs of the people were to be taken into consideration, the commodities absolutely necessary to the life of the country and its economic rehabilitation." Kayden emphasized this point since, "the leading principle is to extend the kind of economic assistance which would enable the people to help themselves." He placed priority on sending liberal quantities of tools and hardware supplies to alleviate the severe shortage of basic implements. With regard to clothing and boots Kayden specified that it was the needs of the "common people—peasants, lumbermen, trappers etc." that should be considered and not the "standards of the town people."

The research bureau's report estimated the basic needs for a population of a thousand persons in Siberia. This fascinating report was a preliminary effort on the part of the American policymaking apparatus to investigate and evaluate social and economic conditions in the Siberian society. As an examination of the basic consumption needs of the Siberian population the report demonstrated the Wilson administration's desire to cultivate a harmony of interests between America and this developing frontier society. Moreover, Kayden's notes made further assessments of the social and economic merits of sending certain types of goods in preference to others.

The report consisted of the following categories of articles: foodstuffs, agricultural implements, trappers' implements, lumbering implements, carpenters' tools, blacksmiths' and machinists' tools, fishing implements, hardware and building supplies, household utensils, and miscellaneous items that included soap, and kerosene.

The report's recommendations and Kayden's notes illustrate the social characteristics America wanted to cultivate in Siberia's population. For example, the report advised that cobbler shops be organized in the towns to facilitate the efficient repair of footwear supplied by America. To instill efficient repair practices into these operations the report suggested the shops be modeled on the "existing American military standard." However, Kayden opposed the shipment of dairy and agricultural machinery, such as separators, churns, and pails to the Siberian cooperatives. He objected that the "Natives fully organized for [the] task. Give them only what they can't get; they will do the rest provided transportation facilities permit." In the pressing matter of agricultural machinery Kayden was emphatic that America "send *no* machinery now. That would be required for spring sowing and harvest; not now. It is imp[ortant] to send soft iron, sheet iron, and tool steel and let the peasants make their own plows etc. during the winter months. They know best. They can make tools and hardware goods and suit their own needs. *Send soft iron, etc.*"[39]

These preliminary discussions were the basis upon which the United States established the Russian Bureau of the War Trade Board. On October 10 detailed instructions were cabled to August Heid, who became the Russian Bureau's field manager at Vladivostok. As International Harvester's marketing representative in Siberia, Heid was particularly qualified for the task.[40] The board indicated to Heid that this program merely constituted a "provisional plan" in which the U.S. government would permit the licensing of exports required by the Siberian population and their distribution under War Trade Board supervision.

In accordance with Wilson's stipulations, the State Department and War Trade Board designed the program to promote private commerce with Siberia, supplemented by a modest $5 million revolving fund furnished by the government. A large quantity of goods existed in the United States that had been manufactured for export to Russia, as the American-Russian Chamber of Commerce petitions had been indicating since early summer. To determine the character and quantity of goods available in the private sector, the War Trade Board would now publicly announce its intention to consider export licenses. The War Trade Board believed this announcement would encourage exporters to file a large number of applications and thereby supply the data needed to evaluate the availability of goods in the private sector. Information from the American-Russian Chamber suggested a large number of applications would be forthcoming when the War Trade Board announced it was again considering licenses. The chamber was anxious to cooperate with the program, and indeed the War Trade Board depended on the organization for much of the data it required.[41]

The $5 million governmental subscription was to be used only for the purchase of goods the private sector was unwilling to export in view of the risks involved, or because the War Trade Board's regulations were considered too stringent. Shipping space to handle approximately fifteen thousand tons was to be made available in the beginning of the program, which, hopefully, would be increased over time. In the meantime much of this tonnage would be required for the transportation of military supplies to the Czech forces and for railroad materials ordered by John Stevens. A loan of $7 million was made by the United States to the Czecho-Slovak government, which was now officially recognized by the Wilson administration.

As the program developed, the War Trade Board planned to distribute goods only on the recommendations of its representatives in Siberia. Licenses would be granted on conditions that gave these representatives "effective control of the manner, place, and terms of sale," as well as the type and quantity of goods.[42] Heid was instructed to consider certain factors in the exercise of his regulatory control. First, he had to ensure that goods were sold on equitable terms that still allowed the exporter to make a reasonable profit, with due regard for risk. Profiteering had to be prevented so that the American program could not be discredited with the charge of exploitation. The War Trade Board suggested that exploitation could be avoided if goods were sold through the reputable Siberian cooperative societies.

Moreover, the military situation had to be followed closely by the War Trade Board representatives to make sure the civilian population received supplies wherever Allied forces operated. This would help foster friendly relations with the population and enhance Allied prestige. In particular, supplies had to be available for the people who lived in areas where the Czechs operated, or who lived along the routes by which supplies for the Czechs were transported. Wilson agreed to furnish the $5 million supplemental fund to meet this contingency, since under American assumptions, the whole program hinged on the Czechs' popularity.

When barter was employed to facilitate exchanges, goods should be acquired that would otherwise be available for Germany or that were needed in the United States. But since Russian organizations would also have to establish credits to pay for American goods, the War Trade Board was ready to grant import licenses for products of the cooperative societies or other private interests. Still, priority should be given those Russian goods that were actually needed in the United States.[43]

Finally, Heid was authorized to select American agents and to assign them to the important population centers along the Trans-Siberian Railroad. Their duties would be to investigate and report on local needs and the reliability of local purchasing bodies. These agents would also collect information on local products that could be used in other parts of the country by either the civilian population, or Allied military forces, or that could be exported.[44]

Important stakes were involved in the controversy between the State Department and the War Trade Board on the one hand and the Commerce Department on the other. The Commerce Department's arrangement with the Zakupsbyt threatened to compromise America's policy objectives in Siberia. While it was the Commerce Department's function to promote American commerce abroad, its initiative toward the Siberian cooperative societies did not take into consideration the numerous hazards that could undermine a program of commercial assistance under highly unstable conditions. The complex diplomatic and economic challenges that confronted American assistance policy in Siberia required careful control over exports to ensure that the distribution of American supplies furthered the administration's overall policy objectives.

It was for this reason that the State Department and War Trade Board gave priority to supplies for Stevens and the Czecho-Slovaks, who would necessarily lay the groundwork for an effective program of commercial assistance. In early October 1918, before the Russian Bureau program had even been announced, Ambassador Roland Morris informed the State Department that the United States should not attempt to undertake extensive commercial operations for the winter months. Because of the disruption of commercial activity along the Trans-Siberian railway, he recommended that railroad operations had to be reorganized first.[45]

Above all, as the fall progressed, American policymakers were increasingly preoccupied by the contest with Japan for control of the Trans-Siberian railway system, a question that had to be resolved before any significant supply efforts could be undertaken inland. A satisfactory agreement with Japan over this issue became the most critical question as winter approached since Japan's stranglehold over the Chinese Eastern Railway even prevented the transportation west from Vladivostok of the supplies Stevens had ordered for the line.[46]

In contrast, as late as the end of August 1918, the State Department's main antagonist in the controversy, Stanley Cutler, chief of the Bureau of

Foreign and Domestic Commerce, remained unreconciled to Wilson's subordination of economic assistance to support for the Czecho-Slovak troops. At this time Secretary Redfield actually reminded Cutler that he did not feel he could take any steps toward furnishing assistance to Siberia without the president's approval, because only "he understands the situation fully."[47]

The conflict that pitted the State Department and the War Trade Board against the Commerce Department boiled down to the question of establishing priorities in the shipment of goods to Siberia. While the Commerce Department and War Trade Board were considering the same types of goods for shipment to Siberia, the War Trade Board was specifically preparing a priority list to ensure that the most beneficial goods were allocated for the limited shipping space it would receive in November and December of 1918. A memorandum that summarized the policy behind the War Trade Board's initial commercial arrangements with the Zakupsbyt emphasized that the War Trade Board would specify the character of goods shipped to Siberia on the basis of negotiations between its representatives at Vladivostok and those of the Zakupsbyt in order "to insure—so far as possible—the purchase of those supplies to which the War Trade Board will be able to give shipping priority."[48] In the first months of the program much of this tonnage had to be reserved for the railroad and for the Czecho-Slovaks, and these requirements were still being determined. For instance, it was not until the end of October that the War Trade Board received Stevens's recommendation that it immediately ship 10,000 gallons of valve oil, 700,000 gallons of car oil, and 250 tons of cotton waste packing for use on the railroads.[49]

Throughout October, Stanley Cutler, who continued to brood over the War Trade Board's incursion on his initiative, criticized the board for the slowness with which he felt it was moving on announcing the materials it would license for export to Siberia. In late October Vance McCormick explained to Cutler that the board was preparing a licensing system that would involve a priority rating of various commodities.[50] In fact, the War Trade Board's decision to assemble a priority list was consistent with the advice of Ambassador Morris and August Heid, the Russian Bureau's field manager, that only limited supplies could be furnished to Siberia during the coming winter.

Closely linked with the question of priorities, the War Trade Board was preoccupied with maintaining tight supervision over the whole process of distributing American goods in order to prevent the exploitation of the Siberian population. But during the summer the Commerce Department's efforts to circumvent the supervision of the State Department and War Trade

Board threatened to expose the administration's assistance policy to a host of abuses. It was unlikely that a Commerce-run program would adequately control the distribution of supplies, and it would probably have to depend on Russian intermediaries. Without strict regulation over distribution the United States could not protect Siberian consumers from speculators, or, in general, from the decline of ethical business norms that inevitably take place under crisis situations.

There had even been some question in the mind of Stanley Cutler over whether trade commissioner Preston was making adequate provision for the supervision of American supplies. In late July he cabled Preston with the inquiry, "what distribution have you planned and what guarantee against enemy advantage. We cannot put our goods into hands of private traders without strict supervision."[51]

But the War Trade Board was concerned that American assistance could also inadvertently become exposed to abuse for political or financial gain if it gave preferential treatment to specific cooperative organizations out of failure to carefully scrutinize the recipients or the terms of contracts. As a case in point, the War Trade Board delayed its initial contract with the Zakupsbyt and its agent, the Narodny Bank, for this reason. Although the board approved in principle the importation into the United States of five hundred thousand dollars worth of furs, which the Zakupsbyt consigned to the Moscow Narodny Bank, as late as October 22 it had not granted import licenses or announced the proposal. The board had put the arrangement on hold "pending study of other applications to import furs, as Board in this particular transaction does not desire its action in respect to Narodny Bank to be preferential in character, and it is possible that within certain limits as to amounts, importers generally will be allowed to bring in furs, if they will submit to same terms proposed by Narodny Bank."[52]

By establishing priorities on the basis of the most badly needed supplies, the Wilson administration also hoped to restrain unrealistic expectations among the Siberian population, as well as speculative practices. For instance, American interests would not be served if the Commerce Department promised the Siberian cooperatives large quantities of expensive agricultural machinery, which it was then unable to deliver, regardless of the reason.

It is clear that from the middle of the summer American officials, especially Commerce Department trade commissioner Preston, had been building up expectations among the cooperatives that a large percentage of the exports would consist of agricultural machinery and twine. As late as the middle of September, Rueben R. MacDermid, a reputable American merchant at Vladivostok, indicated that the cooperatives were still clinging to this false impression when he reported to consul John Caldwell that the cooperative societies "will probably not be able, so far as my investigations at home showed, to get all the agricultural machinery they want, as that amount is tremendous, nor as quickly as they want it, since the steel and iron supply is limited for such manufacturers, but the foundations for business of 1919 and onward can be laid now."[53]

Finally, in view of the United States's problematic relations with Britain and Japan, a program run by the Commerce Department would fuel the already-intense economic rivalry that existed with the Allies, at a time when Wilson was attempting to cultivate the Allies' cooperation over the program of intervention. Japan, whose occupation of the Trans-Siberian Railroad enabled it to dictate the success of any assistance efforts, was particularly sensitive about American economic influence in Siberia. Indeed, a principal goal of Foreign Minister Gotō's Siberian policy was to check American economic penetration in the region. Since the spring of 1918 Japan had been very concerned about rumors over the likelihood that the U.S. government would finance ambitious economic ventures in the Russian Far East. In May Ambassador Kikujirō Ishii reported rumors from Washington of an American plan to spend billions of dollars to provide agricultural machinery to Siberia.[54] In view of these suspicions, Japanese officials would have been alarmed if they received any inkling of the Commerce Department's proposals from late June for a government-financed commercial assistance program of $100 million.

So deep was Japan's mistrust of American motives that its worst fears seemed confirmed when Wilson announced his intention to create an economic commission in his July 17 aide-mémoire. Many officials in Japan's foreign ministry viewed this declaration as the beginning of a bitter struggle for economic supremacy in Siberia. On July 26, in a meeting between government ministers and bankers, the Japanese government sponsored the formation of a syndicate of industrialists who would attempt to obtain concessions in Siberia with the support of financial subsidies from the government to the extent of 20 million to 30 million yen.[55]

The conflict between the State and Commerce Departments for control of the commercial assistance program was therefore rooted in important policy considerations. The State Department's successful struggle to place the assistance program under War Trade Board jurisdiction is itself crucial to understanding Wilsonian conceptions of the reconstruction process in Siberia. By providing the Siberian population with an infusion of basic manufactured goods that were in particularly short supply during the winter months, the War Trade Board hoped to reduce speculative pressure on prices caused by severe shortages of these necessities. This, in turn, would help stabilize the currency and restore a basis upon which more extensive commercial operations with the cooperatives could be undertaken in 1919. Meanwhile, in the critical early stages of reconstruction, this plan was purposely designed to limit the possibility that the U.S. government would be promoting American commercial interests at the expense of supplying the Siberian population's immediate needs. Finally, by fostering a more stable commercial environment, the administration hoped to bolster in the population the quality of industriousness and a capacity for self-government. Therefore, the Russian Bureau program demonstrates how the Wilsonians attempted to harmonize American interests and values with a practical appraisal of existing conditions in Siberia. The preoccupation of the State Department and the War Trade Board with the potential complications associated with an assistance program proved to be well warranted, for during its brief and troubled existence the Russian Bureau's operations were handicapped by the disruptive forces afflicting Siberia.

6

✦

A Stillborn Program:
The Russian Bureau,
October–December 1918

The United States's commercial assistance program required cooperation from the Allies and more stable conditions in Siberia than existed there in the fall of 1918. Indeed, insurmountable problems caused the American initiative to miscarry in its preliminary phases. The Russian Bureau of the War Trade Board was effectively undermined by the Allies' rival plans, contradictions within America's currency proposal and by deteriorating conditions in Siberia. When the Armistice occurred, which eliminated the German threat, American policymakers had concluded that reconstruction in Siberia would be stalled until communications along the Trans-Siberian Railroad were dramatically improved.[1]

On September 21, Lansing advised Wilson that, before commercial assistance could proceed, a practical medium of exchange had to be established. Even though the United States planned to operate the commercial program on a barter basis, some type of currency was required to demonstrate the amount of purchasing power a party had from the sale of its commodities. Great distances would exist between the sites of the actual exchange of goods, since most parties would not purchase commodities at the same location where they sold commodities. For that matter, direct exchanges of commodities between parties would rarely take place. Seasonal cycles of trade also complicated barter exchange, since harvests and their income were realized during the fall, yet peasants needed to purchase manufactured goods throughout the year. Consequently, some form of circulating medium was required even though transactions were to approximate a condition of barter as much as possible.[2]

Monetary questions quickly arose after the decision to introduce Allied troops in Siberia during July. On July 21, Adm. Austin Knight cabled Washington that the impending military expedition to support the Czecho-Slovaks would create a monetary crisis in Siberia. Banking facilities were nonexistent, and the better ruble issues were scarce as a result of hoarding. Rubles at that date were worth 10 cents but were subject to extreme fluctuations. Knight suggested that rubles be purchased in Shanghai, Tientsin, Peking, Mukden, Changchun, and Harbin, where considerable currency had accumulated. He also recommended that the National City Bank or American International Corporation establish a branch bank at Vladivostok to handle deposits and issue currency. A virtual "currency famine" existed for rubles in smaller denominations, which would make it difficult for the army to pay the sudden influx of enlisted men. Rubles could be purchased at the aforementioned centers, as well as New York, but their price would be considerably higher than the rate at Vladivostok.[3]

Breckinridge Long immediately sounded a warning in regard to any monetary plans for Siberia in a memorandum dated July 23. The paper rubles that would be used by the military and civilian forces who entered Siberia had depreciated to varying degrees—in some cases to the point of being worthless. Germany had bought large quantities of rubles in neutral countries and was rumored to have printed a great many more paper rubles from the dye allegedly in its possession for the production of old ruble notes. The face value of the rubles held by Germany was estimated to be $400 million. If Allied forces restored confidence in the ruble as a medium of exchange, its value would rise accordingly, and "Germany's wealth will be increased by just that much, estimated in 400,000,000 units." Long believed it was necessary to further depreciate the value of the existing rubles. Otherwise, windfall gains might accrue to Germany and greatly enhance its ability to purchase control of Russian assets.[4]

Germany hoped to derive considerable strategic benefits from its ruble holdings during the war as well as in the long run. Its effort to accumulate ruble holdings not only threatened to establish its predominance over Russia's banking and industrial structure, but these assets also had a direct bearing on Germany's ability to prosecute the war. For some time Germany had been endeavoring through various means to accumulate imperial rubles. In April 1917, the German governor-general demonetized the ruble standard in Poland and authorized the exchange of ruble notes into Polish loan bank certificates through banks under German control. Since 1917, it had also been buying up imperial rubles in the neutral Scandinavian markets. Moreover, under the supplementary agreements to the Brest-Litovsk Treaty, Russia was obligated to pay 6 billion marks in gold and in Russian State Bank notes of older issues, principally in denominations of fifty, one hundred, and five hundred rubles. Finally, after its reopening in the spring of 1918, the German consulate in Moscow released a circular to Russian citizens announcing its intention to accept rubles for safe deposit in the German Imperial Bank. William Huntington, the American commercial attaché of the Commerce Department, brought this to the attention of the War Trade Board after he returned from Moscow in September 1918. From his first-hand knowledge of events in Moscow Huntington related that

> the financial section of the German Consulate in Moscow had been doing a land office business in accepting deposits of money and valuable[s] and in transmitting funds to Germany for safe keeping. He states that for weeks carriages were lined up before the German Consulate with persons awaiting their opportunity to hand over their funds. With the terror prevailing in Russia even the German Government bank represented security.[5]

William H. Owen, a member of the War Trade Board in Scandinavia, suspected that Germany was using rubles to expand the bank credit available within its own economy. He speculated that "it seems ridiculous, but nevertheless not far from true, that a great part of the German loan bank notes in circulation in Germany are covered with Russian State Bank ruble notes as security."

Owen was also certain that Germany expected a future Russian government to repudiate Kerensky and Bolshevik money, leaving the greater part of the negotiable Russian currency in Germany's hands. Owen thought Germany was anticipating that Russian holders of industrial securities would be inclined to sell their assets at low prices for these cash rubles, given the complete disappearance of banking credit. Alternatively, they might be willing to accept this cash as indemnification for Bolshevik nationalization of their property after a bourgeois government had been restored to power.[6]

Germany's extensive financial operations in the imperial rubles gave a definite urgency to the currency questions associated with economic assistance for Siberia in 1918. Long proposed that a new ruble be issued at a fixed rate in exchange for the existing rubles in Asiatic and European Russia, which were not under German influence. The Narodny Banks could be used to issue the new rubles in exchange for the old rubles in areas east of the Ural Mountains, while an embargo was placed on all rubles that passed into Siberia from European Russia. Old rubles should be presented to the Narodny Banks for redemption in new rubles during a specified period of time, after which, the embargo could be discontinued. Long sent a copy of this memorandum to Assistant Secretary of the Treasury Russell C. Leffingwell, on July 25, and the State Department also raised the subject with the Federal Reserve on August 9.[7]

The Treasury Department discussed these financial questions with Russian ambassador Boris Bakhmetev and the Russian embassy's financial attaché, Serge Ughet, around the middle of August.[8] On August 21, after consultations with Treasury Department officials, Vladimir Novitskii of the Russian embassy and the American banker Samuel Bertron, Bakhmetev presented the State Department with a currency plan to facilitate the commercial assistance program. Two important considerations guided the recommendations embodied in this program. First, no currency procedures should be adopted that would hamper both the future stabilization and the consolidation of Russia's monetary system. Second, the value of Germany's large ruble holdings should not be augmented. Three types of monetary procedures could be employed in Siberia: the existing rubles, foreign currency, and special bank notes or certificates denominated in rubles.

The Russian embassy–Treasury Department proposal rejected the possibility of using the existing rubles, because the unrestricted issuance of paper money had caused a rapid depreciation in its value, stripping it of the stable qualities required of a standard of value. Allied troops would have a difficult time buying commodities with the ruble, since the Siberian population considered them to be practically worthless. Conversely, any stabilization of the ruble would only strengthen Germany's financial leverage over Russia.

Foreign currency should not be introduced, because the population was unfamiliar with foreign values and because, "in the future, such a course would be bound to cause difficulties to the Government of Russia." Not only would the future government have to establish a new national currency unit, but it would also have to remove foreign currency from circulation. The government would then be faced with the difficult, and possibly hazardous task, of reasserting Russian sovereignty, because the foreign medium "might become a familiar instrument of purchase and exchange and the value of which besides is totally independent and is beyond the authority on the part of any institutions in Russia." In other words, foreign currency zones should not be allowed to develop, because this process would transform whole regions into spheres of influence for other powers. Hard foreign currencies should not be introduced into Siberia, because they could "be diverted into German channels."

The Russian embassy's plan, which was endorsed by the War Trade Board and the State and Treasury Departments, called for the production of special certificates denominated in ruble values to be issued in connection with all Allied activity in Russia. This proposed monetary system was only intended to serve as a temporary measure and was specifically not meant to constitute a general settlement for Russia's problems. Only the future national government of Russia would have the authority to resolve the country's myriad monetary problems. The introduction of this new exchange medium was motivated strictly by the practical objective of facilitating Allied economic assistance. Popular confidence in these ruble certificates would stem from their effective purchasing power, which was tied to the availability of imported Allied goods. The quantity of new notes should be determined by the actual demand for exchange media stimulated by economic assistance. The Russian embassy proposal presumed that an inter-Allied financial institution would manage the currency and that it would operate under the auspices of a "governing" inter-Allied economic commission that would extend assistance to the Siberian population by supplying goods on a "fair cost basis" and by extending the necessary commercial credits. However, by this time, the Wilson administration was drawing back from an inter-Allied commercial venture in light of its suspicions about the British government's preemptive commercial plan.

An Allied or American bank was to act as the financial agent for the economic commission. Its stock would consist primarily of subscriptions by the allied governments or the United States, such as the $5 million fund allotted to the Russian Bureau. The Treasury Department assumed this capital stock would be invested in commodities and the currency issued by the bank would be redeemable only in commodities imported by the Allies. It was believed this commodity-backed currency system could retain a stable purchasing power. Nevertheless, in the Russian embassy–Treasury Department proposal, part of the stock was expected to consist of foreign currency. Because imports to Russia would greatly exceed Russian exports during the program's early stages, the Allied bank would essentially provide credit to importers in dollars, other foreign currencies, or the commodity-backed notes. This department would also provide the currency needed to pay Allied troops.

The commodity-backed notes were not intended to immediately replace the existing rubles, because importers, whether individual peasants, municipalities, zemstvos, or cooperatives, might only be able to offer paper rubles as security against imports payable in foreign currency. In these cases, rubles could be accepted as collateral. Their exchange rate with foreign currencies could be settled in the future after a national government had consolidated the monetary system and determined the relative value of these current paper rubles.

Yet, as reconstruction progressed, it was hoped that transactions in the present ruble would be reduced to a minimum as the population gained confidence in the new notes.

While the new bank notes were not to be regarded as legal tender, the Russian embassy–Treasury Department plan envisioned a significant role for these temporary certificates. They should adopt standard ruble denominations and their value should be determined by establishing their exchange rate with foreign currency. A central premise of the plan stipulated that this rate should be based on the ruble's prewar value. By attaching the ruble's prewar value to these certificates, Russia's economic links with gold-standard countries like the United States could be preserved. It was hoped that the certificates would, after a certain period of time, be favored by the population "as a generally recognized exchange media [sic]" because of their effective purchasing power. Furthermore, it was expected that the certificates would assume the role of a parallel currency to be accepted by municipalities, zemstvos, railways, and banks in payment of taxes, transportation fares, and postal telegraph services, and so forth. The prospect that these certificates would evolve into a medium of "general character" was to be encouraged. In this capacity they could act as a nucleus around which a future national government of Russia could restore the gold standard. When the time arrived to establish the value of the depreciated revolutionary rubles in relation to a new national unit, the ruble certificates would "constitute a well-established standard" through their fixed valuation with foreign currency. While in circulation though, the ruble notes should not be freely convertible with foreign currency even though their value was established in relation to foreign currency. This provision was required to prevent them from being utilized by Germany. Convertibility with foreign currencies could only take place under the authority of the Allied bank and must be subject to the existing Allied regulations. In the future, the Russian national government could assume control of the Allied bank. At this time, the ruble certificates could be recalled in exchange for a consolidated national currency or redeemed in foreign exchange at face value.[9]

By the end of August then, American policymakers recognized that complicated monetary difficulties would have to be overcome if the commercial assistance program were to succeed. Thus, even before Wilson had decided that the War Trade Board would coordinate the commercial program, the Russian embassy, and the State and Treasury Departments had begun to develop plans for a temporary currency for Siberia.

During August, Admiral Knight received advice from American banking representatives with regard to the severe shortage of small ruble currency.

William Anderson of the International Banking Corporation (IBC) suggested that Allied war notes be printed in ruble denominations of one, three, five, ten, and possibly fifty kopeks. These notes would then be put into circulation in exchange for ruble notes of larger denominations, which were more plentiful. Knight objected that this plan would require lengthy negotiation by the Allies. He preferred that an American bank or the U.S. government issue the required notes at once. Anderson thought this unilateral course would violate Russian law, but Knight believed the critical monetary situation outweighed legal questions.

American authorities at Vladivostok particularly wanted an American branch bank established to serve their financial requirements. Since large amounts of more reliable ruble issues were being hoarded throughout Siberia, the establishment of a National City Bank branch would draw out these sums and relieve the currency shortage. While Anderson believed it would be easier to establish a branch of the IBC, the National City Bank already had Russian branches and it had the confidence of the Russian public. Anderson inquired of the National City Bank whether it had the prerogative to open a branch at Vladivostok under its agreement with the imperial government.

On August 23, the National City Bank wired Anderson that it would open a branch at Vladivostok pending the authorization of the minister of finance. Anderson did not think this reply resolved anything because there was presently no Russian government. In a cable to the IBC, Anderson reported that "prospects for [a] branch [are] very uncertain" because of the risks posed by present circumstances. He nevertheless added that it held "great possibilities in the future." Under the circumstances, he suggested that the IBC attempt to obtain a guarantee against potential losses on exchange rates of approximately $2.5 million from the U.S. government. Furthermore, all of the financial arrangements of the army and navy should be transacted at a rate of exchange set by the IBC.

In the meantime, Anderson recommended that some responsible authority immediately issue small ruble denominations in exchange for larger denominations. Since long negotiations would delay this course of action, Anderson asked whether the City Bank could issue the notes in the name of the U.S. government. Alternatively, he asked whether an agency like the Red Cross could be persuaded to undertake the cost of such an issue.

Anderson learned that the Russian banks at Vladivostok, such as the Russo-Asiatic Bank, could not be counted on to issue the emergency notes. In fact, the Russian banks were held in very low esteem by the public, doing virtually no business in August except for current accounts. The

Russo-Asiatic Bank was charging 1 percent commission on deposits and it would pay out only 250 rubles a week on current accounts. A Japanese bank, called the Matsuda Bank, was doing a small amount of business in Vladivostok. This bank was supposedly a branch of the Chosen Bank "in disguise," which had introduced the yen into northern Manchuria.

Anderson concluded that the National City Bank should establish a branch bank at Vladivostok. It would be "cordially welcomed" and would likely acquire large deposits, because the Russians were awaiting the opening of the "first reliable bank." The funds of the branch bank could be used to restore commercial credit, particularly with the cooperative societies. Anderson believed Vladivostok would have "a great and prosperous future" as the source of transshipment for Siberia's potentially immense export and import trade. Siberia was "raw and undeveloped," but it undoubtedly had "great potential wealth and under wise and liberal laws would offer a great opportunity to capital." Only the "strong socialistic element" was a disquieting feature, but even this problem was discounted as more of a passing concern in as much as "the working people here had not experienced the evils of Bolshevism."

Anderson thought it was likely that the Allies would either stabilize Siberia quickly, or that Vladivostok would become an important military base after the introduction of Allied Expeditionary Forces. In the first instance, Vladivostok would become a center for Siberian trade, while in the latter case business would be stimulated by the restoration of monetary services for the Allied forces. Anderson predicted that, when Japan introduced its military forces, it would almost assuredly open a government bank, "and it would appear to be almost a necessity for us to do likewise" in order to satisfy the requirements of the U.S. troops, the Red Cross, the YMCA, and other government officials.[10]

Although Anderson's recommendations were advocated by all of the American officials at Vladivostok, the State and Treasury Departments urged the ruble certificate plan on the Allies throughout September and October 1918. These departments were anxious to coordinate financial procedures among the powers to prevent them from developing preferential spheres of influence. For this reason, the State Department did not take any steps to encourage the establishment of an American branch bank at Vladivostok in these two months. Nevertheless, by September Japan and Britain had quickly moved to introduce their own currency plans in their prospective spheres of influence.

In August, the Japanese military began to introduce the yen into Siberia by circulating headquarter notes redeemable in yen. These notes were ostensibly intended to finance Japan's military requirements because of the scarcity of small ruble denominations. This development had ominous implications for Russian sovereignty, since Japan had introduced the yen into Manchuria by the same method.

Likewise, in the faraway Archangel district of northern Russia, Britain decided to implement a monetary program that would establish its sphere of influence in that region. During mid-September 1918, Britain announced that it planned to issue a new ruble currency for Archangel and Murmansk, which would alleviate the shortage of circulating medium in the area. Britain justified this initiative on grounds that the growing cost of Allied expenditures and local administrative expenses could not be met by the depreciated value of the existing rubles. To address this problem Britain proposed to dissociate the currency of north Russia from the rest of the country by issuing a new ruble based on a paper pound in London. A conversion office would be attached to the Provisional Government and would work under the guidance of a British financial advisor. This office was authorized to issue and redeem these notes at a fixed rate of 40 rubles to the Pound. Britain claimed this program would enable the Allies to pay cash for their military expenditures and to supply a stable currency for commercial activity. It was also said to offer a quicker and less complicated means of establishing a stable monetary system in north Russia in contrast to a complicated inter-Allied plan. The British government planned to purchase a large number of these rubles in the coming months.[11]

This program carried the seeds of British supremacy in the region, since other nations would have to finance their trade with north Russia through sterling exchange. Britain scarcely concealed its desire to establish a sphere of influence in north Russia. After Ambassador David Francis suggested that the reserve be held in New York as well as in London, Francis O. Lindley, the British high commissioner for north Russia, bluntly informed him that Britain expected America and Japan to settle financial matters in Siberia between themselves. Lindley believed his government was "wedded" to this plan and would insist on its adoption because Britain was a large creditor of France and Italy.[12] Unexpectedly, one week later, Britain agreed to modify its plan to provide for a reserve in dollars at New York. This provision would make it possible for American exporters to be paid in dollars rather than in sterling and for America to buy rubles through the deposit of dollars at a fixed rate in the reserve fund at New York. But Lindley exposed Britain's desire to steal a march on its American competition when he casually told Francis that a financial expert was already en route to north Russia to begin the monetary program immediately. The French ambassador was not told of Britain's plans, because France was working on its own plan for an Allied bank.[13]

Arthur Crosby of the Treasury Department, who was a delegate to the Inter-Allied Council on War Purchases and Finance, pointed up the inherent dangers of the British program from London on September 23. He warned that if each Ally operated independently, as Britain was in north Russia, "there would soon develop competition for exploiting the Russian field as rapidly as that field is pacified by Allied and American forces." Unilateral action by any power would give it a commercial advantage over the others even though stabilization of the country was a result of the combined efforts of the participating governments. Crosby cut to the heart of the matter when he emphasized his "somewhat rooted objection to financial arrangements that will result in the interlocking of international finances after the war." Instead, the United States "should avoid anything in the way of general endorsements of currencies, or other instruments of credit." Conversely, Crosby did endorse the principle underlying the Russian embassy–Treasury Department program when he recommended that the United States could "enter a combination in which the specific amount of the obligations of the United States, or of its cash resources, should be pledged to support any necessary issues in Russia during a period of military operations in which our government may join. Our part in the final liquidation of such obligations would be measured wholly by such participation as we may agree to."[14]

Crosby indicated that France might also object to Britain's independent course. On September 17, the French government proposed the establishment of an inter-Allied bank that would receive assets deposited by the Allied governments and that would issue special currency denominated in rubles. This agency would enable the Allied forces to purchase supplies in Siberia. Crosby had just spoken with a financial agent from the French Treasury who was unaware of Britain's initiative "and presumed that his Government's proposition would initiate the whole subject."[15]

On October 5, the State Department presented the British embassy with its objections to Britain's plans for a north Russian currency. The United States opposed Britain's proposal, because the "problem in connection with Russian currency both in north Russia and in Siberia is practically identical." In both cases, the question was one of creating a circulating medium that would be accepted by the population. For a currency to be accepted at its nominal value, it would have to be backed by commodities "on the spot" to demonstrate its effective purchasing power. A currency issued under British auspices and tied to sterling was unacceptable then, because whatever circulating value it acquired would arise from the presence of American and French goods as well as British.

Above all, if the Allies introduced any new currency, it should be easily convertible into a future national currency system by a Russian government.

Indeed, the American position was essentially concerned with maintaining parity between any new currency and gold. Originally, the ruble had a gold value of fifty cents, but it was now selling at from ten to fifteen cents. The State Department memorandum proceeded to emphasize that "if a new and distinctive issue of rubles, backed by commodities, is now put out on the market at what the old rubles are selling, it would be necessary ultimately to redeem that ruble at a face value of 50 cents which would involve considerable and unnecessary losses."[16] If Britain and the other powers introduced distinctive currencies into various parts of Russia at the market rate, a future national Russian government would have to incur great financial losses to redeem these issues at par with gold. In effect, this situation would hinder Russia's return to the gold standard and disrupt its trade with gold-standard countries like the United States. Therefore, from the American standpoint it was desirable to establish similar currencies in north Russia and Siberia, "so that the systems established may fit into each other and be taken over subsequently by any stable Russian government."[17]

America's strategy for countering the Allies' rival economic initiatives was disclosed during a War Trade Board meeting on October 4. At this meeting, chairman McCormick related the State Department's position with regard to joint commercial and monetary endeavors in Russia. McCormick told the board that the State Department was opposed to the creation of an inter-Allied trading company at Vladivostok that would administer the distribution of supplies among Siberia's civilian population. Nevertheless, the State Department did intend that representatives from the associated governments be admitted on the American company's board of directors. This gesture to Allied sensibilities was necessary, because commercial assistance in the Archangel district was being administered on an inter-Allied basis, with Britain, France, and the United States sharing the cost of relief measures there. Consequently, "it might become a matter of some delicacy and difficulty to insist upon a different principle of organization and procedure at Vladivostok." Despite its opposition to a joint commercial program, McCormick reported that the State Department desired the creation of an inter-Allied banking organization at Vladivostok. This agency would manage the "financial aspects of the transactions involved in the delivery of supplies to Russia at that port."[18]

It is clear from this proceeding that the State Department did not want American commercial assistance associated with the Allies' suspect activities in Siberia. Lansing had actually been quite explicit on this point with Japanese ambassador Ishii in late June when the administration's plans for an economic mission were otherwise in the formative stage. At that time, when Ishii had inquired about the prospective American economic commission that would engage in barter with Siberia, Lansing told the ambassador that it would act from purely humanitarian motives and that it would be a strictly American venture. He then explained to Ishii that "if it were made up of Japanese, the Russians would suspect it of political designs, and if it were made up of Englishmen, they would suspect it of commercial ambitions."[19] Yet, it was important that the Allies participate in a joint note-issuing financial agency. This bank would safeguard American objectives in Siberia amid the separate Allied commercial ventures. As the sole authority through which notes were issued and through which credits were furnished to importers, the bank could retain regulatory control over the Allies' commercial relations with Siberia as well as facilitate the integration of these notes into a future national monetary system.

Britain tried to assuage American objections to its north Russian currency plan in a memorandum of October 16. Britain claimed it had considered the possibility of issuing its new ruble at the gold value of fifty cents. However, it was convinced that great difficulties would arise if the value of the new unit diverged greatly from the value of the present currency. These new notes would clearly state that they were redeemable at the rate of 40 rubles to the pound. This declaration released the participating governments from any obligation to redeem the notes at par. Britain also reasserted its right to issue these notes because it was primarily responsible for Allied operations in north Russia. For the same reason, the United States would be perfectly justified in taking the lead in Siberia. Finally, too much time would elapse before an inter-Allied currency could be issued for all of Russia. Immediate action was required in north Russia to prevent disaster. Consequently, a plan "of experimental character and limited application" was needed to meet urgent military exigencies. Britain hoped the United States would agree to the plan as an emergency measure, particularly it if was "done without prejudice to later developments or to any subsequent scheme on permanent lines which may eventually be reached by the Allies."[20]

The State Department chose to interpret this statement as an acceptance of the American position on the currency question. First, the department assumed that Britain's memorandum confirmed its intention to establish an inter-Allied currency as soon as possible, and second, that British authorities had only resorted to this plan because they found it impractical to use existing issues for immediate requirements. With these stipulations, the United States was willing to defer to Britain provided that the currency was only of an emergency character and that it could be redeemed within a limited period.[21]

A consensus in favor of a temporary currency plan prevailed at a conference of Allied financial delegates in London on October 26. The conference rejected an inter-Allied note issue because of the time it would take to settle the details. A solution was reached for its "simplicity and speed," which authorized France to make an emergency note issue in Siberia similar to Britain's in north Russia. Since France had to finance the Czecho-Slovak troops, its expenditures would be greater than that of Britain or the United States. France would furnish the other governments with its notes in exchange for their currencies at the existing exchange rate. Although the American advisory counsel, Paul D. Cravath, had no instructions, he consented on the condition that this initiative would only be a temporary expedient and that it could be superseded by more permanent measures after a greater degree of stability was restored in Siberia.[22]

The U.S. government was not satisfied with the decision of the Allied conference regarding currency questions. Crosby and Cravath were instructed by the Treasury Department to reject the conclusion of the conference and to press for the acceptance of an inter-Allied currency. In the meantime, the State Department believed the critical shortage of small ruble denominations in Siberia could be met by an immediate emergency measure. Prior to the overthrow of the Provisional Government, an order for Russian bank notes had been placed in the United States. These notes had been produced and were now ready for shipment pending a War Trade Board license. The Russian embassy and the State and Treasury Departments all agreed that small denominations from this issue could be exchanged in Siberia for existing rubles of larger denomination when presented in the proper amounts. They also believed this temporary expedient could satisfy the monetary requirements of Britain, France, and the United States in Siberia without resorting to the British or French plans. This procedure could be used until the commodity-backed inter-Allied ruble was introduced. To further the American position in the controversy over Siberian currency, the State Department hoped to continue discussions in Washington rather than London or Paris.[23]

Nevertheless, at the beginning of November, Britain, France, and Japan continued to signal their uncooperative stance toward the American currency proposal. A summary of the situation was prepared for the War Trade Board on November 2 by John Foster Dulles. In this memorandum, Dulles called attention to the fact that the Allies had never stated their acceptance of the American proposal for an international ruble. Instead, Dulles believed these governments were "independently exerting every effort to preempt the field wherein they are operating by new issues of currency bearing the character of the respective nations under whose auspices they are issued." Since the rubles Britain produced for the Archangel district had already been printed, the State Department doubted whether the purely emergency character of these notes was even designated on their face. Above all else, Britain was clearly attempting to play the United States against Japan and France in Siberia while it consolidated its own currency zone in north Russia. American resentment toward Britain's strategy was manifested in Dulles's comment that "It is evident to us from our conversations and from exchanges of notes with the British that they desire to work toward the establishment of certain spheres of influence in Russia and that they desire a free hand in Archangel, leaving the United States to work out with Japan and France the question of which of those governments shall take the lead in Siberia."[24] Thus, even before the Armistice of November 11, the Russian Bureau program was crippled by Allied resistance to the plan for an international note issue.

Shortly after the Russian Bureau's inception it became clear that conditions in Siberia would drastically limit the effectiveness of the commercial assistance program itself. For commercial assistance to be rendered on any significant scale, Siberia would have to export its own commodities to finance imports. However, the dislocation of production in Siberia left the region with few products that it could sell in America.

By November 1918, Washington was gaining a fuller appreciation of the degree of economic dislocation in Siberia. On November 1, the State Department sent the War Trade Board a memorandum by Vladimir Novitskii of the Russian embassy concerning economic conditions in Siberia. Novitskii's facts were supplied by the various branches of the Russo-Asiatic Bank scattered throughout Siberia. A bleak reality emerged from the bank's reports; between Vladivostok and Omsk there were no available supplies of exportable commodities, like grain or hides. Vladivostok was dependent on Manchuria for its food supplies. Chita had no stocks of grain or hides for export, and it was receiving an insufficient supply of foodstuffs from Manchuria. Mining operations in the vicinity had also ceased. Leather, soap, and furs were still being manufactured at Irkutsk, but these goods were not available for export. Krasnoyarsk had little manufacturing to begin with, and no products were available for export. It was only at Omsk that plentiful supplies of grain began to appear as well as stocks of hides, bristles, wool, and horsehair.[25]

On Armistice Day (November 11, 1918), Heid cabled Washington with facts that were cause for a serious reevaluation of the Russian Bureau program. In late October, the board had requested Heid to consider the purchase, on credit, of some goods in China and Japan. His response from November 11 called into question the efficacy of commercial assistance at that time. The Russian Bureau did not have an organization sufficient to distribute the merchandise from China and Japan.[26] In reply to the same issue on October 21, Heid advised that it would take "some months" to establish an organization that could adequately distribute and control these purchases. He emphasized that a competent organization was necessary to regulate commercial transactions; otherwise, "only confusion will be added to the already confused conditions and the object of our work will be defeated and loss of time and money incurred." Heid also advised against these purchases, because Japan and China had no price controls. Furthermore, goods from these countries could not be distributed in Siberia before February, at which time American goods could also be distributed.[27]

Heid's remaining points in his November 11 cable raised more serious questions for American policymakers. Transportation facilities were in a "disorganized condition," which effectively prohibited the movement of goods inland from Vladivostok. Also, while there were shortages of clothing and foodstuffs, it was becoming evident that there was no immediate risk of suffering among the people in Siberia's northern regions. Suffering would exist primarily among prisoners and refugees. Next, reliable sources indicated that speculation was hampering the bureau's regulatory functions. In some cases, even cooperative societies were known to obtain goods for profiteering. Finally, it was clear that workers and farmers had actually hoarded a substantial amount of currency. This meant that hardship did not exist for lack of a circulating medium. Rather, it was the breakdown in transportation that had disrupted production and distribution. By this time, Washington was well aware that rehabilitation of the Trans-Siberian railway system was the prerequisite for Siberia's reconstruction.[28]

Britain and Japan must ultimately bear a great deal of responsibility for this deterioration of conditions in Siberia. The military policies of these powers quickened the pace of social disintegration in Siberia during late 1918. By late August, it was clear that Wilson's gamble of using the Czecho-Slovaks as a vanguard for commercial assistance had failed. Britain encouraged Japan to turn the expedition into a large-scale intervention with the aim of restoring an eastern front. What is more, the Czecho-Slovaks had become embroiled in the Russian civil war west of the Ural Mountains. This could only bolster Britain's efforts to maintain its position in southern Russia. Inevitably, by late September, the Czech forces west of the Urals were in jeopardy from advancing Bolshevik forces. However, they refused to withdraw out of loyalty to the Russians who had supported them. Wilson and Lansing were therefore placed in the unenviable position of having to tell the Czechs that they would not receive American supplies unless they retreated east of the Urals. Moreover, after Adm. Kolchak's Omsk regime was established with British connivance in November 1918, Gen. William S. Graves, head of the American Expeditionary Forces, wanted the American troops entirely withdrawn from Siberia. Graves recognized that the presence of Allied troops, especially American, only abetted the Omsk government's repression of the Siberian population.[29]

But by this time, the success of the administration's Siberian policy had come to rest on the fate of the Trans-Siberian railway system, and at the end of October, a showdown was brewing with Japan over control of the Trans-Siberian railway system. Between late summer and December 1918, Japan choked off the modest amount of American commercial assistance to Siberia. Since the end of the summer, Japan had made a determined effort to undermine John Stevens's managerial authority over the Chinese Eastern and Trans-Siberian railways. Significant operating improvements on the Chinese Eastern Railway had been achieved under Stevens's authority after the arrival of George Emerson's Russian Railway Service Corps at Harbin in March 1918.

But the Allies proceeded to use the military intervention to whittle away at Stevens's position. In August, a Bolshevik force defeated Japan's puppet, the disreputable Cossack leader G. M. Semenov, in the Trans-Baikal and drove him back into Chinese territory.[30] Japan seized this opportunity to occupy the whole Chinese Eastern Railway with a force of twelve thousand troops. After Japan's resolve to control the line became clear, Stevens sought diplomatic support from the State Department to strengthen his authority over the whole Trans-Siberian railway system. By early September, the Japanese military had begun to displace Stevens entirely when it placed all Siberian railroads under military control.[31]

By the end of October Japan's military was poised to absorb the Chinese Eastern Railway into its Manchurian sphere of influence and thereby strangle America's Siberian policy. In a memorandum of October 28, based on cables from Ambassador Roland Morris, Miles warned that divided operation of the railways would doom American reconstruction efforts, because "the successful operation of the railways is fundamental to all our plans to assist the Russian population." The situation required an agreement for joint Allied supervision of the Trans-Siberian railway system under Stevens's direction; the United States supported Stevens as an accredited representative of the legitimate Russian government.[32]

War Trade Board chairman Vance McCormick also expressed to Lansing his concern over Japan's efforts to disrupt America's commercial assistance. He reported that plans were "fully matured, and in part in operation" for the shipment of supplies to the civilian population of Siberia, the Czecho-Slovaks, and to John Stevens for the Trans-Siberian railway system. But Japan's large expeditionary force obstructed these operations. Through its occupation of the Chinese Eastern Railway and parts of the Amur railroad line Japan controlled the westward movement of freight to exclusively promote its own trade at the expense of other foreign goods.

McCormick believed that great stakes hinged on the success of America's program in the interior of Siberia. He revealed the potential scope of American ambitions in Eurasia when he stated, "I am convinced that the most effective areas in which to distribute supplies are in the western portions of Siberia, where we will be close enough to impress the great mass of the Russian people located in European Russia." Thus, the commercial assistance program for Siberia must be seen as an important element in the Wilson administration's grand liberal-internationalist strategy. To protect the railroad and the shipment of American supplies, McCormick recommended that American troops be sent as far west as Omsk. This suggestion was not considered in view of the strong objections made by General Graves and Secretary of War Newton Baker to any expanded role for the American troops in strife-ridden Siberia.[33]

The ambitions expressed in McCormick's memorandum would not have surprised the Japanese, for they perceived the historical continuity of American policy in the region. In November, Foreign Minister Gotō told Ambassador Morris that Japan considered Stevens's role on the Trans-Siberian railway system as analogous to the purpose behind the Knox Neutralization Plan of 1909. This American initiative had proposed a six-power loan to China to finance its purchase of the Russian-owned Chinese Eastern Railway and the Japanese-owned South Manchurian Railway. Secretary Knox viewed China's redemption of these railroads as the foundation of the Open Door in the region. The existence of an intense Japanese-American rivalry in this developing region by 1919 was therefore rooted in Japan's recognition that Stevens merely represented a new agent of this long-standing American objective in the Far East.[34]

Throughout October, reports from Vladivostok had increasingly cast doubt on the wisdom of introducing any new currency—even of a temporary character. On October 6, Ambassador Morris informed the State Department that the existing ruble was "accepted everywhere throughout Siberia and is preferred to all other forms of currency." American forces at Vladivostok were able to obtain all the supplies they needed with the ruble. Moreover, the earlier fear that Japan might introduce the yen into eastern Siberia had not materialized. Japanese authorities had no success with this policy as they had had in north Manchuria. Morris reported with confidence that no yen circulated in Vladivostok and that attempts by Japanese military authorities to use yen in areas where their forces operated "has been bitterly resented and I understand that they have decided to discontinue it." The Russian State Bank was even considering plans to alleviate the shortage of small ruble denominations by issuing notes of small denominations against notes of larger amounts.[35]

This view was confirmed by John Sukin, from the foreign ministry of the short-lived provisional Siberian government based at Vladivostok. In October, before it was absorbed by Admiral Kolchak's Omsk government, this predominantly Social-Revolutionary government was considering a currency plan that was very similar to the Russian embassy–Treasury Department proposal. As part of this fragile government's efforts to curry favor with the United States, it claimed to have abandoned its plans for devaluation of the present ruble currency and for issuing more valueless paper money. However, Sukin advised that if the international ruble plan was administered by an Allied bank, it might meet with opposition from the Siberian authorities. He recommended that Russian feelings would have to be considered before any decisions were made. Therefore, the foreign ministry of the Siberian government urgently requested that Allied financial representatives be sent to Vladivostok to negotiate this question.[36]

Morris believed a National City Bank branch at Vladivostok would perform a more useful role than the introduction of new currency by the Allies. American goods would not be attracted to Siberia, given the risks involved with exchange rates, unless the U.S. government encouraged a branch bank to open there. A political incentive also existed for such action, as the Allies were planning to open branch banks at Vladivostok in the immediate future. Britain's Hong Kong and Shanghai Bank was expected to open a branch at Vladivostok on October 19, while Japanese and French banks were also preparing to open branches soon.[37]

August Heid agreed that the U.S. government should encourage the National City Bank to open a branch at Vladivostok. All "classes" of the Siberian population, but especially the peasantry, held large sums of rubles. These funds were hoarded because of the uncertain status of the Russian banks and because of their unwillingness to arrange foreign exchange. An American bank that agreed to accept deposits at a fixed rate of exchange would quickly attract millions of rubles. In turn, the reestablishment of a fixed exchange rate with the dollar would encourage trade with the United States. Under these conditions, American exporters and Russian buyers could determine prices on a more stable basis. Heid recognized the risks involved for a bank that attempted to operate in Siberia under the prevailing circumstances. Nevertheless, he believed the value of the ruble had bottomed out and that any improvement in confidence would raise its value. But he thought it would be necessary for the U.S. government to assist the bank by guaranteeing the value of the depositors' savings, because the Allied governments subsidized financial services for their nationals. Heid concluded by pointing out that "large British and Japanese firms cooperate with those banks under their Government control."[38] Shortly after this, the National City Bank opened a branch office at Vladivostok.[39]

Following the Armistice, which signaled Germany's collapse, American planners had to reevaluate their plans for an alternative currency in Siberia. An interesting debate arose when, on November 16, War Trade Board representative William Owen suggested that the Allies announce their intention to no longer accept Kerensky or imperial rubles. Owen believed this step would undermine Germany's efforts to acquire Russian assets by causing a collapse of the ruble market. He recommended this course because the Bolsheviks were printing these issues in unlimited quantities, which undermined Russian finances. If this step were taken Russian property owners might stop selling their assets to Germans, because the Russian notes would no longer appear to have any worth.[40]

Back at the War Trade Board, serious objections were being raised against Owen's recommendation. Lt. Landon K. Thorne, who had been temporarily assigned to the War Trade Board from army ordnance as an expert on currency, now expressly counseled against any plans to discredit the Kerensky and imperial ruble currencies. Thorne opposed this step on grounds that it would "impose hardship" on the Russian masses who accepted these issues because of their relatively stable value. This policy would not even reduce the amount of depreciated paper money that existed in Russia, since the Bolsheviks would merely counterfeit other issues. Finally, this draconian measure would make it even more difficult for a future government to retire the old currency, because cancellation of these stable issues would undermine the confidence of the masses in paper currency. Consequently, Thorne advised that Russian currency should not be "tampered with" until a stable government adopted a uniform system for devaluation of the existing currency.[41]

Thorne proceeded to express strong misgivings about the temporary ruble plan itself. On December 10, he warned that the certificates' acceptability with the Russian population would be limited if they were only convertible into commodities and not currency as well. He doubted the certificates would be a suitable means for extending loans, unless American goods were specifically desired, in which case the goods should be advanced directly. For those who were not dealing with American merchants, the certificates would only have purchasing power at par if the bureau redeemed them in currency.[42] John Foster Dulles, assistant to Chairman McCormick, agreed that the notes should be redeemable at par, but he added that this provision had been rejected by the Treasury Department after much discussion.[43] The

Treasury's objections to convertibility were not explained but were probably based on the concern that, if the certificates were made convertible with other currencies, German interests or the Bolsheviks could make use of them. For instance, the original Russian embassy proposal stressed that free convertibility should be prohibited to prevent "German affiliations" from using the notes.[44]

On December 14, Thorne marshaled his arguments in a detailed memorandum that recommended that America's currency proposal be abandoned. Thorne clarified the issue by stating that the object of American policy was to facilitate Russian-American trade and not to establish a new currency. Indeed, the American proposal did not adequately address the question of creating a medium that would circulate among the Russian population. In any case, the proposal would have been received with hostility by the Siberian population, as had Japan's efforts to introduce the yen, unless it was to be administered by a Russian agency. Thus, the sole purpose of those certificates was to supply the Russian population with a means with which to pay American exporters.

But the ruble certificates were not even suited to this purpose. When issued in payment for Russian goods, the certificates bore a close resemblance to dollar drafts; in effect, they represented credit extended to American buyers of Russian goods! For a volume of these certificates to be outstanding and thereby constitute a circulating medium, Russian exports would have to exceed the importation of American goods to Russia. Yet, it would be exactly under these conditions that American goods would not be available to demonstrate an effective purchasing power for the certificates. As a result, the peasantry would lose confidence in the certificates, and they would be discounted. Speculators would likely acquire the certificates in order to purchase American goods cheaply, whereupon these unpopular notes would finally be removed from circulation.

Thorne explained that what Russia needed was credit because it would be importing far more than it could pay for with its own exports. Since the only time when the Russian Bureau certificates would function at all was in the hands of Russian importers, he concluded that actual bank credits were what was required. Credit could be effectively extended only to organizations such as cooperatives and municipalities that had the machinery to collect exports and to distribute imports. These organizations would quickly use whatever credit they obtained to purchase imports. It was not realistic to expect individual peasants and small merchants who were not exporters to obtain the certificates necessary to purchase American goods.[45]

Within two days, Thorne's arguments had prevailed at the War Trade Board. On December 16, Henry Van Sinderen approved a cable Thorne drafted, which informed representative Owen that "the issuance of a new certificate [was] not considered feasible at present." Thorne's closing comments on the American currency program demonstrate that this misconceived plan was devised in response to Germany's financial ambitions in Russia. He confirmed that Germany's holdings of approximately two billion Russian State Bank notes "have been the basis of much of the discussion relative to the restoration of the Russian currency." His opposition to the temporary certificate plan notwithstanding, Thorne acknowledged: "It is obvious that the rehabilitation of the Russian monetary situation would not only be of great economic benefit to Germany but would also materially increase her hold on Russia. It seems to me that if arrangements have not already been made, that the surrender of these notes in addition to the Russian gold should be made."[46] Van Sinderen noted that this question should be brought to the attention of Chairman McCormick, who would be advising President Wilson at the Peace Conference.[47]

In the final assessment, the American plan for a temporary ruble certificate was doomed by the conflicting aims it was designed to achieve. On the one hand, it was necessary to undermine the value of Germany's menacingly large ruble holdings; on the other hand, the United States wanted to introduce a new currency that would both circulate at par and facilitate trade between Russia and America. Thorne's criticisms demonstrated the incompatibility between these objectives—the plan would create neither a functional currency nor promote American exports to Russia. Yet, while the American currency proposal was never viable, it was based on the authentic concern over German, as well as Allied, manipulation of Russian currency. It should therefore be evaluated in this broader context. The Wilson administration's stubborn advocacy of its inter-Allied currency plan and its refusal to acquiesce in the Allies' alternative currency plans can be viewed as a holding action against the forces of dissolution. In view of the vacuum that existed after the Provisional Government's collapse, the stalemate produced by this vigilant Open Door diplomacy may have helped prevent the rival powers from rapidly dismembering the Russian Empire.

By December 1918 the rapid deterioration of conditions in Siberia had already overwhelmed the modest Russian Bureau program. The dimensions of the crisis in Siberia were graphically depicted by E. A. Brittenham of International Harvester in a letter from Vladivostok in early 1919. Brittenham illustrated the extent of economic dislocation in Siberia through his account of the pilgrimages peasant representatives had made across Siberia to Vladivostok in quest of agricultural machinery. International Harvester officials had interviewed "most every society and institution East of the Ural Mountains that were ever interested in the machine business and a great many new societies that have sprung into existence since the revolution." Many parties representing small groups of farmers had even made the arduous journey across Siberia to buy equipment for themselves. A particularly desperate image is conveyed by Brittenham's revelation that "peasants have come to us all the distance from the Ural Mountain districts in the hope that they could get machines and twine and repairs for the coming season." Yet among these travelers, the speculators, "both Jew and Gentile," far outnumbered the legitimate producer interests. Most of these journeys had been initiated on the basis of rumors that grossly exaggerated the extent of assistance that would be forthcoming from the United States. Many of the parties who arrived at Vladivostok were "fully convinced that they had only to place their requirements with Allied official organizations here, and all requirements would be forthcoming. Many small dealers, private buyers, and speculators, came to us from the interior, quite convinced that we had warehouses full of machines, repairs, and twine which were ready for distribution."[48] It was a "staggering blow" to these Russians when Harvester officials told them the company was only selling machinery on a commercial basis and not as part of a large governmentally financed relief effort. Most of these visitors never returned. Some officials from the more prominent organizations returned to negotiate terms that called for International Harvester to assume most of the risk. These representatives claimed their main financial problems were due to difficulties in arranging exchange in dollars. However, after the Russians urged the Harvester officials to accept payment in rubles, it was discovered that they were unable to make even the necessary deposits in rubles.

Those relief efforts that were undertaken were merely preyed upon by the Russians who resorted to unscrupulous business practices under the pressure of worsening economic conditions. For instance, the Narodny Bank, the principal intermediary in the assistance program, had become involved in a bitter rivalry with its constituent credit societies over the financing of purchases with International Harvester. Brittenham thought it was possible this dispute would result in the severance of ties between the bank and the credit societies. It had become almost impossible for companies such as International Harvester to transact business under these conditions, because Russian organizations had forsaken ethical business practices. Brittenham recognized this was an inevitable response by the Russians to instability, since "they all seem to anticipate worse days ahead, and during such anticipation the feeling of self preservation to the degree of 'dog eat dog' controls their actions."

In his final thoughts, Brittenham linked the fate of the rich western Siberian region to an immediate reorganization of the Trans-Siberian railway system, which had become its virtual lifeline. Under the present circumstances, few goods could be shipped to Western Siberia in time to meet the needs for the 1919 harvest. This region's purchases of agricultural machinery would require the Trans-Siberian's maximum commercial capacity for the whole year, and this proportion was being reduced by military requirements. Brittenham declared that this situation prevented "any program being carried out for the extensive relief to Western Siberia, until the railroad is restored and operated on a different basis." He warned that, unless the line was reorganized soon, "we may expect a complete collapse of the railroad in the next few weeks."[49]

In 1919 the preservation of John Stevens's authority over the Trans-Siberian railway system moved to the forefront of America's Russian policy. Stevens would retain this pivotal role until October 1922, when he was finally withdrawn from the Chinese Eastern Railway.

7

❧

An Insoluble Dilemma:
Economic Assistance
and the Kolchak Government

The year 1919 was pivotal to the Wilson administration's reconstruction program for Siberia. In February the United States reached a tenuous inter-Allied agreement for supervision of the Trans-Siberian railway system, which was placed under the operational control of John Stevens. This agreement required the Allies to cooperate with Stevens and to furnish a modest financial contribution that would cover emergency expenses. In practice, the competing interests of the participating powers severely limited the effectiveness of the agreement.

Beyond this inter-Allied agreement, the Wilson administration also contemplated a strictly American plan for facilitating general economic reconstruction in Siberia, which would be financed by an unprecedented foreign assistance program. Throughout the first half of 1919, the American mission at Paris worked under the assumption that the administration could obtain a large appropriation from Congress for Russian assistance, after Wilson had successfully negotiated a peace treaty and a League of Nations structure with the Allies. However, the president's political fortunes declined at home as the peace treaty encountered stiff opposition in the Senate. As Wilson's domestic political prestige eroded, any chance of obtaining a congressional appropriation for Russian assistance disappeared.

Finally, the rapid deterioration of conditions in Siberia overwhelmed the assistance program in its early stages. The reactionary policies of the

Kolchak regime intensified social and economic instability in Siberia and worked against American reconstruction initiatives. As if the Omsk government's corruption and incompetence were not enough to overcome, Japan purposely exacerbated these conditions by its support for the bandit Cossack leaders and by the persistent efforts of its military to monopolize the Chinese Eastern Railway.

The negotiations over inter-Allied control for the Trans-Siberian railway system began in September 1918. It quickly became apparent to Roland Morris, the American negotiator and ambassador to Japan, that British acquiescence encouraged Japanese intransigence in the negotiations over control of the Trans-Siberian railways. A week before Morris and Japanese representatives concluded a tentative agreement for operation of the railroads, Britain notified the State Department that it would take a neutral position in the negotiations between the United States and Japan. Rather than support the State Department's plan, which would place Stevens in charge of the railways, Britain declared that it "would prefer that the United States and Japanese governments should arrange the question of actual control, since they are primarily interested, and His Majesty's Government will fall in with any agreement that may ultimately be reached by these two Governments."[1] This statement gave a clear message to Japan's General Staff that the American plan would receive no backing from the Allies.

Following these diplomatic exchanges, the Japanese government announced that it would not accept Stevens's undivided control over the Trans-Siberian system. In early November, Foreign Minister Viscount Yasuya Uchida suggested that the plan could be amended to the General Staff's satisfaction if a Japanese engineer shared the director-generalship with Stevens. Uchida rationalized this alternative on grounds that joint management would smooth relations between Stevens's personnel and Japan's military. But the motives of the General Staff were less benign. It really intended to effect a division of the railway system. The General Staff wanted jurisdiction over all the railways east of Irkutsk, giving it complete control over all access into Siberia's interior. Therefore, while Stevens would have authority over all railroads west of Irkutsk, the effectiveness of his efforts would be completely dependent on Japan's administration of the connecting lines to the east.

Not surprisingly, Stevens found Uchida's compromise completely unacceptable. While Stevens was prepared to include a Japanese engineer on his staff, an equal division of authority between them would undermine his status as representative of the Russian people. Moreover, since the large number of Japanese troops were the real authority in northern Manchuria, the Japanese engineer would inevitably become the dominant figure, while Stevens would be forced to share responsibility for actions he did not approve.

Morris believed Britain's neutrality had emboldened Japan to make such a counterproposal. Uchida's remarks regarding the lack of interest Britain and France had exhibited in the negotiations over the railroad led Morris to conclude that "I am sure that this belief has given the General Staff added confidence."[2]

But the political maneuvers Britain engineered in Siberia during early November 1918 altered the stakes involved in the railroad issue. The coup of November 18, 1918, which installed Admiral Aleksandr Kolchak as leader of the Siberian government at Omsk, took place with British support. A regional Siberian government under British influence served Britain's objectives of weakening the Russian Empire and of building its sphere of influence in the regions surrounding Russia proper.

Kolchak's coup caused friction with Japan, which was attempting to tighten its grip over the area east of Lake Baikal. Japan had been using the Cossack troops of G. M. Semenov to favor its own commerce in northern Manchuria and the Russian Far East at the expense of the other powers. Hence, Kolchak's regime aroused deep suspicion on the part of the Japanese because he constituted a rival for their clients, such as Semenov. Furthermore, Japan's representatives in Siberia were concerned that Kolchak's government would grant exclusive economic privileges to Britain.[3]

Kolchak's emergence had provocative implications in light of the bitter relations he had with the Japanese military and the Cossacks. In May 1918, Kolchak had been made administrator of military affairs for the Chinese Eastern Railway by Dmitri Khorvat in a reorganization of the company's board of directors. Japan had supported this initiative in an attempt to transform Khorvat's administration into a shadow government under its influence. But Kolchak had upset these designs when he opposed Japan's intervention in the Russian Far East. He quickly severed all relations with the Japanese military mission because of its support for Semenov. At the end of June, Khorvat, with Japan's backing, removed Kolchak from the position he had held for only five weeks. Kolchak immediately turned to his Russian allies and the British in order to challenge the Japanese clients.[4]

On the eve of Kolchak's coup, Britain suddenly began to take an interest in the operation of the Siberian railways. To ensure the viability of Kolchak's regime in central Siberia, Britain had to secure his supply line eastward along the Trans-Siberian railway system. From Tokyo, Ambassador Morris reported on November 8 the concern of British ambassador Sir William C. Greene that Japan's support for the Cossacks' banditry east of Lake Baikal "would lead to the disintegration of Siberia." Morris used this opportunity to impress upon Ambassador Greene the advantages of the American plan, since Stevens's personnel represented the "centralizing force in Siberia." At the time, Morris believed he had convinced the British ambassador of the merits of the American plan, and Greene expressed his intention to abandon the neutral position he had been taking.[5]

While the British government was concerned about Japan's objectives in the Russian Far East, it had its own plans for operating the Trans-Siberian railway system. By December, in contrast to the American proposal for operation of the Siberian railways, British engineer Col. Archibald Jack suggested that L. A. Ustrugov be given administrative control of the railways. Ustrugov had been appointed manager of the Trans-Siberian system by the czarist government, and, accordingly, Kolchak's Omsk government made him minister of communications. Morris believed the head of Britain's military mission to Russia, the arch-conservative Gen. Alfred Knox, and the high commissioner Sir Charles Eliot had influenced Jack's position, because, until recently, Jack had "zealously" supported the American plan. In Morris's view, these officials had been obstructing American proposals for economic assistance since the summer and had "consistently advocated military and financial support to the promoting of a central Siberian Government."[6]

Necessity forced the Omsk officials to accept Stevens's control of the railroad in mid-December. They surmised that Stevens's prestige might offer the Omsk regime its biggest advantage in its struggle to transport military supplies for western Siberia past the Japanese and Cossack forces who blocked railroad transportation east of Lake Baikal. Pressure from Stevens virtually ensured that Omsk officials would see things his way, for he threatened to cancel orders for desperately needed lubricating oils unless the Omsk regime accepted his terms for managing the railway system.[7]

By the end of December, after prolonged negotiations with Japan, Morris reached a settlement that he believed would give Stevens sufficient operational control. In the final agreement, the Allies permitted Stevens to become president of a Technical Board, a position in which he would be authorized to administer the technical operation of the railway subject to the general supervision of an Inter-Allied Railway Committee composed of representatives from the Allies and the United States. In this capacity, Stevens could issue instructions to the Russian managers regarding technical matters, and he could appoint assistants and inspectors who would serve under the board's jurisdiction.

Yet the agreement qualified Stevens's power in some important respects. It also established a Military Transportation Board that would coordinate military transportation under the instructions of the appropriate Allied military authorities. The effectiveness of Stevens's authority would always be contingent on the degree of cooperation he received from the various Allied military officials, because the agreement specifically placed the railroads under the protection of the Allied military forces. When he assigned experts to any of the stations, Stevens would be required to take into account the "interests" of the Allied powers who were in charge of those stations. Moreover, the agreement also stipulated that the Russian managers or directors would remain at the head of the different sections of the railroad and they would continue to exercise the powers conferred on them by existing Russian law.

Stevens was still not entirely satisfied with the extent of his powers as president of the Technical Board or with his formal subordination to the Inter-Allied Railway Committee. Nevertheless, Morris convinced the State Department and the American mission to the Paris Peace Conference that the agreement granted Stevens the necessary authority to manage the Siberian railways without jeopardizing the cooperation of the Russian officials and the Allies. Stevens would later admit that the inter-Allied Committee had been devised to function as a "cloak" for his Technical Board.[8] In mid-February 1919, Britain, France, the United States, and Japan officially approved the Inter-Allied Railway Agreement.

Following the inauguration of the inter-Allied agreement, problems immediately arose for Stevens that would foreshadow the trials of the next three years. China balked at the railroad plan, arguing that it was entitled to assume control over the Chinese Eastern Railway because of the collapse of the Russian administration. The United States countered China's claims to the Chinese Eastern Railway by declaring that the inter-Allied agreement was designed to preserve all existing treaty rights, Russian rights representing the primary claim in this case. Chinese officials grudgingly acquiesced in the inter-Allied agreement, but they would attempt to assert Chinese control over the line as soon as the opportunity presented itself. Chinese claims on the line were particularly problematic for the United States, since officials like Minister of Communications Tsao Ju Lin were under Japanese influence. Therefore, while America wanted China's participation in the railroad administration, China could never be allowed to assume control over the Chinese Eastern Railway lest its corrupt and incompetent officials become tools of Japanese ambitions.[9]

An even more serious dispute arose between Stevens and Japan's representatives over supervision of the Chinese Eastern Railway. Stevens informed the Japanese that he planned to give Japanese experts supervision of the Amur Railroad and the Changchun-Harbin section of the Chinese Eastern. He distributed the Railway Service Corps across the main line of the Chinese Eastern and Trans-Siberian railways, where they would introduce a unified system of train dispatching. In keeping with the provisions of the inter-Allied agreement, Stevens intended to attach Japanese experts to the corps so they could learn American methods and thereby assume supervision over some divisions of the line. Stevens had no objection to delegating supervisory authority to Japanese operators as long as they functioned in harmony with Open Door principles. Needless to say, Japanese representatives who wanted sole supervision over a substantial portion of the Chinese Eastern Railway remained "greatly dissatisfied" with Stevens's plans.

Despite these difficulties, the United States was anxious to get the railroad plan under way. Yet, emergency funds were needed immediately just to begin operations. These funds were required to pay arrears of wages to employees, to pay wages and salaries in the near future, and to purchase equipment. Ambassador Morris suggested that Stevens's position would be strengthened if America made such a temporary advance. While the State Department agreed that it would probably be necessary for the Russian Bureau to make an initial advance to Stevens, it nevertheless believed that it would be a mistake for the United States to unilaterally finance the Siberian railways. Instead, the Inter-Allied Railway Committee should determine what financing was necessary and each nation should then contribute its quota to the general pool. A future Russian government would be obligated to repay these loans to the Allies.[10]

From Paris, Lansing and McCormick agreed with the State Department that a comprehensive inter-Allied financial plan, equally distributed among the Allies, should be adopted for the Siberian railways. In the meantime, McCormick recommended that the Russian Bureau make a temporary advance of $1 million to Stevens.[11]

On January 24, the State Department warned the American mission that Congress would not look favorably on any plan that required further appropriations for Russia. Congressional Republicans were expected to attack every aspect of the administration's Russian policy, which was quite vulnerable after the cessation of hostilities.[12] For instance, the Russian Bureau had already begun to draw fire from the House of Representatives. In mid-January, Iowa representative James W. Good questioned the legality of the $5 million appropriation the administration gave the Russian Bureau, without congressional approval, from the $100 million fund for National Security and Defense. Good especially criticized the bureau's open-ended certificate of incorporation, which gave it the power to engage in a practically unlimited range of economic activities in Russia, which, he emphasized, could conceivably involve billions of dollars.[13]

As a result of the opposition the administration encountered from Congress in obtaining the $100 million Food Bill for Europe, the State Department frankly doubted its chances of receiving the large appropriation that would be necessary to undertake the railway plan.

In spite of the State Department's recommendations, Wilson and his advisers were determined to convince Congress that assistance for the Siberian railways was a vital national interest. On January 31 the American mission sent lengthy instructions to acting Secretary of State Frank Polk that demonstrate the significance it attached to establishing the Open Door in Siberia. Polk was authorized to hold a confidential meeting with congressional leaders at which he would explain the president's objectives in Siberia. He was instructed to emphasize the "strategic importance" of the Trans-Siberian railway as a communication link between Russia and the United States. The line facilitated American economic assistance to Siberia "where the people are relatively friendly and resistant to Bolshevik influence."[14]

Above all, the mission earnestly counseled Polk to impress Congress with the importance of the administration's hard-fought Inter-Allied Railway Agreement. He was instructed to review in detail with Congress the administration's struggle to prevent Japan's monopolization of the Chinese Eastern Railway subsequent to the intervention of the previous summer. The unwarranted size of the Allied military intervention in the Russian Far East was a consequence of Japan's desire to seize the railroad. Therefore, in the mission's view the successful conclusion of the railroad agreement "can properly be described as a very important and constructive achievement which may be of inestimable value to the people of Russia and to the United States as well as the world in general, provided they are followed through, thereby giving practical effect to the principle of the Open Door." But to put this plan into effect Congress would have to appropriate funds for the United States's share. If Congress favored the plan, the emergency advance to Stevens could immediately be arranged through the Russian Bureau.[15]

The State Department responded to this instruction with a very discouraging assessment of the political climate in Congress toward the Russian question. At a cabinet meeting on February 4, the opinion was unanimous that Congress could not be approached at that time for any further foreign appropriations—particularly for Russia. Polk was convinced that, in light of the difficult fight for the $100 million Food Bill for Europe, the administration's vague proposals for assisting the Siberian railroads would receive no consideration. Since even supporters of the Food Bill had complained about the lack of information provided them on that issue, it would be hopeless for the State Department to present a case for assistance to the Siberian railroads when it could supply no estimates.[16]

The State Department's difficulty was compounded by the apparent inability of the administration to define its Russian policy to the satisfaction of the public and Congress. The United States's program of economic assistance for Siberia was implicitly designed to undermine bolshevism. Yet, as a matter of policy, the president wanted to avoid taking a public position toward that regime. In early January when Wilson was attempting to arrange the Prinkipo Conference for the purpose of reconciling the different Russian factions, he commented to Lansing, "I still see no great advantage to be derived from words and public statements in the matter of Bolshevism." Wilson then expressed an integral assumption of his world-view when he concluded with conviction that "the real thing with which to stop Bolshevism is food."[17]

Accordingly, the Wilson administration's policy toward Siberia during 1919 was to assist the reconstruction of Russia's civil society, rather than intervene in the chaotic political environment born of war and revolution. Wilson's enduring faith in the efficacy of liberal capitalism led him to conclude that bolshevism was a symptom of social and economic malaise and should be treated as such. For Wilson, an American policy designed upon liberal principles would perform the greatest service to the Russian people. American assistance to the Siberian railroads was intended to achieve such liberal ends by restoring the necessary preconditions whereby the Russian people themselves could reconstruct their society.

Wilson's liberal historicism also informed his decision not to declare an overtly anti-Bolshevik policy, because he understood that intervention only exacerbated the radical phase of a revolutionary cycle. As N. Gordon Levin has argued, this assumption motivated Wilson's attempt to convene the Prinkipo Conference in January 1919. Wilson's gambit was based on the recognition that fear of foreign intervention created popular support for bolshevism. Moreover, by pressing for a negotiated settlement rather than a military solution, which would work on behalf of Russia's reactionaries, Wilson hoped to limit the Allies' influence over Russia's political evolution. In other words, Wilson's effort to sponsor negotiations between the Russian political factions was an attempt to undercut the Bolsheviks' moral influence without aiding reaction. Therefore, Wilson's unsuccessful pursuit of a non-interventionist settlement in early 1919 was calculated to promote a liberal world order conducive to American national interests.[18]

Mounting congressional opposition to the American involvement in Russia by early 1919 would create serious complications for any new policy initiatives the Wilson administration would propose for Siberia. Wilson's refusal to declare a position toward the Bolshevik regime left the administration vulnerable to domestic political attack because of the presence of American troops in north Russia and Siberia. The United States originally sent troops to Archangel as part of the Allied effort to bolster anti-German groups. After the Armistice, these troops became involved in the civil war against Bolshevik forces who were attempting to overthrow the Provisional Government of Nikolai V. Chaikovskii, which remained in control around Archangel. In response to the public outcry over American deaths at Archangel, congressional Republicans, led by Hiram Johnson, demanded the immediate withdrawal of American troops from north Russia. Public outcry over these casualties was particularly vehement because the administration gave no explanation for their presence in north Russia after the Armistice. On February 15, the administration narrowly defeated a Senate vote sponsored by Johnson that called for the withdrawal of American troops from Archangel; Vice President Thomas R. Marshall cast the tie-breaking vote.

Unfortunately, while the north Russian expedition had become irrelevant to American policy, the controversy it had engendered now jeopardized the Siberian program because American troops were required on the Trans-Siberian Railroad. The mere presence of American troops placed some restraint on the depredations Japan's military and the Cossacks were committing against person and property. Yet, the administration could not take this matter publicly to Congress without aggravating relations with Japan. Polk concluded that "any attempt to commit Congress to a definite policy on the Siberian railroad, which is only part of the whole Russian problem, would be hopeless until some definite information could be given them on the whole subject." Vice President Marshall believed that if the Russian question were thrown into Congress at that time, it would probably jeopardize all appropriation bills.[19]

Congressional objections against the appropriation of funds for the Siberian railroads reflected the lack of precedent for extended foreign assistance commitments not connected directly to national defense. The unease with which Congress was responding to the new global responsibilities the administration was thrusting upon it can be perceived in Polk's assessment of congressional sentiment. Based on the advice he had received, Polk was convinced that it would be hopeless to approach Congress with any proposal to finance the Siberian railways at that time "in its present mood when it is badly frightened over the amount of money we are spending and when it is so completely at sea as to what should be done in Russia." In view of this discouraging assessment, Polk recommended to the American mission on February 4 that the compromise agreement for management of the Siberian railways be formally accepted by the United States "and then take our chance later on [of] our being able to get Congress to assume the responsibility." Then, if Congress refused to accept a carefully worked plan that required a definite amount of funding, the administration could place the onus of responsibility on it.[20]

Meanwhile, War Trade Board officials were considering a method whereby the Russian Bureau's anomalous status could be resolved to the benefit of the administration's reconstruction program for Siberia. Conditions in Siberia had brought the bureau's commercial activities to a standstill. Furthermore, the bureau's trading function had become redundant because private trade could now supply goods far in excess of what could be distributed in Siberia in view of the lack of shipping and the disruption of the Trans-Siberian system. Under these circumstances, War Trade Board officials were particularly hesitant to maintain stringent regulations on private trade and to place a government agency in competition with the private sector, if only nominally.[21]

Beyond these domestic considerations, the United States could not effectively regulate Allied commerce—which may have been the determining factor. If War Trade Board regulation of American trade with Siberia were maintained, Allied commerce would have an advantage. British and Japanese traders would be inclined to purchase American goods for resale in Siberia at significantly higher prices, which would tend to harm the credibility of American trade.[22]

In view of these developments, near the end of February, the War Trade Board suggested to Vance McCormick at Paris that the Russian Bureau's capital be reduced to $1 million and the balance of $4 million be returned to the president's fund. This fund would constitute a more appropriate source from which Stevens could be advanced the emergency fund of $1 million.[23]

Far from abandoning the objective of supplying the Siberian cooperative societies, the War Trade Board was contemplating an alternative means of financing commercial assistance. On February 17, William R. Stanert of the War Trade Board informed Basil Miles that the Russian Bureau was discontinuing its efforts to finance the Siberian cooperatives on credit. Instead, the War Department would assume this task by selling army surplus to the cooperatives on credit.[24]

These financial maneuvers were almost certainly motivated by the immediate need to create a fund from which Stevens could draw. Since no hope existed for obtaining a congressional appropriation for Stevens, the War Trade Board may have been anticipating a situation in which the Russian Bureau's capital was the only fund available to finance the American share of the Inter-Allied Railway Agreement. As a by-product of these moves, the politically controversial capital fund of the Russian Bureau quietly passed out of existence. Conversely, the sale of War Department surplus on credit presented little political risk, since this arrangement would require no new appropriations and because these types of goods would be a less conspicuous form of competition with the private sector. In this reformulated version of the reconstruction endeavor, the Russian Bureau's infrastructure of marketing agents would continue to mediate exchanges with the Siberian cooperatives; now they would be agents of the War Department.

In March, the administration's Russian policy was overtaken by a financial crisis that demonstrated the foresight of the War Trade Board's measures. On March 15, Stevens informed the State Department that the Inter-Allied Railway Committee would immediately need an emergency Allied credit of at least $20 million.[25] Stevens based this figure on an estimate of the minimum necessary financial assistance the Trans-Siberian system would require from foreign sources in the short term.

Sir Charles Eliot, the British representative on the Inter-Allied Railway Committee, immediately contested Stevens's financial policy by introducing a counterproposal from the British War Office. This plan called for the Allies to undertake the complete financing of the Trans-Siberian railway, including the collection of its revenues. Any deficits resulting from this arrangement would be equally shared between the governments represented on the Inter-Allied Railway Committee, while any profit accruing from Allied control over the railroad system would be returned to the Russian administration. A financial sub-committee consisting of representatives from Britain, France, Japan, the United States, and the Russian administration would supervise the expenditure of the Allied funds.

Stevens's Technical Board immediately lodged serious objections to the British proposal. It argued that in conformity with the Allies' declared policy of nonintervention with Russia's internal affairs foreign financing should be restricted to the acquisition of foreign supplies, to the expenses of Allied supervision, and to emergency needs. If the Allies did not confine their financial commitment within these parameters, it would be impossible to fix limits on the habitual internal deficits of the Russian railroads.

The Technical Board emphasized that the Allies would undermine the financial independence of the Trans-Siberian system if they assumed complete responsibility for its financing. For instance, the board pointed out that in 1919 the Trans-Baikal, Tomsk, and Omsk sections of the railroad would run operating deficits of about 500 million rubles. The Amur line needed 300 million rubles for its completion and another 50 million for its annual operating deficit. Beyond these huge liabilities, the cost of rehabilitating the railroad system west of Omsk could not even be estimated, though it would run into enormous sums.

Yet, the British proposal had even more troubling political implications. While the Allies would assume responsibility for the total deficit, the plan had no provision for strengthening the Technical Board's administrative control over the railroad system. Indeed, this financial guarantee would actually remove any incentive for the profligate Russian administration to implement efficient practices. Under these circumstances, the Russian administration could easily become perpetually dependent upon foreign financing, jeopardizing Russian sovereignty over the system.[26]

On April 4, the Russian Chairman of the Inter-Allied Railway Committee, L. A. Ustrugov, presented a variation on the British plan. In his proposal, an Allied banking group or consortium rather than the Allied governments would finance the Trans-Siberian railway system. Russia would participate in this consortium as owner of the railway system. If deficits resulted from this arrangement, they would be charged to Russia but without interest![27]

Charles H. Smith, the American representative on the Inter-Allied Railway Committee, sponsored the Technical Board's proposal for temporary financing of the Trans-Siberian railway system during the committee's discussions on the issue. On April 8 Smith persuaded his colleagues to adopt the temporary procedure on grounds that the Technical Board's plan would meet the "urgent and immediate" needs of the railway system. He insisted that Ustrugov's proposal be shelved because it would require extensive study both by the committee and the various Allied governments.[28]

Even this minimum estimate of the railroads' financial requirements must have caught the State Department off guard because the War Trade Board was only then formally releasing the $1 million emergency fund to Stevens. The War Trade Board's instruction to Stevens stated that no additional funds would be forthcoming from any department of the U.S. government. Instead, it expected that until congressional appropriations were obtained Stevens could draw upon payments made to the Russian Bureau from its sales of goods to the Siberian cooperatives. In other words, it was thought that in the short run Stevens could tap into the bureau's revolving fund.[29]

An equally pressing financial crisis followed directly on the heels of Stevens's request for emergency funds. On March 21 the State Department informed the American mission that the Russian embassy was nearly bankrupt. At that time, it had cash assets of $8 million and materials worth $25 million, which consisted of railway equipment, boots, and shoes. However, the embassy's debt to the U.S. government and to private American creditors, principally the National City Bank, totaled almost $73 million. These obligations were scheduled to come due between April and July 1919. Most of this debt consisted of National City Bank loans from 1916 of $11 million and $50 million, which would mature on May 1 and July 10, respectively.

If the United States and the National City Bank collected these debts when due, not only would the Russian embassy be bankrupt, but its material assets would have to be attached and sold to help pay this debt. In view of this impending crisis, the State Department inquired of the American mission whether Wilson wanted Russian cash and material assets protected and whether he wanted the Russian embassy maintained in the United States. If Wilson approved the measure, the State Department would have to intervene to protect the Russian embassy's cash assets from private creditors until about July 1920. Wilson would also have to approve the postponement of interest collections on Russian obligations held by the Treasury Department.[30]

At the heart of this gloomy financial picture lay the vital question of financing the Siberian railways. On March 28, in a cable prepared by Basil Miles, the State Department stressed to the mission at Paris that Russian reconstruction depended on rehabilitating the Trans-Siberian railway system, which urgently required the $20 million fund. Miles emphasized:

> This question of finance strikes at the root of our whole undertaking in Siberia. The Department has believed the only solution of the Russian problem to be an attempt to restore normal conditions of economic life. The railway plan is the only sound attempt thus far launched. If it collapse[s] through mere failure of financial support, as seems not unlikely, the result will be disastrous. The effect would spread beyond the limits of Siberia. Moreover, by natural force of circumstances the result would lead to Japanese intervention on a scale which would eclipse all further efforts by other powers, including ourselves.[31]

The State Department identified three possible sources of American financing for the railroad: a congressional appropriation, a private loan through the China Consortium banking group, or recognition of the Omsk government in order to formally extend it a loan for restoration of the railways. Furthermore, the State Department also requested the mission's views on the long-term question of devising a permanent plan for financing the Siberian railways.[32]

This crucial question of finding a means to finance the Siberian railways was the most important factor in the administration's debate over recognition of Kolchak's regime. Conservative internationalists at the State Department were undoubtedly more predisposed than Wilson to recognize Kolchak as a defender of "order" against bolshevism. Yet, as Miles demonstrated, conservative American officials were also primarily interested in rehabilitating the Trans-Siberian as requisite for initiating Siberian reconstruction. To illustrate this point, when the Japanese military continued to cause problems following the inauguration of the Inter-Allied Railway Agreement, Miles drafted a State Department message instructing Ambassador Morris to make clear to Japan that in our opinion the situation has changed since we cooperated in sending troops to assist [the] Czechs. The adoption of [the] railway plan marks this change. Our efforts should now be directed to restore the railways. This is an economic and peaceable undertaking which calls for military activities only for policing and for protection in cases of actual necessity. In the opinion of this Government our two military forces should now be employed exclusively in assisting the inter-Allied committee and the boards subordinated to it under the plan proposed by Japan. Such an interpretation modifies our previous understanding and presents a new phase of assistance in which we can achieve success best by emphasizing the purely economic and practical character of our purpose.[33]

During the spring of 1919 Miles's attention had become so focused on the Russian and Siberian railroad question that one State Department insider remarked that it had become "his chief hobby."[34] Hence, the State Department's readiness to urge recognition of Kolchak in the spring of 1919 should be attributed primarily to its concern over the critical state of the Russian embassy's finances and to its appreciation of the increasingly uncooperative drift of the Republican Congress.

Wilson's instinctive reservations against recognition of Kolchak's government could only have been strengthened by the views of Roland A. Morris, the American ambassador to Japan, who was assigned to observe Siberian conditions. Morris, whose judgment Wilson particularly trusted, added his commentary to the recommendations of Ernest Harris, the American consul general at Omsk, who favored an immediate de facto recognition of Kolchak. In mid-April Morris counseled against even a de facto recognition of the Kolchak government because he had serious doubts about its chances for survival. While Morris agreed with Harris that "encouragement and friendliness" should be extended to Kolchak, he felt this should continue only so long as the "attitude" of his government warranted American support.

But in contrast to the staunch anti-Bolshevik Harris, Morris did not agree that financial assistance should be given to Kolchak. Instead, he emphasized that a direct Allied loan to the Trans-Siberian Railroad was essential. Morris's views, which were communicated to the American mission near the end of April, were consistent with the position Wilson would adopt toward Siberia.[35] Wilson would also consider the question of financing the railroad as a matter of overriding importance and separate from the question of Kolchak's recognition. The differences that existed between Wilson and the conservative State Department officials over America's official position toward Omsk should not obscure the fact that Wilsonians and administration conservatives were both searching for a method to finance the all-important railroad.

However, in its preoccupation with the unprecedented tasks of peace-making in the spring of 1919, the American mission at Paris was slow to appreciate the magnitude of the financial crisis facing the Siberian railways. The mission affirmed Wilson's desire to maintain the Russian embassy and to protect its cash and material assets, provided they could be utilized in Russia. Yet, Wilson insisted that these Russian assets could only be furnished to the Trans-Siberian railways on terms that did not imply recognition of the Omsk regime. On these conditions, Wilson directed the State Department to lend its good offices for the conservation of Russian assets. But the mission underestimated the seriousness of the Russian embassy's financial condition, and it misunderstood the needs of the Siberian railroads. The mission believed $6 million would be sufficient to pay the embassy's maturing interest payments and its expenses for the next year. Moreover, it mistakenly believed the embassy's $25 million of supplies could be used to furnish all of the $20 million emergency fund for the Siberian railways. To the extent that these supplies were not suitable for the Siberian railways, the mission believed they could simply be sold and the proceeds utilized.[36]

In suggesting this arrangement, the American delegation hoped to obviate dangers they perceived in the proposed plan for inter-Allied governmental financing of the railways. By supplying the railway's needs entirely from the embassy's own assets, the mission now hoped to postpone inter-Allied financing until a permanent plan for operation of the railways could be devised. This plan would solve a number of problems American policy faced in Siberia: it would facilitate the constructive use of Russian assets in America while avoiding the "political implications" associated with recognition; it would defer Japanese financial and political participation in the management of the Siberian railways; it would delay the need for American financial participation at a time when it would be difficult to obtain; and finally, this plan would tend "to preserve the integrity and independence of the Trans-Siberian for the benefit of such Russian Government as ultimately may be recognized." The mission even broached the possibility of using this arrangement to establish American trusteeship, in equity, over the railways. In exchange for the $20 million advance, which, after all, could only be preserved for Russia through the good offices of the U.S. government, the mission thought it would be desirable to receive the securities, or obligations, of the railroad. These securities would eventually be delivered to a Russian government or used in connection with the settlement of Russian loans held in the United States.[37]

These ambitions were quickly dashed by the bleak figures reported by the State Department. The $6 million in cash assets that the Russian embassy reported to its credit as of March 1, would be reduced to about $1 million by May because of shipping costs and payments made on old contracts. Payments for these purposes would further reduce this amount in May. Meanwhile, the Russian embassy scrambled to obtain an extension on the due date of the National City Bank loan of $11 million, which required additional interest payments. Stop-gaps would not suffice beyond mid-July when additional large interest payments to the bank would come due, bankrupting the Russian embassy. The Treasury Department's willingness to defer collection of past and present due interest on the governmental loans would therefore be of little help. Finally, the State Department took pains to emphasize to the mission that the Inter-Allied Railway Committee urgently needed $4 million in cash and that the railway supplies, which constituted assets of the Russian embassy, were not suited to Stevens's needs.[38]

By early May, the American mission had finally come to grips with the seriousness of the Russian financial situation. On May 5 the mission informed the State Department of the approach it wanted to take for dealing with Russia's critical financial situation. It believed the problem had to be resolved as two distinct issues: financing the Trans-Siberian Railroad, and protection for Russian assets in the United States in a manner that would ensure the most beneficial use for all concerned interests. First, the mission impressed upon the State Department that it should obtain a "substantial" appropriation from Congress for the Siberian railways at the "earliest possible occasion." Similar to its detailed cable of January 31, the mission expected the State Department to emphasize the critical economic role of the Trans-Siberian railway system. In the meantime, the mission approved the transfer of the Russian Bureau's funds for Stevens's use. Reciprocally, Secretary of War Baker had agreed to the War Trade Board's plan of furnishing the cooperatives $3.5 million in credits directly from the War Department for the purchase of army supplies. This arrangement freed the Russian Bureau's remaining $4 million to serve as the American share of the $20 million cash fund. In addition, because China had difficulty in providing its share of the emergency fund for the railways, the mission hoped that the War Trade Board's assets could also cover its share.[39]

These arrangements were completed in mid-June, but not without opposition from House Republicans who, noting the administration's desire to follow up this emergency arrangement with a more comprehensive financial plan for the Trans-Siberian railways, accused the president of drawing Congress into an open-ended commitment to this vast system.[40] Frank Polk cautioned the mission that congressional Republicans would make a political issue out of the transfer of Russian Bureau funds to the Siberian railways, although he agreed it was an urgent matter.[41] While aware of these dangers, Vance McCormick nevertheless urged Clarence Woolley to transfer the Russian Bureau funds; the mission strongly believed "the financing of the railways seems so constructive and important an undertaking that it should be proceeded with irrespective of the possibility of political attack."[42]

The mission also favored conservation of Russia's material assets for use in Russia on grounds that this would serve the best interests of both Russia and the American creditors. Accordingly, the mission approved the department's recommendation that the Treasury defer collection of past due and present interest on government debt and that its good offices be used to postpone the maturity of private debt, provided arrangements could be made for the interest. Even then, there would be considerable doubt the embassy could meet the interest payments on this private debt.[43]

In May, when Wilson could devote more attention to the Russian question, the views of Roland Morris and Aleksandr Kerensky reinforced his predisposition against recognition of Kolchak. On May 4 Kerensky gave his views to an unidentified member of the American delegation at Paris. Kerensky expressed confidence that the Bolsheviks would be overthrown in a few months. However, he feared a more repressive government could succeed the Bolsheviks because Britain and France were supporting reactionary elements around Kolchak. To counteract these reactionary tendencies, he recommended that America and the Allies require Kolchak to respect basic democratic principles as the condition for recognition of his regime as the Provisional Government of Russia. Kolchak should be willing to meet the following conditions: the restoration of civil liberties for zemstvo and municipal organizations, the reorganization of his cabinet as a coalition, a promise to convene a Constituent Assembly as soon as possible, and guarantees for peasant land holdings and the rights of workers.[44]

In a reply to inquiries from the mission, Morris confirmed Kerensky's opinions about Kolchak's regime. He recommended that recognition be postponed until Kolchak's government defined its policies and ceased its reactionary behavior.[45] Following this report, Wilson instructed the State Department to send Morris on a fact-finding mission to Omsk. The State Department indicated to Morris that the president would rely on his recommendations in formulating the American position toward Omsk.[46]

By May 20, Wilson was prepared to adopt Kerensky's demands, including the establishment of regional democratic assemblies, as the conditions under which further support could be extended to Kolchak. However, he remained unwilling to recognize Kolchak's as an all-Russian government.[47] Kerensky's conditions were embodied in an inter-Allied dispatch of the Council of Four to Kolchak on May 26, 1919. Vance McCormick and Secretary Lansing were encouraged about the prospects that this initiative would result in recognition of the Omsk government. Furthermore, since the U.S. government had postponed the collection of interest payments owed the Treasury, they now hoped the financial collapse of the Russian embassy could be averted until the administration enacted a general assistance program on the basis of Ambassador Morris's reports. Thus, the recommendations of Morris would play a critical role in determining whether the administration would undertake more extensive diplomatic and financial commitments toward the Omsk government.[48]

Although Kolchak responded only in general terms to the Council's dispatch of May 26, the Allied leaders nevertheless declared his statement satisfactory and the basis on which he could be given further support. By this time, Wilson's doubts about the Omsk government must have increased as first reports of Kolchak's military reverses began to reach Paris. In any case, near the end of June, Wilson made it abundantly clear to the State Department that the council's reply to Kolchak did not imply recognition but only assistance to the extent that each nation's legislation permitted. This meant that Wilson's continued unwillingness to recognize Kolchak disqualified the Omsk government from generous Liberty loans; supplies could be furnished to his government to the extent that it could pay a certain amount directly in cash.[49] However, political considerations motivated the State Department to support arms shipments to Kolchak. In March Polk reminded the American mission that following the introduction of American troops into Siberia, the State Department considered it appropriate to support the Russian embassy's efforts to ship rifles to the Russian forces. More important, he added, "in our efforts to aid the Czecho-Slovak armies it seemed proper to cooperate in measures to strengthen the Russians who were acting with them." In view of these political considerations, when Kolchak assured the Allies that he would support democratic reforms in his June message, Wilson could not deny him military support against the Bolshevik's conventional military forces, particularly after the United States had given the Czechs $7 million the previous summer. Wilson had to accommodate Kolchak because the American economic assistance program would require cooperation from the Omsk government. If the United States proved unwilling to furnish any military supplies to the Omsk regime at this point, it would relinquish what political influence it had with that regime to the other powers.[50]

Thus, by the end of June, Wilson had demarcated clear limits on the extent to which his administration would support the Omsk government. In contrast, he remained committed to obtaining a substantial appropriation for the Trans-Siberian railway system, which he considered an entirely separate and overriding issue from the recognition of the Omsk government. On June 23 Wilson and McCormick discussed the central importance of the railroad to America's Far Eastern policy. McCormick emphasized to Wilson "the difficulty of furnishing money unless you could recognize some governmental obligation, particularly in Siberia for railroad development." Wilson agreed that the issue was urgent, but, instead of recognizing Kolchak, he told McCormick that he planned "telling Congress the whole story and said he would appeal for funds upon his return, as he also recognized the opportunity of a great constructive program in aiding Russia through [the] Siberian road and keeping [an] open door by preventing Japan from creating [a] sphere of influence and monopoly [in] Siberia, which will also jeopardize Chinese interests."[51] Like the State Department, Wilson recognized that the Siberian railroad system played a pivotal role in Far Eastern questions, since the fate of Manchuria hinged on preventing Japan from controlling the Chinese Eastern Railway.

As they began to consider plans for a comprehensive reconstruction program in Siberia, it is important to note that Wilson and the American mission intended that the operation be financed and managed by the United States alone. In a memorandum to Wilson dated June 21, Herbert Hoover, director of general relief for the Supreme Economic Council, recommended that the United States serve as an "economic mandatory" for the Russian Empire. Hoover emphasized that this endeavor could not be organized on an inter-Allied basis because of the "conflicting financial and trade interests" involved. When Hoover discussed his statement with the president and Vance McCormick on June 23, Wilson concurred with "Hoover's statement that Russia could not rehabilitate itself without economic aid, which should be given without political interference; that it was impossible for an inter-Allied body to give such aid without getting mixed up in politics to some extent." McCormick also agreed with this assessment.[52]

The opposition of the Wilson administration to a comprehensive inter-Allied loan for the Siberian railway system reflected a well-founded mistrust of the Allies' motives. After the Technical Board rejected the British War Office proposal, which called for the Allies to assume complete financial responsibility for the Siberian railways, Britain gradually withdrew its promise to contribute its share of the $20 million emergency fund. Britain was evidently dissatisfied with the Technical Board's decision not to place restrictions on the expenditure of the emergency fund in any one country—since three-fourths of the foreign purchases would necessarily have to come from America. In late May the British representative on the Inter-Allied Railway Committee informed Charles Smith that Britain would be willing to contribute its $4 million share, but he then suggested that for the remaining subscription "each country might advance money only for whatever materials [were] bought therein."[53] But through August, only the United States placed its $4 million subscription with the Inter-Allied Railway Committee; China managed to put up five hundred thousand dollars. Then, in mid-August 1919, Britain abruptly reneged on its promise to contribute its share. Smith learned from a Foreign Office representative that Britain "felt that she had already advanced her share in bacon and locomotives and did not care to do more at present."[54]

In light of this action, it would seem that Britain's original desire to have the Allies take over the complete financing of the Siberian railways was motivated by the desire to obtain preferential commercial arrangements with its client, the Omsk government. Britain probably entertained hopes that a large financial commitment to the Trans-Siberian railways could be tied to the purchase of British railway materials. This objective was undermined when Stevens forced the adoption of the limited American proposal for emergency Allied financing, which placed no restrictions on where the funds could be spent. When it became apparent in late summer that the Omsk government would most likely collapse and that there would be no prospect for commercial gain, Britain decided to withhold its contribution entirely.

Wilson's ambitious plans for an American loan to the Siberian railways were communicated to Morris by the State Department on July 11. Placing special emphasis on restoring the railway system, the department instructed Morris to estimate the financial requirements for "a comprehensive plan for economic reconstruction in Siberia and ultimately for European Russia."[55]

Eleven days later, on July 22, in response to a Senate resolution from June 27 that inquired about the presence of American troops in Siberia, Wilson sent a message to the Senate explaining his Siberian policy. After an extensive review of the Siberian intervention, Wilson emphasized that American troops should continue to protect the railroad from "partisan bands," a clear reference to the Japanese-supported Cossacks. Wilson stressed to the Senate that Russia's participation in the war had been of incalculable value to the Allied cause, and that Russia now desperately needed economic assistance to prevent the spread of further chaos and to begin the process of reconstruction. He maintained that the United States bore a heavy obligation to protect the Trans-Siberian system, since it was not only the main transportation artery for Siberia but also the only means of access to European Russia.[56]

Ambassador Morris arrived at Vladivostok on July 10 and began to travel west in accordance with his instructions to evaluate the Omsk government. On his approach to Omsk, Morris discovered to his surprise that the Kolchak regime completely lacked popular support and was backed only by "a small discredited group of reactionaries, Monarchists and former military officials." Moreover, the Czecho-Slovak troops were becoming restless with their situation; their discontent was fueled in no small measure by their disillusionment with Kolchak's regime. They would have to be repatriated to their homeland after November. All Allied representatives and moderate Russians with whom Morris conferred believed the Czechs' withdrawal would bring about an uprising against Kolchak.

Without even making a thorough evaluation of conditions in central Siberia, Morris immediately identified five major reasons why Kolchak failed to win popular support for his government: popular distrust for the Cossack leaders of Eastern Siberia who ostensibly represented him; the inability of the Russian military and civil officials to in any way amend their reactionary views or practices; the government's failure to implement constructive economic and financial measures, while it condoned rampant speculation and corruption by its officials; the resentment by the peasantry against an extremely harsh system of conscription; and the suppression of all local self-government in the urban areas. This report was repeated to the American mission at Paris.[57]

After discussing the situation with Admiral Kolchak, Morris and the pro-American foreign minister, John Sukin, agreed that certain of the Omsk government's policies had to be addressed: the supervision of the railway, which principally involved enforcement of the Inter-Allied Railway Committee's operational authority and protection of the line, for which the Czechs had been responsible; credits for military supplies and commercial assistance; Red Cross relief; the German-Austrian prisoners; and a bill of rights.

Morris elaborated on the latter point, which underscored the basic dilemma confronting the attempts of the administration to undertake a reconstruction program in cooperation with the Omsk government. Morris suggested to the State Department that it would be necessary for Kolchak to issue a carefully prepared statement in which he promised to guarantee certain fundamental individual rights. He believed "much of the discontent with the present Government, the demoralization and panic, is in my judgment due to the utter insecurity of person and property." The reconstruction process could never commence while "all over Siberia there is an orgy of arrest without charges, of execution without even the pretense of trial, and of confiscation without color of authority." In conclusion, Morris expressed to the department his view that the United States should not invest great hope in the Omsk government.[58]

None of the problems Morris observed during his fact-finding mission to Omsk could be resolved independently of the transportation question.

The success of the Wilson administration's assistance program for Siberia hinged on Stevens's ability to reconcile the region's pressing commercial transportation needs with the Omsk government's military program. To facilitate cooperation with the Russian and Allied military forces, the Technical Board conceded priority to military transportation, although railway materials received precedence over everything else. Stevens's principal challenge lay in overhauling the existing system of car distribution, which had contributed to the disruption of railway operations. Since the March Revolution of 1917, the Trans-Siberian Railway had operated under a complicated system whereby the authority to distribute cars was divided among the military, the commercial transportation committees, and the local transportation officials. Both the military and civilian transportation committees were authorized to distribute cars by issuing instructions to the local railway officials whose responsibilities were limited to the movement of trains and maintenance of the line.[59] As long as wartime conditions existed military transportation received priority over civilian traffic. By the spring of 1919, the competing demands of the various committees and the combined burden of Russian and Allied military forces had brought about the complete disruption of railway operations.

In May the Technical Board tried to reduce military interference with railway operations by requiring the Military Transportation Board to place all orders through the central railway administration. This central authority would then issue instructions to the local railway officials regarding military requirements. By routing all military requests through the Central Transportation committee, Stevens hoped to insulate the local line authorities from military pressure and encourage them to assume more responsibility for the railroad's operations. Stevens planned to exercise the Technical Board's supervision over this whole process by assigning Maj. F. B. Parker as general superintendent to the Central committee, and by attaching the Russian Railway Service Corps to the local Russian line administrations—George Emerson as chief inspector would coordinate their work.[60]

Beyond facilitating better coordination between the Russian bureaucracies, Stevens also attempted to use Emerson's corps to decentralize Russian railroad operations. Since Stevens did not believe that lasting improvements in transportation efficiency could be achieved without limiting bureaucratic interference with the local railway administrations, he assigned Emerson's approximately 150 technical and operating specialists the task of introducing the dispatching system across the Trans-Siberian from Vladivostok to Omsk. Under this system dispatchers who were distributed across the line expedited train movement on the basis of detailed reports regarding traffic conditions received by telegraph or telephone. If successfully introduced, this decentralized system would effectively shift operational control from the Ministry of Communications to the parallel network of Russian dispatchers. Benjamin O. Johnson, Stevens's Omsk district inspector, would later make the point that the dispatching system "to all intents and purposes ran along parallel to the Russian organization."[61] As one American inspector noted, "when the Russian Chief Dispatchers are installed they will serve as a buffer between outsiders and the dispatchers."[62]

Emerson's inspectors immediately discovered they would receive no cooperation from the Russian military authorities. At major terminals, particularly Vladivostok and Harbin, military station commandants ignored the inspectors and demanded transportation directly from the local railway officials. Problems with the Russian military command were compounded by the arbitrary behavior of the Japanese military and their Cossack clients who routinely commandeered transportation in open defiance of Allied regulations.

Throughout June, Minister of Ways and Communications Ustrugov refused to authorize the Allied Resolution from May 27, which required the Military Board to transmit all requests for transportation through the civilian transportation officials under the supervision of Emerson's inspectors. Ustrugov's silence undermined the inspectors authority; their instructions were conveniently ignored by Russian railway officials because they inevitably conflicted with the myriad Russian laws and regulations governing railroad operations. In July Emerson repeatedly met with Ustrugov, urging the minister to endorse the resolution. Ustrugov demurred, claiming the government could not enforce the inter-Allied agreement because it could not control the Japanese or Semenov.

But Ustrugov's ministry also hindered the Technical Board's work in the case of purely technical issues that were not subject to the arbitrary whims of the military officials. The minister gave only equivocal support to the inspectors endeavors to expedite repair and maintenance procedures. Ustrugov and his bureaucracy were suspicious of the Technical Board's efforts to decentralize control over technical matters for the same reason they opposed the dispatching system. The extensive rules and laws regulating technical matters helped perpetuate the power of the ministry's bureaucracy. Reviewing the failure of the inter-Allied Agreement in December 1919, Johnson commented that "the Department of Ways of Communications including all the heads of railway service, constituted under Mr. Ustrugoff the most weighty political element in Siberia." Johnson added that "Mr. Ustrugoff's declaration to his organization, 'Save Russian Railways for Russians,' sounded patriotic enough, but back of it, was as we all know, the fight by Ustrugoff to maintain the old railway regime of Russians, with all that went with it in authority and Power."[63] Faced with the open hostility of the Russian and Japanese military officials, and the passive resistance of the Russian railway officials, the Technical Board would only achieve limited success, except on the Chinese Eastern Railway where officials, such as Chief Engineer D. P. Kazakevitch, cooperated with the inspectors.

But the Omsk government's complete disregard for social reconstruction is best illustrated by its unwillingness to stabilize its currency. Since it had come to power in the fall of 1918, the Omsk government had resorted to the printing press to pay its administrative and military costs. This reliance on monetary inflation to pay its expenses created a powerful incentive for its czarist civil and military officials to engage in widespread graft and speculation. Currency stabilization was crucial to the reconstruction process, because the collapse of the ruble made it difficult to pay railroad workers wages and hindered cooperative associations and the Trans-Siberian railway from concluding credit arrangements with foreign suppliers. Accordingly, shortly after its formation, the Technical Board decided that its first task had to be the stabilization of Siberia's currency. At the request of the Technical Board, the Inter-Allied Railway Committee enlisted the services of a British financial expert who drafted a monetary plan in cooperation with Allied and Russian bankers.[64]

On May 5, Smith cabled the committee's unanimous recommendation to Washington. This plan consisted of two phases, the first of which addressed the creation of a stable currency and the second of which devised a method whereby credits could be extended to the Omsk government and other institutions in Siberia. Initially, the committee's plan required the Omsk government to replace all of its currency notes and bonds with the American Bank Note Company's issue of 500 million rubles, which had originally been printed for the Kerensky government. As Charles Smith, the American representative, emphasized, this technically well-printed currency would inspire confidence on the part of the population, in contrast to the Omsk government's poorly printed and easily counterfeited currency. Small denominations were particularly needed, since their absence contributed to higher prices. The committee believed substitution of the new currency for the old should take place at par. While these new notes would be legal tender, there should be no promise for their redemption in gold, since this obligation could only be assumed by an all-Russian government. This reservation could be clearly stated by a surcharge stamped on each bill. To ensure an adequate supply of currency the committee recommended that existing Kerensky notes should continue to circulate. It should only represent legal tender on the basis of its daily market rate with the new American Bank Note Company currency. Finally, the Omsk government would need to publish a monthly statement on the quantity of new notes in circulation. This provision, together with the replacement of all Siberian currencies by the necessarily finite quantity and high quality American Bank Note Company's issue, demonstrated the committee's intention to control the regime's currency emissions.

In the plan's second phase, the committee suggested that the Allies provide a gold credit to the Omsk government and other reliable institutions for the purchase of necessary foreign supplies. This foreign credit would be required to bolster the new ruble's stability, which could then be used exclusively for circulation in Siberia. Otherwise, if this new ruble were used in foreign exchange, it would quickly depreciate because of Siberia's unfavorable balance of trade.

For these financial measures to succeed, however, the committee stressed that it must also supervise Siberia's imports to ensure that Western commercial assistance would be used exclusively for the restoration of normal economic conditions. Accordingly, it recommended that one financial expert from each Allied power be assigned "to aid the Omsk Government properly in carrying out its part of the program." These experts would give the committee extensive oversight of the Omsk government's financial activities since they "should be allowed to make regular reports to and consult with the Inter-Allied Committee which shall be granted the privilege of discussing all financial questions with the government before any final decision is made on any question which the Allies may be interested."[65]

In particular, the committee hoped to exercise control over the government and private institutions, such as the cooperatives, in order to limit their use of foreign exchange to "actual needs." As an alternative to the experts, the committee suggested that this supervisory function "might be delegated to the government bank, or else an Allied bank." Existing organizations, like the Russian Bureau, should continue to function in order to assist both the export of raw materials from Vladivostok and the purchase of imports. These regulatory powers would give the Inter-Allied Railway Committee capabilities similar to those envisioned for the proposed inter-Allied bank the previous fall when the United States supported the Russian embassy's plan for a temporary ruble scheme. From a broader perspective, the committee's functions resembled those of the international banking consortium, which supervised foreign loans for China; moreover, it should also be viewed as a forerunner of the Marshall Plan.[66]

While the Inter-Allied Railway Committee prepared these financial recommendations, the United States renewed its efforts to provide the Siberian cooperatives with commercial assistance. It would now be even more difficult for the administration to furnish Siberia with commercial credit because the precipitous decline of the ruble created increasing chaos within the Siberian economy. Although War Trade Board export regulations with Siberia had been lifted after the Armistice, the administration still intended that the Russian Bureau personnel supervise commercial assistance with Siberia.

In March 1919, the State Department informed August Heid that the Union of Siberian Creamery Associations and the Union of Siberian Cooperative Unions (*Zakupsbyt*) had applied for credits to purchase army surplus from the War Department on credit, the method that had been proposed by the War Trade Board in February. Similar to the concerns that preoccupied the War Trade Board in the fall of 1918, the State Department wanted assurance on the following points: Were these organizations really active? Could assisting them disrupt political stability? What suggestions could the Russian Bureau offer for supervising these arrangements? Did the bureau think any other organizations should be included in the plan?[67]

Heid responded with a generally favorable assessment of the Union of Siberian Creamery Associations. While Heid could not determine the politics of its officers, he believed the peasant membership of the Creamery Association made it a desirable recipient of American assistance because they "generally stand for equitable land distribution and improved educational facilities, freedom of the press and religion, and general enactment of laws to assist improvement of social and civic conditions." Nevertheless, Heid did recommend that credits be given to the Creamery Association on the basis of a fixed profit to contain part of the overhead salary expense that resulted from the organization's large number of highly paid officers.[68]

By the end of April, the War Trade Board officials in Washington and Heid had established the terms upon which the War Department surplus could be sold. Patterned on negotiations with the Siberian Creamery Association, the general regulations were consistent with the administration's policy that only the most pressing needs of the population be met first and that all necessary steps be taken to prevent speculation or favoritism by the cooperatives. The Russian Bureau would attempt to supervise the association's purchases at each stage of the process: it would regulate the sale price on the basis of a profit not to exceed 10 percent; and it would require that the association only sell goods to actual consumers, including nonmembers, and not to middlemen for resale. American agents would have to supervise distribution, and the bureau would be furnished detailed lists of requested commodities and their specifications in order to help it determine priorities.[69]

These conditions formed the basis for three identical $5 million contracts the War Department concluded with the Central Union, the Siberian Creamery Association, and the Zakupsbyt in late June 1919. At this time, the War Department announced that it would furnish as much as $25 million worth of supplies to approved cooperative societies.[70] These negotiations had taken on even greater urgency in light of the cooperatives worsening financial condition due to the deterioration of railroad transportation, the collapse of the ruble, and the lack of Russian exports. War Trade Board planners hoped that if the Russian Bureau could establish reasonably effective supervision over the distribution of necessities and "if enough are sent into Siberia prices will be regulated automatically."[71]

By late September, Heid informed Washington that these commercial arrangements could not be carried out because "the entire machinery of commerce is wrecked." Without doubt, Japan bore a great deal of responsibility for creating these conditions. Its support for the Cossack leaders was largely responsible for obstructing railway traffic between Vladivostok and Irkutsk. The shortsightedness, incompetence, and corruption of the Omsk government caused a great deal of instability in its own right and certainly did nothing to mitigate the region's problems. In resignation Heid explained: "There is no prospect of early rehabilitation, on the contrary the large issues of new Siberian currency to meet expenses of military railroads and general government budget accelerate and increase devaluation. Credits are impossible, the Cooperatives can not safely accept rubles in payment for commodities."[72]

Any chance for promoting social and economic reconstruction in Siberia rested on the willingness of the Omsk government to implement the Inter-Allied Railway Committee's financial recommendations. Instead, the regime sacrificed the welfare of the Siberian population to its single-minded quest for a military victory over the Bolsheviks. Not only did the government subject the population to brutal acts of repression in its pursuit of a military solution, but its economic practices exacerbated instability and hardship. On May 28 Ernest Harris, the American consul general at Omsk, reported news that contradicted the Inter-Allied Railway Committee's financial recommendations. In a conference with Foreign Minister Sukin and Finance Minister I. A. Mikhailov, Harris learned that the Omsk government no longer believed a pressing need existed for the rubles printed by the American Bank Note Company. The Omsk government officials explained that while the notes had been needed six months ago, the government had now practically completed preparations for the printing of "a very much larger sum than had been ordered in America." Supposedly, Omsk might be interested in using the American notes as an all-Russian currency in the future after a constituent assembly decided to establish a permanent currency.[73] This announcement, coming on the heels of the Inter-Allied Railway Committee's recommendations, indicates the Omsk government probably balked at the committee's financial recommendations.

Charles Smith, the American representative to the Inter-Allied Railway Committee, attributed the railroads' financial difficulties largely to the government's unwillingness to stabilize its currency. He asserted that, two months after the committee's proposal had been submitted to the Omsk government, the memorandum "had hardly been read."[74]

The Omsk government's overissuance of currency had particularly deleterious effects on the Chinese Eastern Railway. Within the Chinese Eastern Railway zone, Omsk government currency depreciated sharply because the railroad was the only major outlet for the currency.[75] In late July, workers on the Chinese Eastern, who could no longer buy anything with the virtually worthless Omsk currency, initiated a general strike, which paralyzed the line. Because Russian railway workers along the Chinese Eastern purchased their necessities from Chinese merchants who refused to accept Omsk currency and because Chinese workers preferred Chinese currency, the Chinese representative on the Inter-Allied Railway Committee proposed that the railroad adopt the Chinese silver dollar. The Russian administration and the non-Chinese members of the committee flatly rejected this suggestion because it would result in the displacement of the ruble from this international corridor and because it would effectively dissolve Russian authority over the line. In early August, the Technical Board temporarily alleviated the problem when it used $550,000 in gold from the committee's funds to purchase Romanov rubles, which enabled it to meet the July payroll.[76] Smith told Washington at the time of this payroll crisis that this precarious financial situation existed because of the refusal of the Omsk government to follow the committee's May 5 recommendations.[77]

Smith related that the Omsk government's monetary practices were no more responsible in areas that lay under its direct control. When workers on the Tomsk Railroad threatened to strike because the government had not paid them for an extended period, Omsk cabled the dubious reassurance to the Technical Board that it would soon meet the payroll because the government printing press had been repaired and the necessary sums could simply be run off![78]

In July the Omsk regime's military fortunes began to decline rapidly as the Bolshevik forces advanced through the Urals, capturing Chelyabinsk and Ekaterinburg. These setbacks gave Stevens's Technical Board an opportunity to demand reforms from the Omsk regime as a precondition for additional financial support. In mid-July Ambassador Morris agreed to personally discuss the Technical Board's problems with Kolchak. Morris also reassured Stevens confidentially that the U.S. government would only consider aid requests from the Omsk regime if Kolchak's officials cooperated with the Technical Board.[79]

Shortly after this, Emerson appealed directly to the Allied diplomatic corps when Ustrugov ignored a Technical Board resolution that limited transportation privileges for military commanders. Emerson's protest prodded the Allied representatives at Omsk to inform Kolchak's council ministers that the Allied credit to assist the railroad (to which, of course, only the United States and China had actually contributed!) would be withdrawn unless the Omsk regime enforced the railway agreement.[80] This ultimatum induced the Omsk regime to concede the Inter-Allied Railway Committee's principal demands: it suspended the laws governing technical standards, and it ordered military authorities to observe the Technical Board's procedures for obtaining transportation.[81]

As a prerequisite for additional credits, the Allied diplomatic corps also urged the Omsk officials to enact a series of financial reforms. On July 30, Ambassador Morris participated in a meeting with Allied representatives and Russian officials during which Finance Minister Mikhailov outlined steps his government would take in order to receive foreign credits. It is likely that the pro-American officials, Foreign Minister Sukin and Vladimir Novitskii, who had served as the financial delegate to the Russian embassy in Washington, were instrumental in formulating this program since Mikhailov knew little about finance himself.[82]

The ministry's program addressed three main problems: the reform of monetary circulation, the resumption of payment on Russia's foreign debt, and measures to be taken for the acquisition of foreign credits. As a precondition for further foreign support, the government would undertake monetary reform to ensure the severance of its currency from that used by the Bolsheviks, and it would attempt to unify its monetary tokens by exchanging all existing currencies in the areas under its control for new Russian State Bank notes produced by the American Bank Note Company. The government would also strive to improve the technical quality of the currency it printed in small denominations to prevent counterfeiting. After the completion of these reforms, the emission of currency would be subject to public control.

Next, the ministry recognized that the Kolchak government's willingness to resume interest payments on the nation's foreign debt would be a condition for any significant amount of assistance from the Allies, let alone recognition. It therefore proposed to issue an interest-bearing script as reassurance to French, British, and American private creditors of the Omsk government's intention to cover unpaid interest. After attempting to satisfy the Allied representatives on these two issues, Mikhailov hoped the Allies would agree to grant the Omsk regime substantial Allied credits for war matériels, railway supplies, and for general economic assistance.[83]

For Ambassador Morris, however, the question of embarking on a large-scale foreign assistance program for the Omsk government remained problematic. His evaluation of the regime in early August exhibited a great deal of ambivalence. This was a result of the difficulty he had in resolving the administration's desire to assist reconstruction in Siberia with his recognition that the presently constituted Omsk government was fatally flawed.[84]

On August 4, Morris reported to the State Department his belief that the government had "moderately liberal and progressive" intentions, but that it was ill-equipped for the task of governing the region. Morris considered Kolchak personally honest and patriotic but completely lacking in administrative ability or an appreciation of the social, political, and economic problems that confronted his government. Likewise, he thought the civilian Council of Ministers was a committed, politically moderate body but inexperienced and inefficient. While the military would obviously continue to pose great difficulties for the civilian officials, Morris nevertheless expressed confidence that if the government survived, it would honor its promise to convene a constituent assembly. In Morris's view, administrative shortcomings largely resulted from the failure of the government to represent the truly organic institutions in the region, such as the zemstvos and municipalities, which left it with little effective authority. This weakness gave the reactionary and corrupt military officials a free hand to engage in ruthless and indiscriminate acts of repression against the civilian population.

Morris captured the essence of the dilemma American policy faced in Siberia when he attempted to summarize the strengths of the Kolchak regime, for he could not really find any. He concluded that "however helpless this Government has proved, no alternative is offered around which those opposed to Bolshevikism might rally. The choice which confronts every moderate in Siberia is between Kolchak and Bolshevikism."[85]

Morris continued to wrestle with the issue over the next several days as he prepared his recommendations. Without endorsing any further support for Kolchak's government, he frankly informed the State Department that the existing government could not withstand bolshevism. No amount of assistance could save the government unless fundamental changes in the personnel and the methods of government were enacted. Still, he clung to the idea that with perseverance and patience the Allies could shape the Omsk government into a bulwark against bolshevism. This would necessarily be a long and difficult task, and, in the meantime, the government would have to survive its present crisis.

On August 11, Morris recommended that the Allies essentially assume trusteeship over all facets of the Omsk government in order to make it worthy of further foreign assistance. Morris's recommendations covered three broad categories: the amount of credits needed by Kolchak and the civilian population, assistance for the operation of the railroad system, and the need for extensive Allied supervision over all assistance furnished to Omsk.

First, Morris thought that if the government survived its present military crisis during the next months, it should be accorded formal recognition as the Provisional Government of Russia in order to facilitate the substantial assistance that would be required. This assistance included: $90 million for military supplies; $70 million for commercial assistance; $20 million for the Inter-Allied Railway Committee, plus an additional $15 million to cover its expenses and salaries—credits totaling nearly $200 million. The second recommendation urged steps that would be necessary to maintain communications between Vladivostok and Omsk. This would require a continuation of the inter-Allied agreement, an addition of 40,000 troops to replace the departing Czechs, and the $20 million credit that the other powers had been slow to furnish.

In his third point, Morris stipulated that these recommendations were contingent upon the establishment of an extensive network of Allied supervisors who must ensure that the credits were efficiently used and the supplies distributed honestly. An Allied military supply committee should be authorized to appoint at least three hundred military inspectors to supervise the delivery of military supplies. Likewise, a committee of commercial experts should establish a corps of Allied inspectors who would oversee the distribution of goods consigned to selected Siberian firms and organizations. Fourth, Morris believed the United States should appoint a diplomatic representative "at the seat of the Kolchak government" who would be assisted by experts in commercial affairs, finance, labor relations, and agriculture. In other words, this representative would occupy an advisory status within the Omsk government similar to the position John Stevens held with the Trans-Siberian railway system.[86] These conditions were tantamount to Herbert Hoover's recommendations to Wilson in June that the United States must establish an "economic mandatory" over Siberia.

Political realities at home made it impossible for the Wilson administration to consider a commitment of this size to the Omsk government. On August 25 the State Department informed Morris that the question of recognizing the Omsk regime had become moot, because the United States could not furnish the support Morris thought necessary. Public opinion and the mood in Congress would not support any further commitment of American troops to Russia. Furthermore, no credits could be extended to Kolchak for military supplies or for commercial assistance without authorization from Congress. Any action by Congress depended on whether Wilson presented an assistance program then being prepared by Vance McCormick on the basis of Morris's reports. This endeavor had to be put on hold until the administration obtained ratification of the peace treaty—itself a hopeless battle that would drag on long after conditions in Siberia had deteriorated beyond help.

But even if the Wilson administration had been able to act on Morris's recommendations, Omsk lacked the capacity and willingness to accept the American ambassador's stringent terms for assistance. Indeed, Morris's visit to Omsk in August only caused new tensions between the United States and Kolchak's regime, as the desperate Russian officials alleged that the ambassador had agreed to recommend new credits unconditionally. Foreign Minister Sukin actually told Emerson that Morris had agreed to support a suspension of the railway agreement until the U.S. government recognized the Omsk regime, granted it financial assistance, and replaced the Czecho-Slovaks with American troops. Sukin rationalized that these steps would give Kolchak the prestige necessary to assert authority over the factions working against his regime; then it would be possible for the government to enforce the railway agreement.[87]

Meanwhile, Emerson's inspectors had become thoroughly disillusioned by pervasive Russian opposition to the rationalized repair procedures and the dispatching system. It should have come as no surprise to Stevens that the Russian civil and military authorities would stubbornly resist his efforts to undercut their authority by introducing American personnel and operating methods. To this extent, Stevens and his advisory personnel must share some of the blame for problems they encountered with Russian officialdom, for the Americans undoubtedly offended Russian sensibilities in their efforts to drastically overhaul Russian railroad practices. As a case in point, Benjamin Johnson believed the Technical Board had made a mistake in attempting to circumvent the transportation bureaucracy. During his tenure as chief inspector of the Omsk district, Johnson achieved better results by attaching the Russian dispatchers to the office of the Russian division chief of transportation. Merging the dispatching network into the existing bureaucracy encouraged Russian officials to cooperate with the American innovations by giving them a stake in the new system while it enabled the inspectors to supervise operations more effectively.[88]

Regardless of any tactical mistakes Stevens may have made in implementing the railroad agreement, these errors were ultimately overshadowed by the inhospitable political environment the Great Power rivalry fostered for all American initiatives in Siberia. British and Japanese support for their military clients in Siberia only strengthened the reactionary elements who opposed the American assistance program. For instance, the independent-minded British consul at Vladivostok, W. O'Reilly, believed his government's policy had been too accommodating to the Omsk regime. O'Reilly thought that British High Commissioner Sir Charles Eliot had been "too much taken up with the idea of pleasing the Omsk Government at all costs, regardless of their real interests, and also of our position in the eyes of the population generally, who are the permanent factor in the situation." In contrast, O'Reilly believed American policy had been unfairly criticized by Omsk officials because "Washington would not let them [the American troops] go beyond railway guarding" and because the Americans "did not agree with old regime[s] bullying of the population."[89]

As Kolchak's position grew more critical in the fall, State Department experts vigorously lobbied Wilson and Lansing for a de facto recogniton of the Omsk regime. Basil Miles, probably the main advocate of recognition, considered this action necessary in order to prevent Russia from being absorbed into the economic orbit of Germany or Japan. Miles reiterated the principal concern of American policymakers when he emphasized that "to my mind we must get appropriations from Congress for a general plan to assist in economic re-construction in Russia."[90] Near the end of September before resigning from the State Department, Miles pleaded with his superiors to furnish Kolchak's regime additional support, warning that if the United States did not do something for Russia "the alternative is to let others act who are willing to do so—which would leave Siberia to the Japs."[91]

Following Wilson's stroke in late September, Secretary Lansing, who temporarily assumed authority for policy decisions, expressed the hopelessness of the Russian situation. Whereas Miles's passion for Russia had undoubtedly begun to cloud his judgment of the Omsk regime, Lansing had to face the inescapable fact that "responsible government" could never be based on the "corrupt and incompetent, and to a large extent reactionary" civil and political officials who surrounded Kolchak. This regime, Lansing emphasized, had managed to alienate the Siberian population in less than a year, particularly the zemstvos and cooperatives "which being democratic in principle are best representative of the popular will." Lansing anticipated that the Czecho-Slovak's evacuation would force Kolchak to withdraw his government to Irkutsk, where he might be compelled to seek Japanese assistance.[92]

When Kolchak's collapse became imminent in late November, the State Department explained to Morris why the administration must continue to support the regime's survival, albeit in a reorganized form. American officials were essentially concerned that if Kolchak was replaced, a pro-Japanese government could quite possibly succeed him. Recently, a visiting Japanese publicity agent from the Japanese Parliament had suggested to Smith at Vladivostok that Kolchak would soon fall and that Japan and America should sponsor Russian self-government through the zemstvos and cooperatives. While on the face of it the State Department welcomed these sentiments as perhaps representing a new departure in Japanese policy, it nevertheless feared it could just as well be "a disingenuous attempt to obtain [our] support for the elimination of Kolchak." Therefore, "in the interest of securing as orderly a succession of government as possible," the United States favored a reorganization of the Omsk government along democratic lines—which Kolchak had pledged to the Council of Four in June—"rather than a complete break with the past." While the presently constituted Omsk government itself stood in the way of reconstruction, the Wilson administration did not want to risk its succession by a regime oriented toward Japan.[93]

The position of the Omsk regime grew critical in October when White resistance collapsed along the Tobol River, leaving Omsk defenseless before the Red Army. Meanwhile, growing uncertainies over the fate of the peace treaty threatened any further initiatives the administration might have wanted to undertake in Russia. But these grave setbacks did not weaken the State Department's resolve to assist economic reconstruction in Siberia. On the contrary, during November Dewitt C. Poole, the new Russian division chief, prepared a lengthy report urging the U.S. government to underwrite a large-scale reconstruction progam for Siberia. Secretary Lansing submitted this report to Wilson on December 4.

Poole predicated his recommendations on the conviction that the Russian market, "comprising one-seventh of the land surface of the globe," would have to be integrated into the global economy in order to maintain stable international growth in the postwar period. Accordingly, regardless of the enormous difficulties this unprecedented program would encounter, Poole justified such a commitment as an alternative to leaving the Russian Empire under the control of "adventurous revolutionaries" or a "renascent imperialism which would conspire once more to establish itself in forcible control of the world's affairs."[94]

To meet the emergency conditions in Siberia, Poole recommended that an expanded Russian Bureau be incorporated with a capital of $100 million. While continuing to lend directly to cooperatives, zemstvos, and municipalities, this agency would also assume functions similar to the War Finance Corporation by insuring exports and imports to Russia. Although American policymakers favored the return of economic activity to private channels, Poole's recommendations illustrate how the Wilson administration believed that exceptions to this principle should be made in cases where widespread social and economic instability on the continent could only be alleviated by substantial governmental intervention. A major portion of the bureau's funds would be used to assist the Trans-Siberian railway, which would continue to play the pivotal role in the region's reconstruction.[95]

Events at home and in Siberia had already squelched any potential program of this scope; Poole's ambitous recommendations would never even reach Congress. This does not, however, lessen the importance of his views, for they were consistent with Wilson's position in June. Equally important,

Poole's report enables us to reach broader conclusions regarding the nature of American intervention in Russia during the Revolution and civil war. His recommendations were founded on the widely shared American belief that the Bolsheviks and "bolshevism" were distinct phenomena. In contrast to the small, but dedicated Bolshevik party, which relentlessly pursued its revolutionary goals, Poole defined bolshevism as "a popular state of mind growing out of the war and past abuses." After identifying social grievances as the cause of revolution, Poole reiterated that American policy had been guided by the principle that bolshevism "is obviously not to be conquered by force. It is pre-eminently an economic and moral phenomena against which economic and moral remedies alone will prevail." He considered military measures to be useful only as a "practical necessity, in certain contingencies"; beyond limited purposes, military operations only produced more hardship for the population, thereby fueling social protest and strengthening the Bolsheviks.[96]

While Poole's distinction between the "Bolsheviks" and "bolshevism" is obviously an oversimplification, it nevertheless demonstrates a recognition that the Bolsheviks' success at mobilizing popular support had little to do with their ideological program. Most of the Siberian peasantry lacked any coherent political consciousness; between 1918 and 1920 they simply supported whichever side appeared to offer relief from oppression and material hardship.[97]

Near the end of 1919, the State Department abruptly informed Japan that the United States would withdraw its troops from Siberia, an act that called into question the continuation of the inter-Allied agreement for supervision of the Trans-Siberian railways. Nevertheless, by the spring of 1920, the United States reaffirmed its commitment to maintaining the Open Door on the Chinese Eastern Railway as a link between Siberia and the world market. But in much the same way that the aims of its Siberian policy had been compromised, American efforts to establish an international trusteeship over this line would become hopelessly entangled in the even more complex web of Great Power rivalry in China.

8

⁓

A Critical Juncture:
The Chinese Eastern Railway
in Far Eastern Rivalries,
1920–1922

After the collapse of the Kolchak government at the end of 1919, America's Siberian policy rested exclusively on the tenuous international agreement between the United States, Britain, Japan, and France for supervision of the Chinese Eastern Railway. From 1920 until the end of 1922, when Japan's troops were finally withdrawn from the Chinese Eastern Railway zone and Russia's Maritime Provinces, American policy struggled to establish an effective trusteeship over the line in order to maintain a link between Siberia and the international market.

American statesmen believed that maintenance of the Open Door on the Chinese Eastern Railway would eventually have far-reaching implications for the United States's position in the global political economy. This view was best illustrated by an interview that took place between John Stevens and Thomas Lamont, representative of the American group of the China Banking Consortium, at Mukden in early May 1920. Stevens linked the fate of the Siberian market to the Chinese Eastern Railway. He stressed that Japan posed a great danger to the railroad in its desire to "block the rest of the world from the immense possibilities of trade with Siberia." Stevens earnestly impressed upon Lamont that "if America is blocked out of trade with that immense area it will be the greatest misfortune for our country. We need foreign markets badly and that is the very best of them all—the richest, most prosperous, most able to pay. Japan, if she is not checked in her present plans, will control all Siberia east of the Ural Mountains. Such an outcome would be a world calamity."[1] Stevens's comments emphasized certain factors about Siberia that bear special attention. Siberia's rich natural resources and its relatively prosperous, market-oriented population made the region potentially a much more important outlet for American capital than China, whose poverty and instability limited its developmental potential beyond the environs of the treaty ports. Stevens's views suggest that during this particularly fluid historical period American statesmen perceived a whole new dimension to their long-standing interest in the China market. The Open Door in Manchuria now constituted a bridge to the immense possibilities of the Siberian market.

The divergent interests of the powers in Manchuria isolated America in its efforts to maintain a viable international trusteeship over the line. While the Chinese Eastern Railway was critical to American long-term interests in Siberia, the fate of the line had become caught up in the turbulent crosscurrents of China's warlord era. This era was marked by incipient Chinese nationalism, warring political factions, and an intensified competition among the powers over spheres of influence.

The year 1920 opened with the United States contemplating the withdrawal of the American railroad advisers, who, under the terms of the Inter-Allied Railway Agreement, were supposed to depart with the American troops. The termination of inter-Allied supervision over the Chinese Eastern Railway would have serious consequences since this body represented the major impediment to Japan's ambitions toward the railway.

There were ominous signs that Japan was preparing to make a move on the line. Near the end of 1919 Stevens reported that Japan was attempting to introduce the yen in northern Manchuria through indirect methods. Japan proposed to loan the Chinese Eastern Railway yen for the purchase of Romanov rubles to meet payroll and other current expenses. Stevens believed that since the supply of Romanov currency was too small to provide an adequate circulating medium, Japan actually was attempting to establish the yen in the region.[2] The substitution of yen for gold rubles would be facilitated by the fact that they were approximately equivalent in value, both being worth about 50 American cents.[3] Stevens also thought the Japanese were trying to ply the officials of the Chinese Eastern Railway with yen advances in order to gain special traffic privileges.[4] Stevens urged that a joint Allied loan of about $5 million be made to the railroad before it fell under Japanese control for lack of alternative financing.[5]

Over the next three years, Stevens and his American colleagues on the inter-Allied supervisory bodies consistently opposed Japanese and Chinese efforts to discriminate against Russian currency in the Chinese Eastern

Railway zone. They insisted that the monetary "status quo" be maintained on the Chinese Eastern and its revenues should not be reduced into one currency, rather all circulating specie should be accepted without restrictions. Until June 1920, when the maritime zemstvo government devaluated the badly depreciated Siberian ruble, both the Technical Board and Inter-Allied Railway Committee had attempted to compensate for its depreciation by accepting all currencies, whether Chinese silver, Romanov currency, or the Siberian rubles as payment for railroad tariffs on the basis of the prewar gold ruble. Against this fixed standard the exchange rate between these currencies was then periodically readjusted. This American support for the continued use of Russian currency on the Chinese Eastern Railway served two basic objectives. This policy helped preserve a semblance of Russian sovereignty over the line and it maintained the railroad's links with foreign currencies on the gold standard.[6]

Japanese troop movements in early 1920 were a further threat to the railroad. On the pretext of defending its interests in Manchuria and Korea against bolshevism, Japan's military occupied the Chinese Eastern Railway west of Harbin and the Ussuri Railway; this railway connected Vladivostok with the Chinese Eastern Railway. In the Trans-Baikal region Japanese troops and Semenov's forces were blocking the withdrawal eastward of the Czecho-Slovak troops creating a situation that, under the terms of the Allied intervention, justified a continued presence of Japanese troops in the Russian Far East.

The precarious financial position of the Chinese Eastern Railway was compounded by the Allies' delinquency in paying their military transportation bills; this factor increasingly threatened the solvency of the line. In early May Stevens explained that while the road owed about $5 million, the Allies owed it $6 million. Consequently, if those bills were promptly paid the road's financial problems would be solved. While the United States and Britain paid their bills quickly, Japan was slow and France would pay neither its own bills or those of the Czecho-Slovaks, for which it was responsible. Japan's delinquent payments were particularly a nuisance to Stevens because the road simultaneously owed money to Japanese-controlled coal mines in southern Manchuria. Japanese authorities explicitly considered these coal supplies as a loan, which they consciously used as a source of financial leverage against the Chinese Eastern. Stevens feared that Japan would suddenly demand payment of these bills on threat of a stoppage of its coal shipments.[7]

While the collapse of Russian authority over the Chinese Eastern heightened the danger from Japan after 1919, it also encouraged Chinese aspirations to assert control of the line. The added dimension of Chinese nationalism, which was deeply entangled in factional politics and Japanese intrigue, created another destabilizing factor that complicated American efforts to maintain international control of the Chinese Eastern. Following the collapse of Kolchak's government and in response to General Dmitri Khorvat's announcement that he would himself assume full governmental powers of the Russian people within the jurisdiction of the Chinese Eastern Railway, the Chinese government announced that it would assume governmental power in the zone on the pretext that no outside power could exercise this prerogative in Chinese territory. The Soviet government fueled China's pretensions toward the Chinese Eastern Railway when it formally renounced the rights the previous Russian governments had claimed over the line.[8]

Initiatives by Britain and China during the spring of 1920 appeared to offer the United States renewed hope that the Chinese Eastern could be brought under effective international control. Beginning in February 1920, and continuing through the spring, Britain strongly urged the State Department to continue its participation in the Inter-Allied Railway Committee and Technical Board. Fearing that Japan was about to seize control over the line, Britain recommended that control by the inter-Allied board continue, that operation of the line be conferred to China, and that the consortium, rather than Japan, finance the railroad.[9] Similarly, while China was determined to take control of the line, it requested that Stevens remain in his position, and it asked Thomas Lamont, the American representative of the Banking Consortium, to place the line under consortium jurisdiction.[10]

By mid-May the State Department had reconsidered its decision to withdraw American personnel from the Chinese Eastern Railway. This change in the American attitude had been encouraged by the overtures of Britain and China, and the recommendations of Charles Smith, the American representative on the Inter-Allied Railway Committee. The views of the Russian embassy played a particularly important role in shaping American policy toward the line in 1920. In early May the Russian embassy proposed to the State Department that the Chinese Eastern Railway be placed under the mandate of an international committee in order to protect Russia's existing rights in the line. Financing could then be arranged for the line either by the consortium or by a power acting as a mandatory, on the approval of the international committee.

The Russian embassy justified this arrangement in favor of its claims on grounds that the actual ownership of the line still resided in the Russian government, even though the shares were held by the Russo-Asiatic Bank. This peculiar situation worked to the advantage of the fictitious Russian state. Since the bank held the railroad's stock, the legal status of the line was that of a private concern, even though the bank's control was purely formal.

This de jure private status served to protect Russia's rights since it enabled the line to continue functioning under its legally established Russian administration, regardless of whether a Russian government existed.

After asserting that the Russian government still owned the line, the embassy reminded the State Department to uphold Russia's legal rights in the line. Now, with China threatening to unilaterally repudiate the legal status quo, the Russian embassy was anxious to have the Chinese Eastern Railway placed under a formal international trusteeship. This arrangement would guarantee the existing status quo and thereby lay to rest all uncertainty over the line's legal status. The embassy warned that any change of the railway's status in favor of China would have dangerous implications for the future of the line because Manchuria had become a virtual protectorate of Japan. Under these circumstances control of the line would inevitably pass to Japan.[11]

Meanwhile, the State Department briefly considered an alternative form of trusteeship whereby the Chinese Eastern Railway would be placed under the control of the presently constituted Inter-Allied Railway Committee; the Technical Board would be transferred to China as a mandate. The technical operation of the line would then pass to the Chinese government or a new board chosen by that government with a qualifying provision for review by the Inter-Allied Railway Committee. Under this reorganization plan the troublesome Military Committee would be abolished.[12] The American chargé in Japan, Edward Bell, quickly notified the State Department that Japan would vigorously oppose China receiving a mandate over the Chinese Eastern Railway or the Technical Board. Charles Tenney, the American chargé in China, suggested that if the United States wanted to implement the plan of the Russian embassy, it would be best to continue the existing inter-Allied agreement.

American resolve was bolstered by Britain, which indicated it would support an international trusteeship over the railroad to protect Russia's primary rights in the railway and China's secondary interests. Britain favored placing the line under consortium jurisdiction to control Japanese ambitions, to help stabilize China, and to block the spread of Bolshevik influence. Britain, however, would not press for a withdrawal of Japanese troops from the Chinese Eastern Railway because it had a legitimate security interest in the region. Instead, it suggested that a joint military force of Chinese and Japanese troops guard the line. Nor was Britain willing to back up its position by promising a British financial contribution from the British group of the China Banking Consortium. For the ostensible reason that its banking group had been delayed in completing its arrangements, Britain coyly suggested that the United States and Japan make the preliminary loan to the line.

Britain's position conveniently enabled it to support the status quo in northern Manchuria while avoiding a confrontation with Japan in an area where it had little financial interest.[13]

Despite these reservations, the State Department was encouraged by the prospects that an essential concurrence existed between the United States and Britain with regard to the Chinese Eastern Railway.[14] Up until this time the State Department had hesitated to advocate consortium financing out of concern for jeopardizing the broader consortium negotiations with Japan. As recently as the end of April the State Department had instructed its diplomatic representatives not to raise the controversial issue of consortium financing for the Chinese Eastern Railway at that delicate stage of the consortium negotiations.[15] In view of the likelihood of Japanese opposition and because of the difficulties that would be involved in floating a loan for the Chinese Eastern Railway in the American market, near the end of May the State Department still wanted to postpone consideration of the issue until Thomas Lamont, representative of the American group, could be consulted.[16] Nevertheless, the State Department was already placing a great deal of stock in the support it believed Britain was now prepared to lend on the contentious issue of consortium financing for the Chinese Eastern Railway. The department fully expected Britain to line up French support in order to pressure Japan into accepting the proposal.

Meanwhile the State Department now favored a plan for an international trusteeship over the Chinese Eastern Railway, which probably grew out of the Russian embassy proposal of May 7. By late May the department was considering the possibility of establishing an international bankruptcy commission to administer the line temporarily in trust for Russia. This commission would consolidate functions of the Technical Board and the Inter-Allied Railway Committee. It would assume all the duties of a trusteeship over the line with the exception that it could not borrow money without authorization of the participating governments. Yet the governments would be expected to base their financial decisions regarding the line on the commission's reports and recommendations.

Similar to the question of consortium financing for the Chinese Eastern Railroad, the State Department counted on Britain to support the plan for a bankruptcy commission. A department memorandum from June 15 emphasized that they "quite frankly hoped that we could in the first place come to a full understanding with Great Britain, that the latter would be able to enlist the support and cooperation of France, and that the three powers might then be in a position to bring to bear upon Japan such pressure as might induce it to fall in with the project."[17] By this time the State Department had come to "heartily" endorse consortium financing for the line, even though it had not yet heard Lamont's views on the subject. On June 15 Britain's ambassador to Washington, Sir Auchland Geddes, informed Foreign Secretary Earl Curzon that "they [the State Department] believe, failing some arrangement which will really put Chinese Eastern under effective (?trustee)ship, all that hitherto [has been] achieved for consortium in way of eliminating reservations of special interests will be jeopardized."[18] This comment would seem to indicate that the State Department linked the success of the consortium to inclusion of the Chinese Eastern Railway within its jurisdiction. If too many important properties were excluded from the consortium its effectiveness as an instrument of the Open Door would be seriously compromised.

On June 19 the department informed Ambassador John W. Davis in London that it had urged the American group of the desirability of consortium financing for the Chinese Eastern Railway. It then instructed Davis to remind the Foreign Office that the State Department expected it to take the lead in obtaining French cooperation, both in regard to consortium financing for the line and in encouraging France to pay its transportation bills.[19] Circumstantial evidence suggests the State Department thought a bankruptcy commission could be a lever to extract payment from the Allies for the $5 million they owed the line for transportation of their military forces—particularly France, which was responsible for the Czecho-Slovaks as well as its own forces.[20]

The United States quickly found that it could not count on British support when it came to any revision of the existing arrangement for Allied supervision of the Chinese Eastern Railway. In late June Britain's ambassador to Japan, Charles Eliot, reported that any attempt to link the Chinese Eastern Railway with the consortium would meet stiff opposition from Japan. Japanese foreign minister Uchida explained to Eliot that he could not support such a course for the line because Japanese public opinion would not tolerate it at the time. Following this conversation Eliot recommended to London that Britain should not press the question of consortium financing for the Chinese Eastern Railway for the present.[21] After hearing the same report from the British embassy in Washington, the State Department commented with disappointment that Britain's ambassador gave no reason to believe "that in the near future conditions might be more favorable for a consideration by the Japanese Cabinet of using the consortium for financing the Chinese Eastern Railway."[22]

A week later, Britain gave further indication that it was backing away from the American program for the Chinese Eastern Railway. On July 8 Ambassador Davis in London reported that the Foreign Office had strong reservations about the American proposal for a bankruptcy commission. It was concerned that the creation of such a commission would imply complete insolvency and thereby jeopardize French interests represented in the Russo-Asiatic Bank. Yet, beyond this technical consideration, the Foreign Office argued "that the proposed arrangement appears . . . merely to take us round the circle again into a consortium of a more complicated form which Japan's probable contentions would again block."[23]

Britain's equivocal position toward the Chinese Eastern Railway question was influenced by a broader calculation of its interests in China. On July 7, 1920, Frank Ashton-Gwatkin of the British Foreign Office issued a memorandum analyzing Japan's threat to the Open Door. He emphasized that Japan built its spheres of influence around exclusive railroad privileges such as the South Manchurian Railway. These privileges in turn gave Japanese commerce formidable advantages. But British statesmen directed their attention to Japan's emerging spheres of influence in China proper, which threatened British interests in Central China. Japan's exclusive control over the Tsingtao-Tsinan Railroad in Shantung Province and its embryonic position in Fukien Province straddled perilously close to Britain's extensive interests in the Yangtze Valley. Ashton-Gwatkin suggested that while it might be difficult, Japan could be persuaded to accept nationalization of the railroad concessions in China proper out of a keen awareness for its diplomatic isolation and because it wanted to renew the Anglo-Japanese alliance. As compensation he recommended that Britain should be prepared to concede Japan a special position in Manchuria. Ashton-Gwatkin's justification for this policy manifested a basic divergence of interests between Britain and the United States in China at the time. He concluded that:

> although it is difficult to defend the strict morality of her protectorate in Manchuria, yet the position there is entirely different to that of Shantung. Shantung is in the heart of China, the birthplace of Confucius, densely populated and developed by a highly civilised people. Manchuria is on the outskirts, neglected by the Chinese government, sparsely populated, and low in the scale of culture. Recent prosperity there is due to Japanese enterprise, and although the foreigner may be excluded in spite of his treaty rights, yet the presence of the Japanese has been a benefit to the country. Japan in Manchuria has to a certain extent played the part of Great Britain in Egypt. Even if Japanese influence spreads to North Manchuria and can get control of the Chinese Eastern Railway (which at the present moment seems an object coveted by Japan), such expansion can do very little harm to England nor can it greatly damage China. . . . If a real Open Door can be established in Shantung, Great Britain might be able to view a further extension of Japanese influence

in the Manchurian sphere with equanimity. In any case, Japan's position in Manchuria is a peculiar one, and appears to deserve a certain measure of sympathetic consideration.[24]

Indeed, in October 1921, before the Washington Conference, British foreign secretary Earl Curzon advocated exactly this course to V. K. Wellington Koo, the Chinese minister to Britain. He candidly asked Koo whether it would "not be sound statesmanship to steer Japan away from the great industrial areas of China proper, and push her—so to speak—to the North?" After noting that Manchuria was not part of China proper, but an outer territory, and that even America had recognized Japan's special position there under the Lansing-Ishii Agreement, Curzon suggested to Koo that China should "allow the Japanese to expand, under reasonable conditions, in that direction, rather than to bring them down upon the main body of China."[25]

Britain's indifference to the Chinese Eastern Railway issue was not yet grasped in Washington. By mid-summer 1920 the State Department had linked the possibility of obtaining consortium financing for the Chinese Eastern Railway to a strengthened international control over the line. When John Stevens met Thomas Lamont at Mukden in May to discuss consortium financing for the line, he impressed upon the head of the American group that he must be allowed to manage the property on his own terms if the consortium expected him to remain and to administer the line. In July he made the same point to the State Department when he insisted that whoever undertook control of the Chinese Eastern Railway had to be given "full authority which can be enforced," in contrast to the ineffective inter-Allied agreement.[26] In October, when the consortium finally adopted a position on the Chinese Eastern Railway at its final conference, the influence of Stevens's recommendations was apparent. The consortium group unanimously agreed to provide the line with a $10 million gold loan pending the consent of their respective governments, the condition of the security markets, and provided "satisfactory conditions can be arranged as to security, as to payment of debts due from the Allied and Associated Powers, as to the Allied and Associated Powers undertaking that there shall be no military interference with the traffic of the Railway, and as to the position of the representatives of the Consortium Powers on the technical Board (or other Administrative body) being regularized and stabilized."[27] Aside from the financial conditions demanded by the bankers, the remaining points embodied in the consortium's statement had been insisted on by Stevens: the payment of Allied military debts, the end of interference by the military, and the strengthening of the Technical Board's powers.

Unilateral action by the Chinese government near the end of 1920 inaugurated two years of frustration for American efforts to strengthen international control over the line. On October 2 the Chinese government declared its intention to assume control over the Chinese Eastern Railway by virtue of an agreement it concluded with the Russo-Asiatic Bank. Since Russia could no longer administer the line, China claimed that its ultimate right of sovereignty obligated it to provisionally guarantee security in the region until some arrangement could be reached with a future Russian government that merited recognition. Under this agreement China announced that it would now exercise the right to name the president and four of the railroad's eight members of the board of directors, giving it an effective majority. Furthermore, the railroad would be required to pay the Chinese government the sum of 5 million silver taels, which should have been paid it by the company with the beginning of operations, plus 6 percent compound interest up to the year 1920. Although Stevens immediately obtained reassurances from the Chinese minister of communications that this supplementary agreement would not affect the authority of the Technical Board, this promise would be continuously violated.[28] From this point until the termination of the inter-Allied agreement in November 1922, the Chinese dominated board of directors freely ignored all directives from the Technical Board.

In another development that did not bode well for American policy, Britain retracted all support for the new American initiatives regarding the Chinese Eastern Railway. In late December 1920, the British Foreign Office informed American ambassador John W. Davis that Britain would not support either an increase in power for the Technical Board or a financial reorganization of the line by the consortium.[29]

These setbacks did not deter the newfound American resolve toward the Chinese Eastern Railway. By the beginning of 1921 the State Department had prepared a drastically revised plan for supervision of the railroad. In a clear effort to counter China's official meddling in the railroad's affairs, this new American plan would firmly establish an international trusteeship over the line. Under this plan the Inter-Allied Railway Committee would be abolished and replaced by a powerful Technical Board that would oversee both the technical and economic administration of the railroad. In addition to its existing powers the board would now assume the following responsibilities: the full control over the receipts and disbursements of the railroad's revenues, the power to fix all tariffs, and complete control over all personnel matters. The Russian general manager would be entirely subordinated to the board's authority. The State Department emphasized that the president of the board should be entrusted with as much responsibility as possible—

even going so far as to recommend that he be given the prerogative to act independently of the other board members. If operated by a single powerful head, the State Department believed the railroad would be able to collect the sums due it from the Allies and to earn a profit when trade improved. Finally, as a corollary to the plan, the State Department intended that John Stevens be retained as president of this powerful new board.[30]

The State Department immediately used this proposal as the basis for informal discussions with the British embassy in Washington.[31] Early indications from the British ambassador Sir Auchland Geddes were not promising. In a conference with Secretary of State Colby and the acting secretary of state, Norman H. Davis, on February 24, Geddes would only extend qualified support to the American plan. While he expressed Britain's willingness to follow the American lead, Geddes added that it would not be able to put up any money or to take the lead on the issue. Nor was he prepared to discuss the American amendments to the inter-Allied agreement in any detail. Colby and Davis reacted sharply to Geddes's noncommittal position. They told Geddes that the United States "had taken the initiative already in making this proposal and that we wished to have a frank understanding in the matter, and not expect the British to follow us and then look behind and not find them." Furthermore, the American officials made it known to Geddes that Britain's neutrality would not be appreciated, "that if they attempted to take the role of mediator between the United States and Japan in case [of] any controversy that might arise it would not be the proper way to deal with the subject, but if the two governments should propose the amended agreement to Japan it would probably be accepted gracefully without any difficulty."[32]

Britain would not give a definite reply to the American proposal between January and mid-May 1921. Britain continued to delay its response in spite of repeated American appeals that the United States attached great importance to reaching a prior agreement with Britain before negotiating with the other powers.[33] On May 14, 1921, after having received the views of its ambassadors in Tokyo and Peking, the Foreign Office informed the State Department that it preferred not to raise the issue at all in light of the strong opposition that would be encountered from both Japan and China to any proposals for greater international control over the Chinese Eastern Railway. Therefore, while Britain could agree to the American plans "in general principal [sic]," it would leave the United States with the unpromising task of sounding out the other powers on its own.[34]

The State Department's Far East experts perceived a broader pattern behind Britain's uncooperative position regarding the Chinese Eastern Railway. John V. A. MacMurray, head of the Far Eastern division, believed that

Britain's neutral stance toward the Chinese Eastern Railway signaled a growing divergence of interests between it and the United States over investment questions in the Far East. In an analysis of the Chinese Eastern Railway issue for Secretary Hughes, MacMurray argued that this episode reflected a broader shift in British policy away from the Open Door and toward an acceptance of spheres of influence in China. He suggested that Britain's "practical recognition" of Japan's claim for a dominant position in northern Manchuria coincided with a more aggressive support in favor of the prior concessionary claims of certain British manufacturing interests in China proper against rival American interests.[35]

In fact, in the years preceding World War I, Britain had been retreating from an Open Door for industrial loans in China; instead Britain favored a consolidation of its sphere of influence for industrial concessions in central China. This trend emerged out of the heightened competition between the powers over the growing investment opportunities for industrial activity in China.[36]

Despite this obvious setback to American policy, on his return to Washington in the spring of 1921, John Stevens told the State Department that Britain's support was not vital. He planned to return to Manchuria and "limp along" as best as he could under the existing arrangement until sometime in the future when the United States could exert "sufficient pressure to bring them to accept our views of the matter." Stevens felt there was a reasonable chance he could make the line pay because of its tremendous commercial potential, even with his insufficient authority.[37] Stevens's newfound optimism sprung from the promising increase in the volume of commercial traffic the line was handling by the spring of 1921.

A change in the administration of the Chinese Eastern Railway during the winter of 1921 had also given Stevens and the Technical Board reason to be encouraged. After asserting control over the Chinese Eastern Railway in October 1920, the Chinese government ousted Dmitri Khorvat as general manager of the line. In place of Khorvat, the Chinese backed the appointment of Boris Ostroumov, a reform-minded engineer. For the Chinese, Ostroumov's reformist tendencies and his independence from the Russian railway bureaucracy made him an attractive alternative to Khorvat, who would otherwise continue to be a pillar of Russian national interests in the railway zone. Chinese officials counted on Ostroumov to break the grip the Russian bureaucracy had over the line. Ostroumov's appointment would also be satisfactory to the Russo-Asiatic Bank, the line's financial agent, since he had connections with the Stakheev firm, which owned a majority of the Russian shares of the Russo-Asiatic Bank. Nevertheless, China permitted one of

Khorvat's lieutenant's to be named vice president, since some accommodation had to be made to the Russian bureaucrats who continued to manage the line.[38]

Following Ostroumov's installation as general manager in early 1921, the Technical Board immediately began to implement its own reforms by introducing auditing and statistical procedures for the line. Benjamin O. Johnson, who served as acting president of the Technical Board during Stevens's frequent absences in 1921–22, considered these endeavors crucial to the board's work because the line had never had a budget before. Improved knowledge of the railroad's financial condition would enable the Technical Board to begin placing each department on a sound economic basis.[39]

Meanwhile the Technical Board supported the efforts of Ostroumov and assistant General Manager D. P. Kazakevitch to begin making staff reductions in order to bring expenditures in line with operating income. Proceeding cautiously, the Technical Board and Ostroumov planned to make these reductions proportionately among all levels of employees and in limited numbers over a period of time in order to limit hardship. Johnson also believed the impact of these staff reductions would be quickly mitigated, since he anticipated that the surplus employees would soon be redistributed west when communications with Siberia were reestablished.[40] When Ostroumov's staff cuts met stiff resistance in the spring, resistance that the Russian bureaucracy encouraged in an effort to protect their patronage workers, Johnson urged the general manager to delay any drastic changes in the budget because the recent improvement in earnings would permit the administration to delay staff reductions until 1922. For the remainder of the year, Johnson stressed that it would be more important to establish budgetary principles for the line than to undertake any precipitous staff reductions.[41]

But growing Chinese interference with the line in 1921 greatly hindered the Technical Board's efforts to rationalize expenditures. As quickly as the railroad produced any surplus that could be applied to past debts, Chinese officials pressured the administration for additional funds to support Chinese institutions in the railway zone. These demands reflected the political ascendance of Chang Tso-lin in Manchuria, whose power, and that of his clique, required the maintenance of extensive patronage networks.

While the Technical Board agreed that the railroad had an obligation to pay its share of the cost for local administration, it believed the Chinese submitted highly inflated budgetry estimates, particularly for institutions like the railway police. As a temporary compromise, the Technical Board agreed to make lump-sum payments to the city and settlement police and to the prison. After 1921 however, Johnson insisted that the railway should make no further lump-sum payments for any civil institutions and the Chinese would have to furnish the railway administration with itemized budgets before receiving funds from the railroad. In mid-May 1921 Johnson believed the line could be placed on a sound operating basis by January 1922, if only Chinese influence over expenditures could be reduced.[42]

Nor did the Chinese officials appreciate the importance of preserving the railroad's monetary connections with the international economy. In January 1921 the Chinese members of the board of directors attempted to transfer the Chinese Eastern Railway's operations from a gold basis to China's silver-standard currency. C. C. Wang, the Chinese representative to the inter-Allied committee and member of the board of directors, argued that the line could not be kept on a gold basis because gold rubles constituted no more than 10 percent of the line's receipts. The Chinese claimed that the scarcity of gold rubles made it very inconvenient for the line to operate when its local expenses in fuel and labor were paid in silver.

As acting president of the Technical Board, Johnson opposed this step on grounds that it would have serious implications for the future of the line. He explained that the economy of northern Manchuria was tied to the international economy because of the ascendancy of its bean and wheat exports. Since the price of wheat and beans at Harbin was the European price minus transportation costs, their prices fluctuated with the world price, based on gold, rather than with local demand. Even the local cost of living and the cost of transportation was tied to the international market because the cost of labor, itself determined by the price of wheat and imported clothing, and all the supplies for the Chinese Eastern Railway were purchased from gold standard countries. Hence, if transportation rates on the Chinese Eastern Railway were put on a basis that fluctuated with the vagaries of silver, the region's economic ties with the international economy would be disrupted. Johnson viewed the grievances of the Chinese as a reaction to the recent depreciation of silver, which would abate if the exchange value between gold and silver stabilized.[43] Determined opposition from the Technical Board forced the Chinese to back down in this instance.

In July 1921 the Chinese directors placed the line in immediate jeopardy when they attempted to float a bond issue that would probably end up in Japanese hands. At this time the Chinese majority on the board of directors decided to float a bond issue of 25 million taels, in accordance with the provisions of the amended agreement for control of the Chinese Eastern Railway, which the Chinese government foisted on the Russo-Asiatic Bank in October 1920. About 15 million taels of this loan would be used to cover the railway's debt to China, while the remaining 10 million taels would be used to finance operating expenses.

Stevens and the American diplomatic representatives at Peking quickly moved to block the bond issue because they feared Japanese influence lay behind the transaction. A few weeks earlier the Japanese-controlled South Manchurian Railway Company reportedly offered the Chinese Eastern Railway a loan of 20 million yen. Now the Chinese government planned to issue the bonds on terms that would make them susceptible to appropriation by Japanese interests.

This situation arose as a result of Japan's skillful manipulation of Chinese warlord factions. Part of the issue, 15 million taels, was to be handed directly to China, while the remaining 10 million would be floated in the open market; both issues were to bear 5 percent interest. In the first instance, British and American sources discovered that the bonds issued to the Chinese government would quickly be liquidated, and probably at a discount, for the dubious purpose of raising funds for the military expenses of Gen. Chang Tso-lin's powerful Fengtien clique, which had gained a predominant position in Manchuria with Japan's help. Furthermore, political and financial circles in Peking believed that a good deal of the balance would be turned back to Japan to pay arrears on the notorious Nishihara loans from 1916, which subsidized pro-Japanese factions in China.[44]

The 10 million taels worth of bonds earmarked for the open market were also likely to fall into Japanese hands. The low 5 percent rate of interest on these bonds would make them an unattractive investment for private interests. However, Western sources in Peking recognized that the South Manchurian Railway Company, an agent of the Japanese government, would readily purchase these bonds in order to give Japan a direct financial interest in the Chinese Eastern Railway. In fact, the Chinese ministers of communications and of war exhibited such callous disregard for China's interests in the railway because they held their positions on the basis of pledges to raise funds for military and administrative expenses. After a bitter fight, the Russian representatives on the board of directors only acquiesced to the bond issue when they recognized that the Chinese members would merely find other means for pawning China's interests in the line to Japan.[45]

Stevens adamantly opposed this financial maneuver, claiming the Chinese government must recognize the Technical Board's authority in all matters connected with the railroad's finances. While Stevens recognized that the line needed $10 million to pay debts and to maintain adequate working capital, this situation had arisen because of the Allies' refusal to pay for their military transportation. Under normal operating conditions the railway's revenue would be adequate to meet its operating costs. In Stevens's view the line's current financial difficulties did not justify China's resort to questionable financial practices like the present bond issue.[46]

By the middle of July, the United States managed to exert its influence with pro-Western Chinese officials to defeat the proposed bond issue. Between July 7 and July 15, the American legation at Peking engaged in a concerted effort to defeat the bond issue, supported by a vigorous campaign in the English-speaking newspapers, *The Peking Leader* and *The Peking and Tientsin Times*. In particular, the American chargé, A. B. Ruddock, enlisted C. S. Liu, a Chinese member of the Technical Board, as a lobbyist against the bond issue within the Chinese government. Liu, who had studied in the United States, was also one of the most influential men in the Ministry of Communications. The American position finally mobilized sufficient support among the Chinese officials opposed to Chang Tso-lin, when the legation allayed the concerns of the Chinese premier, Gen. Chin Yun-p'eng; Liu; the minister of communications, Chang Chih-t'an; and the Director General of the Chinese Eastern Railway, Sung Hsiao-lien that the United States planned no permanent internationalization of the line, but rather, that it merely wanted to use the Technical Board as a means of preserving the existing rights of all concerned parties. It was only after these assurances were communicated to the premier that Liu informed the legation the bond issue would be dropped.[47]

However, even Liu refused to give a "blanket assurance" that China would cooperate with Stevens's terms; that as a party to the Inter-Allied Railway Agreement, China recognize the Technical Board's authority over all matters connected with the finances of the Chinese Eastern Railway.[48]

In early August, Minister of Foreign Affairs W. W. Yen revealed why all Chinese officials were sensitive about the continuation of joint Sino-Russian control over the Chinese Eastern Railway. This precedent strengthened Japan's claim for a joint Sino-Japanese railway in Shantung Province, a concern shared by Britain in light of its fears over Japanese penetration in central China. In contrast to the Chinese Eastern Railway, Yen commented favorably on the arrangement China had with Britain with regard to lines such as the Shanghai-Nanking Railway, a Chinese government railway constructed by Britain.[49] Britain agreed to build this line for the Chinese Railway System in return for concessionary rights to furnish the line with British capital and materials. British contractors were effectively given a preference in all orders made for this line because a British engineer had the privilege of supervising the line during the term of the loan.[50] This episode demonstrates how the convergence of interests between Britain's investment sphere in Central China and Chinese nationalism operated to the detriment of American efforts to nominally preserve Russian rights in the Chinese Eastern Railway.

In the aftermath of the bond issue controversy, the question remained of how to finance the Chinese Eastern Railway. At the high point of the controversy on July 13, Yen quizzed Ruddock whether, as an alternative to the bond issue, the United States or the governments represented on the Technical Board would be willing to furnish the needed funds. In late June the possibility of consortium financing had again been raised—this time by the British group. Sir Charles Addis of the Hong Kong Bank and head of the British group learned that the Japanese government had decided to retreat from its previous opposition to Japanese participation in consortium financing for the Chinese Eastern Railway. Addis recognized that China probably hoped to inherit the line from Russia, and he suggested that the powers accept this fate. Addis believed the consortium members "should be content to see the Chinese Eastern Railway merged in the Chinese Government Railways and, in view of the international importance of the line, we would remain willing to render financial support in terms of Article 4 of the Consortium Agreement, i.e. 'on the principle of complete equality in every respect.'" In other words, since Britain held no special interests in northern Manchuria it would be completely willing to see the line come under Chinese control as long as Britain retained equal opportunity to finance the line.[51] This encouraging news finally spurred the State Department to approach Japan with the amended plan of January 13, 1921, for supervision of the Chinese Eastern Railway.[52]

The State Department also brought this matter to the attention of the American group in early August, but they quickly dampened the hopes of the State Department. While J. P. Morgan and Company thought the Chinese Eastern Railway should come under consortium jurisdiction, until the Chinese government decided that it wanted the consortium to function "and until the financial position of the railway itself makes a better exhibit, we think there is little immediate possibility of offering in the United States a loan to this railway." Ever conscious of the need to maintain investor confidence in the financial markets, the American group stressed that it "must exercise the greatest caution and assure itself that" any Far Eastern loan it offered to American investors "shall be based upon sound operation and adequate security." Obviously the Chinese Eastern Railway did not meet these criteria. In a comment that demonstrated the advantages state capitalism had over corporate-liberal America in foreign investment ventures, the American group added that "It is true that in a situation of this kind Japanese bankers are sometimes able to proceed, but only under a guarantee on the part of their government which the American group would deem entirely unfitting to suggest to the American Government."[53] J. Paul Jameson, an American consul on temporary assignment to the State Department, captured the essence of the American dilemma over the railroad with his observation that "if the Group waits for the betterment in operations and earnings of the Railway when the object of the loan is to put it on its feet, there is no chance of a consortium loan, unless some sound security can be found to satisfy the Group."[54] In a letter to the American group, Secretary of State Hughes expressed regret over its decision, reminding the group that "the international importance of the Chinese Eastern Railway is quite obvious, and I hoped that through adequate financial support it might be made an important instrumentality of our 'open door' policy."[55]

In response to an inquiry from the State Department, Stevens indicated the Chinese Eastern had great need for a loan. He estimated the line required about $10 million gold. He believed a mortgage on the line's assets would be a more than adequate basis upon which to secure the loan, since a conservative figure placed its value at $100 million. Once again, however, Stevens insisted that the loan only be granted on conditions the Chinese would inevitably resist. The Technical Board must have sole control over all receipts and expenditures and it must have complete authority over all personnel decisions in order to prevent the Chinese from "loading" the payroll with high positions.[56] Stevens could not have been optimistic that anything would come of his recommendations because he informed the department that all actions of the Chinese government demonstrated its resolve to control the line.[57] After receiving Stevens's suggestions for financing the line, J. P. Morgan and Company dashed any lingering hopes that the American group would extend a loan to the line when it told the State Department that, if China hoped to attract the American investing public, it would likely have to pledge the surplus revenues of all the government railways above the charges on bonds issued for railway construction.[58]

American policy toward the Chinese Eastern Railway was clearly at an impasse by the late summer of 1921. The United States lacked the power to assert the Open Door on this critical communication link amid the divergent Far Eastern interests of Japan, China, and Great Britain. Likewise, the poor investment climate in China deterred American bankers.

The problems American policy faced in the Russian Far East and northern Manchuria typified its overall position in the Far East. The Harding administration sponsored the Washington Naval Conference between November 1921 and January 1922 in an effort to remove an important source of the United States's political isolation in the region. With the Anglo-Japanese alliance up for renewal in 1921, the Harding administration undertook this initiative in an attempt to redress the unfavorable relations of power that confronted the United States in the Far East. Since 1902 Japan's defensive alliance with Britain had given it the freedom to pursue expansionist policies. Even though Britain wanted to maintain friendly relations with its Asian treaty partner, by 1921 it could no longer avoid the threat Japan's hegemonic designs in the region posed for its own interests in central China. Britain now hoped to maintain the advantages of the Anglo-Japanese alliance by transforming this relationship into a tripartite arrangement that would include the United States. These sentiments were expressed to American officials through diplomatic channels in the spring and early summer of 1921.

When the British Imperial Conference called for a discussion on the Pacific and the Far East in early July, the Harding administration quickly moved to organize a conference that would address the whole spectrum of Far Eastern issues. By early September the State Department announced that the agenda of the Washington Conference would consist of two phases: the first would address the issue of naval disarmament, and the second stage would take up Pacific and Far Eastern political issues. During this second phase the State Department would attempt to resolve the whole range of Chinese and Siberian issues, including the Chinese Eastern Railway and the Japanese occupation of the Russian Maritime Provinces.

This division of the conference agenda into two parts was crucial to the American strategy. The American delegation, headed by Secretary of State Charles Evans Hughes, hoped to achieve dramatic success in disarmament issues first, in order to reduce tensions among the Far Eastern powers. Indeed, the United States accomplished its principal political goal, the termination of the Anglo-Japanese alliance, by abandoning its own ambitious naval program and by agreeing not to construct advanced bases in the Philippines and Guam. Following the agreements on naval tonnage and Pacific fortifications the United States persuaded Britain and Japan to replace their alliance with a Four-Power Treaty, which also included the United States and France. Under this treaty the signatories agreed they would attempt to settle Far Eastern controversies through diplomacy and conferences, rather than with force.

The Siberian and Chinese Eastern Railway questions figured prominently in the later stages of the conference. As an international forum the conference setting gave the American delegation a more favorable position for bargaining with Japan and China over these issues in which the United States otherwise lacked leverage. In an important breakthrough for the United States's Far Eastern policy, Secretary Hughes obtained Japan's promise to withdraw its troops from Siberia, offering renewed hope for the Open Door in the Russian Far East. This was a noteworthy achievement because both Japan and Britain had favored exclusion of Siberian questions from the conference agenda.[59]

But America's Siberian policy still hinged on the Chinese Eastern Railway and it would be harder to counteract Japan's manipulation of Chinese factions than to obtain an agreement for the withdrawal of its troops. The State Department hoped that it could use the conference to pressure China into accepting some type of strengthened international control over the railroad. Accordingly, the department requested that John Stevens return to Washington in an advisory role for the American delegation. Stevens's prestige still represented the United States's biggest asset in its struggle against Japanese aggression and against China's intractable position regarding the Chinese Eastern Railway.

Just before the opening of the conference, Japan put forward a new proposal that was designed to encourage Chinese resistance toward the American position. At the end of October 1921, Japan responded to the American plan for enhanced supervision of the Chinese Eastern Railway with a counterproposal that would transfer direct control of the line to the legally suspect board of directors; a body dominated by its Chinese majority.[60] On his return to Washington Stevens vehemently dismissed this new Japanese proposal as "altogether inadmissable" and "not worthy even of discussion." He stressed that what little power the Technical Board effectively exercised under the existing agreement would be "entirely nullified" by the Japanese proposal.[61] In view of his staunch opposition to any increase of Chinese authority over the line, Stevens submitted new recommendations for international control of the line, which differed little from the amended plan presented to Japan in August.[62]

But at the conference the State Department attempted to reach an accommodation with China's unyielding nationalist sentiment regarding the Chinese Eastern Railway. During informal preliminary discussions in Washington, the American delegation learned that the Chinese delegation would oppose any form of international control over the line. In view of this unavoidable opposition of China's representatives, the State Department first tried to maneuver around the fragile Peking government. On December 24, before the Chinese Eastern Railway issue would be formally taken up at the conference, the State Department instructed the American ambassador to China, Jacob G. Schurman, to confidentially broach a new American proposal to Gen. Chang Tso-lin, who for practical purposes governed Manchuria independently of Peking. The State Department directed Schurman to impress upon Chang the need for a "temporary international conservancy" over the Chinese Eastern Railway as the only alternative to Japanese financial control over the line.

This new American proposal for the railroad focused on three principal issues: finance, operation, and police. In its new approach to these issues the department skillfully shifted the machinery for international supervision from management of the line to its financing. It hoped to impress upon

Chang that the railroad should obtain funds from a number of foreign powers or else it would become exclusively dependent on the Japanese. While foreign funds were in use by the railroad their expenditure should rightly be controlled by a board of conservators representing the nations who contributed to the line. Located at Harbin, this body would conveniently replace either the existing Inter-Allied Railway Committee or the Technical Board. To further appease the Chinese, the United States acknowledged that operation should be left in the hands of the Chinese Eastern Railway Company without interference from the conservators on technical matters. However, the American plan qualified this concession with the reservation that the conservancy maintain general control in matters of finance. Finally, the American proposal recommended that a dependable police force be established to protect the railway property and to maintain public order in the railway zone. This force could be composed strictly of Chinese, but the American proposal stipulated that this guard be paid by and remain under the conservancy's control.[63]

After a long visit with Chang on New Year's Eve, Schurman reported to Washington that the governor-general reacted very unfavorably toward the American proposal. Since he did not want to be drawn into a controversy with the Peking government over this issue, Chang simply told Schurman that the question should be handled by the Peking government, not him. Later in the conversation, Chang reminded the American ambassador that, even with his extensive power, he could not afford to support any course of action inimical to Japan's wishes.[64]

Even after the Washington Conference subcommittee on the Chinese Eastern Railway began its deliberations on the issue, the State Department continued to pursue independent diplomatic initiatives in Peking in an attempt to enlist first the Chinese foreign minister and then Britain's support specifically for the conservancy proposal. On January 10 the department instructed Schurman to "present the plan merely as a suggestion ... to avoid the possibility that he [the Chinese foreign minister] will immediately unconditionally reject it."[65] Foreign Minister Yen only promised to confer with the minister of communications on the matter.

Meanwhile, the department directed Schurman to confidentially obtain the British minister's cooperation on this compromise American proposal in order to improve the chances of winning acceptance from the Peking government.[66] Instead, the British minister reported to London that he only favored modification of the existing inter-Allied agreement that would modestly increase the Technical Board's power. Schurman attributed the minister's uncooperative attitude to Britain's "opposition to any general program of internationalization of the railways in China as that would deprive

England of [the] predominant position she now holds in connection with certain railways."[67] In other words Britain opposed any truly effective form of international supervision of the Chinese Eastern Railway since it could potentially be used in the future as a precedent to jeopardize the British investment sphere in central China.

Back in Washington, in the deliberations of the conference subcommittee on the Chinese Eastern Railway, the American delegation found it had little room with which to maneuver between Japan and China. The American delegation would have preferred to transform the existing Technical Board into a "temporary international conservancy" since it could then assert that an American be retained as chairman. Predictably, the Japanese delegate opposed this and insisted that Japan obtain "a position of equality in any international body created at Harbin.[68] In what probably represented a compromise, the subcommittee's final report of January 21, 1922, stipulated that a finance committee, similar to the international conservancy, replace both the Inter-Allied Railway Committee and the Technical Board. Even then, the Japanese delegate to the conference subcommittee indicated that he expected the organization of this committee would require adjustment. Parts two and three of the final report, regarding operation and protection of the line, were virtually identical to the original American conservancy proposal.[69]

Inevitably, the Chinese delegates on the technical subcommittee rejected the final report of January 21 on grounds that it infringed upon China's sovereignty. China would not permit a foreign trusteeship to exercise general financial control over the line and it would not agree to place Chinese police forces under an international body.[70]

Recognizing that nothing more than a stalemate had been reached by the technical subcommittee, Secretary Hughes suggested that a subcommittee of delegates be appointed in an effort to reach an agreement. Further wrangling and numerous compromise resolutions failed to produce any significant improvement over the existing inter-Allied agreement. Once again, the obstructionist positions of Japan and China tended to cancel each other, thereby severely limiting the possibility for an effective resolution of the issue. On the one hand, China opposed any amended agreement for the supervision of the Chinese Eastern on grounds that the original agreement provided for Allied supervision over the whole Trans-Siberian system, which included the sections in Russian territory. On the other hand, the Japanese delegate refused to accept the inclusion of the Ussuri Railway in the discussions. Japan's delegate also objected to an appointed chairman of the Allied board.[71]

In the end, Chairman Elihu Root could only report an unenforceable resolution from the subcommittee, which called for preservation of the rights of all interested parties through better protection of the railway and its personnel, more careful selection of staff to ensure efficiency, and more economical use of funds to prevent waste. In an adjoining reservation, to which China did not agree, the other powers called on China to uphold its responsibility, both for performance of its obligations to the foreign stockholders and creditors of the railway and for it to fulfill the responsibilities of trusteeship China now exercised as a result of its possession and administration of the line.

While these resolutions lacked enforcement power because of China's opposition, Hughes hoped that China's participation in the conference would demonstrate to its leaders the benefits of international cooperation. For all of its shortcomings, he considered the conference resolutions on the Chinese Eastern Railway an important moral achievement. First, general recognition was obtained for continuation of the inter-Allied agreement. Next, the resolution's provision for continuing diplomatic exchanges on the issue left open the possibility that an amended agreement for supervision of the line could still be achieved. Finally, the conference exerted international moral pressure on China to fulfill the responsibilities of trusteeship that it had assumed under the "purported" contract of October 2, 1920.[72] Ambassador Schurman reiterated these sentiments to the Chinese minister of foreign affairs, W. W. Yen, emphasizing that the United States "placed particular stress on the advantage to China and the wisdom of the Chinese Government's assuming of its own accord the initiative in immediately asking the other powers to cooperate in handling the railway problem."[73]

Stevens had a decidedly unfavorable view of the conference resolutions on the Chinese Eastern Railway. He believed the United States should have extracted a definite commitment from Japan specifying the date it would begin the withdrawal of its troops from Siberia. He warned that Japan's continued occupation of Russia's Maritime Provinces and of Vladivostok, even if for a limited period, would enable Japan to redirect freight traffic from the Chinese Eastern Railway to the South Manchurian Railway and the port of Dairen. Since its occupation Japan had consistently pursued this goal by interfering with the operations of the Ussuri Railway, which ran from Vladivostok to the Manchurian border, and by manipulating traffic rates.

Stevens's dissatisfaction with the conference results occasioned another of his frequent threats of resignation. Secretary Hughes, who hardly needed to be reminded of these dangers, asked Senator Elihu Root to explain the situation to Stevens. Clearly irritated by Stevens's attitude, Hughes commented to Root that "he seems to think that we have some way of driving the Japanese troops out of Siberia without going to war. Perhaps you can give him a better understanding."[74] In conversation with Root, Stevens also criticized the conference resolutions for placing responsibility on China for operation of the line. Chinese officials would construe these statements as tacit acceptance that the line belonged to China.[75]

In discussions following the Washington Conference, Chinese officials indicated they had little reason to reach an accommodation with the American position. C. C. Wang, who was made director general of the Chinese Eastern Railway in March 1922, told Schurman that China was content to maintain the existing status quo with the expectation that it would soon reach an agreement with the Soviet government over restitution of the line. In the meantime, the Chinese were content to let the line struggle along financially. Any economies the Technical Board achieved were quickly siphoned off by Chinese officials who continued to establish new patronage positions. If a foreign loan became necessary, the Chinese considered the existing inter-Allied bodies convenient vehicles for facilitating any financial arrangements they would have to make with the powers. Otherwise, the Technical Board still served a useful purpose in as much as both the Chinese and the Russians found it a useful buffer between them.[76]

By the end of May the Chinese officials utter disregard for the Technical Board and their willingness to loot the railroad had convinced the demoralized Stevens that inter-Allied supervision over the Chinese Eastern Railway should be terminated.[77] Under the existing state of affairs, Stevens did not think a financial collapse of the railroad could be averted.

By the summer of 1922, however, the Ostroumov administration's rate policy, not Chinese graft, would be responsible for bringing the line to the brink of financial disaster. While the Technical Board appreciated Ostroumov's aggressive efforts to reduce costs and to remove corrupt officials held over from Khorvat's administration, it increasingly became frustrated with his short-sighted financial practices that undermined the line's solvency. During the winter and spring of 1921, Ostroumov's administration had resorted to deep reductions in transportation rates in order to attract more business to the line. In March 1921 the Technical Board temporarily approved the administration's proposal to reduce rates on bean cake from 1.40 to 1.05 gold rubles per tariff ruble to stimulate the reopening of the bean oil mills in northern Manchuria.[78] Then in July the Technical Board approved another reduction on bean oil and cakes from 1.05 gold rubles per tariff ruble to parity at 1 to 1. The Technical Board approved these measures, pending a reliable assessment of the line's cost structure.[79] After returning from the United States in late June, Stevens concluded that the railway administration had reduced rates too far since March in its efforts to satisfy shippers.[80] In August the Technical Board's financial subcommittee, chaired by the British member, Brig. Gen. W. T. C. Beckett, recommended that an upward revision of the tariff rates was necessary. It had found that the existing estimates of the cost of transportation were flawed because they did not take into account that one-fifth of the railroad's earnings were never actually paid in hard cash. This large shortfall in the line's real income existed as a result of unpaid military bills, amounting to about 10 million gold rubles, and because 40 million rubles consisted of Siberian currency, which the railway had been forced to accept and were now worthless.[81] To rectify the divergence between the line's costs and its income, the subcommittee recommended that the exchange rate between the gold ruble and the tariff ruble be raised from parity on most Manchurian products to 1.20 gold rubles per tariff ruble.

Before leaving for the Washington Conference, Stevens had strongly urged the Technical Board to begin discussions with the administration over the desirability of placing the Chinese Eastern Railway's rate policy on a "scientific basis."[82] Repeated overtures by the Technical Board to devise a systematic rate structure failed to elicit any serious action on the part of Ostroumov's administration.

Predictably, the drastic rate reductions of the winter and spring of 1921 gradually eroded the railroad's improved financial performance, which had stemmed from the increased traffic in early 1921. By August 1921 current indebtedness had actually been trimmed from 8.5 million rubles to about 5.4 million rubles. However, as the line continued to haul freight at rates below its costs into 1922, the administration compounded its errors by utilizing short-term notes and transportation credits, both of which were issued to contractors in lieu of cash. Ostroumov's administration increasingly resorted to these quick-fix financial expedients without the Technical Board's approval, thereby escalating the line's current indebtedness to critical levels by the summer of 1922.

In June 1922 the Technical Board's financial subcommittee warned that the Chinese Eastern Railway's current indebtedness would soon exceed 14 million gold rubles. A major cause of this rapid escalation in current liabilities lay in the Russian administration's heavy reliance on the short-term notes and transportation credits issued to the line's contractors. Because the railroad's persistent financial difficulties prevented it from paying its obligations on time, the notes inevitably had to be renegotiated at high rates of interest. Meanwhile, the transportation credits sacrificed the line's future cash receipts, just as this current debt was rising to dangerously high levels. The finance subcommittee calculated that until the end of October, when another bean harvest would be ready for export, existing transportation credits could be applied to as high a percentage as 41 of the 46 daily car exports—the estimated daily average, leaving the railroad with little income from freight traffic. Even worse, about 2.7 million rubles were overdue to the Japanese-owned Fushan coal mines.[83]

While the financial condition of the Chinese Eastern Railway continued to deteriorate, Japan made no response to American requests for a definite proposal regarding the line. All indications suggested that Stevens's warnings of impending trouble following the Washington Conference were being realized. In early May he reported to Washington the likelihood that Japan's Mitsui and Mitsubishi companies were about to purchase the Ussuri Railway and to change its gauge. He believed the Japanese government stood behind these private companies in order to maintain plausible denial.[84]

On June 30 Stevens's fears were confirmed when he received the shocking news of a distinctly unfavorable rate agreement for the Chinese Eastern Railway, which its directors concluded with the Japanese-controlled South Manchurian Railway during a conference at Changchun. Under the terms of this agreement, the Chinese Eastern Railway relinquished its independence to the South Manchurian Railway by agreeing not to change its own traffic rates without consent of the South Manchurian Railway. The Chinese Eastern was now required to apply a uniform freight rate for both north- and south-bound trips on its Changchun branch regardless of destination—whether north to Harbin or south to the Japanese-controlled ports of Dairen, Yinkow, and Antung. But for no other reason than to force traffic in a southerly direction, the Chinese Eastern Railway had to raise its rates eastward to Vladivostok both from Harbin and from the southern Changchun branch via Harbin by 1.22 yen per ton!

In contrast, the South Manchurian Railway could adjust its rates as it saw fit. These rate agreements were designed to create an advantage for Dairen at the expense of Vladivostok because Japan controlled sea transportation to Kobe from both ports. Not surprisingly, with a monopoly of sea transportation Japan discriminated against Vladivostok by establishing highly variable rates from that port, which created instability for shippers while the rates from Dairen remained stable.

As a result of this agreement Dairen would be able to attract from Vladivostok the rapidly developing bean trade of northern Manchuria. Before 1914, 80 percent of these exports went through Vladivostok, and while this decreased to 10 percent during the war, this figure had risen to 70 percent by mid-1922, largely due to efforts of Stevens's Technical Board. Through its control of sea routes, this agreement virtually gave Japan the power to determine the world price of beans at a time when Europe was becoming a large importer.

In Stevens's view Japan had been able to impose this agreement on the Russian administration because of its gross financial mismanagement of the line. The estimated 14 million gold rubles in short-term notes, including the 3 million yen owed the Fushan coal mines, gave Japan the financial leverage to entice the Russian administration into accepting the agreement with the promise of an advance payment of 1 million yen, without interest. Stevens noted that this amount could have been earned by the railroad with only a slight increase of traffic from 1921 levels. This controversial agreement had been concluded in a single day, without consultation with the Technical Board, in order to present it and the public with a fait accompli.[85]

Following this agreement Japan announced it would begin the withdrawal of its troops from Siberia and the Chinese Eastern Railway zone in accordance with its promise at the Washington Conference. This process would be completed by November 1922. Japan no longer needed to maintain its troops because the Changchun agreement fulfilled its principal objective; it now effectively controlled the Chinese Eastern Railway and the economy of northern Manchuria, ensuring the demise of the Ussuri Railway and the Port of Vladivostok. Japan's withdrawal also set in motion the termination of the inter-Allied agreement and the end of John Stevens's service in Russia.

One possible alternative to the Japanese-imposed settlement existed, and it could have developed from the Technical Board's offers to devise a rational rate structure for the Chinese Eastern Railway. Japan had forced the agreement on the Russian administration in part to protect the South Manchurian Railway from Ostroumov's reckless rate reductions, a practice the Technical Board also condemned. Accordingly, a rational rate structure would necessarily have had to take into account the interests of the South Manchurian Railway. Some insight into the Technical Board's views on this problem may be gleaned from a suggestion made by David B. MacGowan, the American representative on the Inter-Allied Railway Committee, in February 1922. MacGowan proposed a plan whereby the Chinese Eastern and South Manchurian Railways would "pool" the revenues from traffic originating in the rich bean producing areas of northern Manchuria, thereby reducing the intense interline rivalry. To illustrate the advantages of interline cooperation, he referred to the recent precedent of the U.S. Transportation Act of 1920, which gave the Interstate Commerce Commission (ICC) broad power to rationally regulate American railroads in the best interests of the railroads and shippers.[86] Implicitly, MacGowan's plan would have given the Technical Board what Stevens had wanted all along—extensive authority to regulate economic activity in northern Manchuria, transforming the Inter-Allied Railway Committee into an international analogue of the ICC.[87]

Before he returned home, Stevens participated in one last attempt to maintain American influence on the Trans-Siberian Railway. From the spring through November 1922, Stevens, M. H. Bunting, representative of the Baldwin Locomotive Works; Carl Mayer, Commerce Department Trade Commissioner for Siberia; and Russian officials connected with the Chinese

Eastern Railway, all endeavored to arrange barter agreements between the Chinese Eastern Railway and the railroads of the Soviet-sponsored Far Eastern republic. By forging a working relationship between sections of the Trans-Siberian railroad in Russian and Chinese territory these American officials hoped to establish the basis for a future American presence on a unified railroad system.

As far back as January 1920, both Stevens and Johnson had expressed optimism over the possibility that they might develop more satisfactory relations with the coalition revolutionary government that was then in the process of formation than they had ever had with the Omsk government.[88] At the Washington Conference, the State Department demonstrated to the Far Eastern republic the value of American diplomatic goodwill. The United States had adroitly permitted a commercial representative from the Far Eastern republic to attend the conference as an observer in order to bolster the republic's bargaining position in its drawn-out negotiations with Japan over the withdrawal of its troops from the Maritime Provinces. Likewise, the State Department thought the presence of a representative from the Far Eastern republic at the conference might induce Japan and China to make concessions on the Siberian and Chinese Eastern Railway questions. In early December 1921, D. C. Poole suggested that the United States should consider letting the Far Eastern republic exercise Russia's legal rights over the Chinese Eastern Railroad, if the State Department could not obtain a satisfactory agreement for an international receivership over the line. Nevertheless, he indicated this should essentially be used as a ploy since "a suggestion that the United States would be prepared to cooperate with the Far Eastern republic in the operation of the railway might move Japan to consent to a continuance and strengthening of the existing agreement."[89]

The United States also employed this diplomatic card in an attempt to delay the conclusion of any agreement between the republic and the Chinese government over restoration of the Chinese Eastern Railway to China. However, the Far Eastern republic also had its reasons for objecting to the American proposal for expanded international supervision of the Chinese Eastern Railway. Representatives of the Far Eastern Republic told Consul John Caldwell at Chita they feared the presence of an Allied police force for the railway zone because it would be composed of anti-Bolshevik elements. The Bolshevik government and the Republic therefore wanted to settle the line's fate among themselves and China. For their part, the Russian revolutionary governments and China were attempting to preempt Japan's efforts to gain control of the line through its support of Chang Tso-lin.[90]

The barter arrangements concluded in November 1922 between the Trans-Baikal and the Chinese Eastern Railways that developed out of discussions

Benjamin Johnson, Stevens's acting representative on the Technical Board, initiated with officials of the Far Eastern republic in the spring. In early March Johnson reported to Stevens that commercial activity in the Trans-Baikal was rapidly improving. This trend would receive additional impetus when the Far Eastern republic established its control over the whole Russian Far East after the evacuation of Japan's troops. But Johnson thought the poor condition of the republic's locomotives and freight cars would hamper this process. Accordingly, Johnson asked for Stevens's authorization to examine locomotive conditions at Chita and to order as much as five hundred thousand dollars of repair parts for this equipment from Stevens's funds.

Johnson recommended this course of action because in a variety of ways it would strengthen American prestige among the Russian revolutionary governments who were deeply interested in the fate of the Trans-Siberian system. He thought it might persuade the Far Eastern republic and its Moscow backers to support the revised American plan for supervision of the Chinese Eastern Railway. Next, a future Russian government would possibly be more inclined to honor the loans already made to the Trans-Siberian railway if the American engineers demonstrated the "non-political character of our work." Moreover, if the United States assumed a friendly posture toward the republic, it might compel Japan and China to adopt a more conciliatory position toward the regime. This service might impress upon the republic some appreciation for the United States. Finally, in view of the inconclusive results of the Washington Conference, this step would reassure Russians of all political stripes that the United States had not abandoned its commitment to Russia's "reconstruction."[91]

The State Department would not approve any financing for the Trans-Baikal Railroad because virtually all of the Technical Board's funds had already been allocated. Stevens added that the Technical Board would probably require that it be permitted to supervise the use of the funds. Still, D. C. Poole, head of the Russian division, did think Johnson should be allowed to investigate conditions at Chita. He favored this overture because it would create goodwill with the Russians and because it would "emphasize the fact that our interference with the Chinese Eastern Railway is not so much with that railway in itself as with a link of the whole Trans-Siberian system in respect to which our assistance was originally sought by the Russians."[92]

Johnson informed the State Department he planned to deliver the materials to the Trans-Baikal line in a manner that would be consistent with past procedures. The transactions would be mediated through a Russian representative of the Inter-Allied Purchasing Committee at Vladivostok; his receipt would then be accepted as if the materials were destined for the

Ussuri Railway. An American engineer would direct all work done with this material. Johnson advised that this arrangement would secure an "entering wedge into Chita" that would later "cover further assistance and control." For the present any further discussion of Allied supervision would only create suspicion on the part of the Russians.[93]

On his return to Harbin in May, Stevens quickly became an advocate of Johnson's plan for assisting the Far Eastern republic's railways. He indicated that a limited amount of the inter-Allied funds would be required, of which only the American contribution remained. Stevens did not think the Technical Board would approve his use of the funds for this purpose, but for this very reason he thought the "action would have good political effect." If the State Department gave final support to the plan, Stevens would insist on being given absolute control over the expenditures, but if he were not allowed to use these funds he believed his assistance would be of little value.[94]

In mid-summer 1922, M. H. Bunting of the Baldwin Locomotive Works made an extensive tour of the Siberian railways at the request of the Far Eastern republic. During his trip, Bunting observed conditions that led him to oppose a loan to the republic at the time. He discovered that plenty of railroad equipment existed in Siberia; the Chita railway officials simply had no idea what to do with the supplies they possessed. Accordingly, he recommended that experts be made available to the government. With technical assistance, the republic could obtain food, spare parts, and other necessary materials from the Chinese Eastern Railway in exchange for the quantities of Siberian raw materials simply stocked along the railways such as coal, oil, cement, wood, and iron. Bunting proposed that unemployed Russian engineers and mechanics who fled Siberia after Kolchak's fall should now return there to organize workers for the repair of the railways and railroad equipment and for the rehabilitation of the related industries. This work would fulfill an immediate humanitarian function because "these workers would be relieved from the hardships they and their families were suffering and a beginning made in the work of improving economic conditions in Siberia." Stevens concurred with this assessment. He believed the economic recovery of Siberia required "outside brains and organizing ability, which no one in Chita appeared to possess."

A delegation of Russian officials connected with the Chinese Eastern Railway, headed by General Manager Boris Ostroumov, favored the establishment of a joint Russian-American company to mediate the exchange of supplies between the two railroads. But neither Bunting or the American consul at Harbin, G. C. Hanson, was anxious to become involved in a business venture with these Russian railroad officials who had repeatedly demonstrated their administrative and financial ineptitude. Instead, Bunting and

Hanson suggested a trial exchange of a few carloads of Siberian coal for Harbin flour. If these shipments proved successful, an American-Russian company could be established to handle the business, which would also include imported equipment.[95] While this trial shipment did take place, the absorption of the Far Eastern republic by the Soviet government, immediately following the withdrawal of Japan's troops in November, prevented any possibility that this initiative would receive further American sponsorship.[96]

✑

American efforts to establish a more effective form of international control over the Chinese Eastern failed because of the United States's political isolation. Britain played a pivotal role in the struggle for control over the line because its support for the American proposal might have compelled Japan to cooperate as well. However, consistent with its long-standing policy in the Far East, Britain preferred to continue its balancing act between the United States and Japan. Britain clung to the Anglo-Japanese alliance even as it increasingly proved less effective as a restraint on Japanese ambitions in China proper. Yet, the more Britain feared Japanese expansion in China proper, the more willing it was to acquiesce in the extension of Japanese influence in peripheral areas like Manchuria.

Below the surface of these geopolitical calculations, Britain also viewed the American proposal for strengthened international supervision of the Chinese Eastern Railway as having potentially threatening implications for its principal investment interests in China. Britain, it should be remembered, had strongly encouraged the United States to continue its participation in the inter-Allied agreement in the spring of 1920. But Britain quickly backed off when the United States proposed to transform the agreement into an international bankruptcy commission. The creation of a bankruptcy commission for the Chinese Eastern Railway might have set a precedent that would endanger the extensive financial and commercial privileges Britain enjoyed on many railway projects in central China. Moreover, in many of these contracts between Britain and the Chinese government, the railroads themselves served as the security for the loan, a factor that enhanced British leverage over the management of the line during the duration of the loan.

Finally, a convergence of interests between British investment policy and Chinese nationalism added another dimension to this intricate Chinese puzzle that militated against this specific American initiative toward the Chinese Eastern Railway. Although Britain extracted extensive concessionary privileges in its loan agreements for the construction of railroads in China, these lines were nevertheless being built for eventual inclusion into the Chinese national railway system. Therefore, because the United States supported Russian sovereignty over the Chinese Eastern Railway, if only to maintain its independence from Japan, it consequently put itself at odds with both China and Britain, who viewed the continuation of this Russian concession in Manchuria as a pretext for Japan's claim for the same privileges with regard to the Tsingtao-Tsinan Railroad in Shantung.

Conclusion

The American efforts to promote reconstruction in Siberia between 1917 and 1922 confronted insurmountable obstacles, ranging from widespread social and economic instability to irreconcilable conflicts with the Allies. These factors reinforced each other. Russian instability encouraged the Allies to advance their spheres of influence in Russia, as Wilson had warned in his aide-mémoire of July 17, 1918. The British and French desire to use Siberia as a base of military operations, first through their efforts to restore an eastern front in 1918, and then through their support of Kolchak's military campaigns against the Bolsheviks in 1919, only bolstered reactionary political elements in the region. Meanwhile, the tight grip Japan's military forces maintained over the eastern segments of the Trans-Siberian system prevented the huge interior from receiving any substantial assistance. These policies intensified social instability in the region. The Trans-Siberian system could not fulfill the developmental role American policymakers envisioned for it, because the line itself had become a focal point of the international rivalries in Eurasia.

Had it not been for the hardening of Soviet-American relations, American statesmen might have derived important lessons regarding foreign assistance from the United States's involvement in Siberia during these pivotal years. Wilson's own position on the question of foreign assistance evolved considerably in the space of a year and a half, from January 1918 through

June 1919. In response to the risks involved in Russia after the Bolshevik Revolution, International Harvester Company, the principal American corporation with interests in Russia, limited any further Russian business to existing operations at its branch plant at Lubertzy and to exports financed on a strictly dollar basis. This demonstrated that "Dollar Diplomacy," the prevailing American view of the legitimate role of the government in promoting American economic expansion abroad, would be completely inadequate for the extraordinary tasks involved in providing economic assistance in Russia. The Taft administration coined the term "Dollar Diplomacy" to describe the more active diplomatic role the U.S. government had begun to take in promoting American economic interests abroad. Yet this intervention, it must be emphasized, entailed strictly diplomatic support, not financial assistance.

As the crisis in Russia deepened in 1918 and as the Brest-Litovsk Treaty raised the stakes involved, Wilson recognized that an assistance program financed under private auspices would be insufficient to the task, but political realities mandated a strictly supervisory role for the government in any program of assistance. In a compromise engineered by State Department proponents of a more active governmental role near the end of September 1918, the administration appropriated the modest sum of $5 million for emergency situations in Siberia. Administration planners clearly considered this initial War Trade Board program to be an exploratory, yet open-ended, operation. By the spring of 1919, Siberian developments had become so crucial for American statesmen that Wilson and his advisers at Paris decided to undertake a large governmentally financed reconstruction program in the region. But Wilson had to expend his political capital in the battle over the treaty and the League of Nations. In the meantime, the Bolsheviks easily triumphed in Siberia.

Wilson's Siberian policy embodied principles that qualitatively distinguished this era of American foreign relations from the post–World War II period when the United States finally established itself as the dominant world power. By endeavoring to assist the reconstruction of Siberia's civil society, Wilsonian policy played an historically progressive role, in sharp contrast to the policies of the rival powers who essentially sought to undermine Russian sovereignty in favor of their spheres of influence. Had this incipient experiment in social policy been allowed to proceed, it is interesting to speculate whether it might have helped to foster the evolution of a uniquely Russian form of "self-government," something between bolshevism and free market capitalism.

One intriguing opportunity for Soviet-American cooperation arose during 1922 when Benjamin Johnson and John Stevens explored the possibility of providing technical assistance for the Chita Railway with the heterodox Siberian Bolsheviks of the Far Eastern republic. These promising beginnings ended abruptly when the parent Moscow regime reabsorbed the republic in November 1922. While American and Soviet cooperation over the railroad question was motivated chiefly by their common desire to wring concessions from Japan, this brief interlude deserves attention, because the American participants considered their initiative with the Far Eastern officials to be the most favorable opportunity they had had to implement some lasting improvements in the operation of the Trans-Siberian system after almost five years of frustrating relations with Russian, Allied, and Chinese authorities.

In this last decade of the twentieth century, U.S. statesmen must again tackle the enormous problems accompanying the process of reconstruction in Russia. In important respects, the challenges confronting reconstruction in Russia today will be even more imposing than they were seventy years ago, because market mechanisms themselves must be reintroduced in place of the existing command economy.

Today, one fact is increasingly becoming clear, American policymakers must find an alternative developmental model to the current short-sighted, and potentially disastrous, International Monetary Fund (IMF) stabilization policies the West is imposing on the former Russian republics. Recently, Martin Walker, former bureau chief for the *Guardian,* has predicted that the IMF will fail to promote economic development in the Russian republic by prescribing severe restrictions on monetary and credit expansion. These draconian measures will only result in massive layoffs and reductions in social expenditures that will be politically unsustainable. Instead, Walker suggests that a stable market economy can be more effectively developed through a series of practical foreign assistance measures.

First, he urges the West to stop committing the bulk of its financial assistance to the dubious goal of establishing currency convertibility. Western financial aid could be used more effectively in financing interrepublic trade and in developing the transportation infrastructure between the separate republics. Second, he adopts an IMF proposal that recommends that the West redirect its financial assistance toward establishing an interrepublic payments union, similar to the European Payments Union that operated between 1950 and 1958—one of the Marshall Planners' most successful innovations. A payments union, consisting of the Commonwealth of Independent Republics, would encourage expanded interrepublic trade by allowing countries to automatically apply trade surpluses with one country to the purchase of goods from third countries. IMF funds would underwrite this system, since deficit countries would be required to settle their balances partly in hard currency. In principle, a payments union's clearing mechanisms would enable the republics to largely offset deficits with credits, allowing these new states to conserve their hard currency reserves.[1]

Perhaps most importantly, if the United States is committed to assisting Russia through this difficult transition period, American policymakers must make concessions on fundamental issues that were not resolved between 1917 and 1922 and that have subsequently been submerged under the weight of Stalinism and fifty years of Cold War. Specifically, the United States must reduce its relentless pressure to base economic development almost exclusively on privatization and free-market forces. Back in the mid-1950s, none other than Dean Acheson, the principal architect of post–World War II American foreign policy, warned that free trade and private foreign investment alone could not build a stable social and economic foundation in the former European colonies that had recently achieved independence. Echoing Wilson's pragmatic approach to state intervention, Acheson cautioned that

> theory must yield to the exigencies of our own interest. We have a deep interest in the stability and independence of many young governments brought into existence by the newly won independence of their people. Often memory of the past makes them suspicious and wary of foreign help and, so we think, blind to real dangers before them. Of one thing they are acutely aware, the need for economic improvement, increased production, higher standards of life. Private advice and investment can be of great help. But it cannot bring the minimum assistance which, in our own interest, is required. So theory must yield again to the conception, already mentioned, of our government as the whole people organized to do what has to be done. This was the conception behind the Point Four program and the foreign aid programs. Our government carried on these programs, not because it was theoretically desirable for the government to do so rather than private business or private philanthropy, but because they would not be carried on at all unless government did so—and it was, and it still is, essential that this help be given.[2]

Acheson's views from the 1950s are just as relevant to the current challenges American foreign policy faces in Russia. But today, American policymakers assume that the system of multinational corporations, which has appropriated many critical powers of sovereignty from the nation-states, will take the lead in promoting reconstruction in Eastern Europe and the former Soviet republics. And it is increasingly evident that the International

Monetary Fund's prescriptions for quickly creating a stable investment environment in Russia, at the expense of the population's living standards, will be overwhelmed by the magnitude of the problems confronting stabilization in this huge country. These instruments of the international financial system do not take into account the necessity of promoting a stable social order in the new republics, in which economic development is harmonized with the general welfare and functioning democratic institutions. The West must exhibit more flexibility regarding the question of economic reform in Russia if only to prevent a retreat into Stalinism, a renewal of the Cold War, or the threat of atavistic nationalism.

Walker's proposals for assisting economic reform in Russia deserve attention in this study not only for their obvious contemporary relevance, but also because they bear a striking resemblance to principal features of the Marshall Plan and Wilson's assistance program in Siberia. Indeed, these comparisons between distinct periods can help us reach some broader conclusions about American foreign policy in the twentieth century, for perhaps the evolution of American foreign assistance policy from Wilson's period through the Cold War holds the key to understanding both the accomplishments and tragic consequences of American world leadership in the twentieth century. Although the Marshall Plan is associated with the Cold War era, it exhibits more continuity with Wilson's stillborn program in Siberia than with the militarization of American foreign assistance that occurred after 1950.[3] Unfortunately, almost a half century of Cold War has obscured the basic parallels between Wilson's reconstruction program in Siberia and the Marshall Plan. In both cases American statesmen initially focused their efforts on achieving two practical goals: relieving human misery—which they recognized to be the cause of social revolution—and facilitating regional economic recovery, as a stepping-stone to full multilateral integration.

The Inter-Allied Railway Committee in 1919 and the Marshall Planners of the late 1940s both recognized that currency convertibility and full multilateral trade would have to be delayed until functioning regional markets had been reestablished. Indeed, Charles Maier summarized the Marshall Plan by concluding that "the ERP [European Recovery Program] worked primarily by alleviating strategic bottlenecks and foreign-exchange constraints, not by vast infusions of capital"—virtually the same analysis can be made of the program the Inter-Allied Railway Committee wanted to implement in 1919.[4] However, these similarities are not apparent because the realities of American domestic politics forced the Truman administration to justify the Marshall Plan on the grounds that it was needed to counter Soviet aggression. Like Wilson in 1919, the Truman administration could not successfully advocate a large foreign assistance program on its own merits in the face of resurgent isolationism and opposition to any extensive new spending programs. In order to build a domestic political consensus in favor of a large foreign assistance program, the Truman administration had to prepare an ideological climate that greatly exaggerated the dangers of Soviet aggression and subversion.[5] Despite the Marshall Plan's impressive short-term accomplishments, Truman administration officials quickly recognized that the United States must assume extensive global commitments to ensure full multilateral integration and, equally important, a favorable climate for American investment in developing areas. This realization marked a crucial turning point in American postwar policy and in the United States's relationship with the rest of the world. Before World War II, the United States's struggle to promote the Open Door pitted it against rival imperialist systems, as well as radical social revolutionary movements. Following World War II, when the United States no longer faced a challenge from the rival imperialist camps, it began to exercise prerogatives that placed it on a collision course with the emerging national liberation movements in the third world.

The United States's conflict with the third world in the postwar period has had its origins in the specific dynamism and expectations of the American capitalist system. As heir to the British Empire, the United States faced the enormous responsibility of rebuilding the world economy. For the American policymaking establishment this task took on particular urgency in the wake of a fifteen-year crisis period that had shaken the world capitalist order to its foundations. A relapse into economic depression would undermine the legitimacy of America's nonstatist capitalist system. Paradoxically, the United States's productive power and capital resources, which had been greatly augmented by the war boom, made the American economy more vulnerable than ever to depression. This anxiety for the stability of the American socioeconomic order, not hypothetical dangers of Soviet aggression, motivated the Truman administration to undertake vast international commitments by 1950. Indeed, prior to the North Korean attack, the American policymaking establishment, led by Secretary of State Dean Acheson, had already concluded that the United States must assume strategic responsibilities commensurate to its unprecedented industrial and financial power. To sustain its economic growth the United States had to become sponsor and guardian of the global investment system.

Placing western Europe under the American strategic umbrella succeeded in undercutting communist political influence on the continent and it bolstered confidence in long-term foreign investment. However, in much of the third world the task would be much more difficult in view of the popularity of alternative developmental models. During their long struggle against colonial exploitation, many independence movements had evolved strong social-revolutionary, as well as nationalist, tendencies. Ten years of systemic economic crisis in the capitalist world and the ensuing devastation of an imperialist world war reinforced this dual characteristic of many nationalist movements. Not only had Western colonialism been dealt a fatal blow, but free-market capitalism had also forfeited much of its appeal and legitimacy for nationalists in the developing world. For these reasons, national liberation movements became a potentially serious threat to the expansion of a global investment system based on multilateral principles and capitalist enterprise. A third world that placed restrictions or controls on American foreign investment would seriously inhibit the dynamism of American capitalism, forcing the United States itself to adopt statist planning and redistributive policies that would radically transform American society.

The Chinese Communist victory of 1949, and the subsequent North Korean attack in 1950, appeared to confirm the Truman administration's worst fears concerning the Soviet Union and the international Communist movement. From this point forward the United States began to engage in "nation-building" efforts around the world; as a corollary to these open-ended commitments, the United States inevitably placed a growing emphasis on furnishing military assistance to unrepresentative anti-Communist governments, without adequate regard for its effects on individual nations' social order.

Had the American reconstruction program in Siberia been given a chance to develop after 1917, a dialectical tension would inevitably have arisen between the strong ethical inclinations of Wilsonianism, which viewed the developing Siberian frontier as the nucleus for Russian "self-government," and the imperatives of the corporate capitalist order. For this reason, perhaps it has been a misfortune for American political culture and for the United States's foreign relations that an imminent debate over Wilson's reconstruction program for Siberia never occurred in 1919. Nevertheless, the Wilsonian features of the United States's Russian policy may embody important lessons for contemporary American policymakers at a time when the Russian question again calls for far-sighted and principled action.

Notes

Introduction

1. The principal theoretical basis for this study is the article by Karl Kautsky, the preeminent Social-Democratic thinker of the early twentieth century, entitled "Ultra-Imperialism," which argued that interimperialist conflict and its accompanying arms race would soon be replaced by a more rational system based on cooperation between the major capitalist powers. Kautsky had the singular misfortune to publish this article as World War I was breaking out across Europe in 1914. Nevertheless, this analysis is significant, because it was consistent with American efforts to establish economic cooperation between the capitalist powers over developmental questions in regions like China. Since World War II, the United States has presided over a system based on "ultra-imperialist" principles. Kautsky's article was originally published in *Die Neu Zeit,* September 11, 1914. An English translation of this essay first appeared in the *New Left Review* 59 (Jan.–Feb. 1970): 39–46.

This study also shares certain underlying assumptions with the work of world systems theorists who argue that the chief causal factor behind historical development since about 1500 has been the emergence of the world capitalist system, characterized by a division of labor between industrialized and developing regions. Of particular relevance is the work of Thomas J. McCormick, who emphasizes that the United States, as the dominant or "hegemonic" power of the twentieth century, has had a powerful incentive for dismantling autarkic or preferential economic systems in favor of a global environment that allows the greatest possible freedom for trade and investment. For instance, see his "Every System Needs a Center Sometimes: An Essay on Hegemony and Modern American Foreign Policy," in Lloyd Gardner, ed., *Redefining the Past: Essays in Diplomatic History in Honor of William Appleman Williams* (Corvallis: Oregon State Univ. Press, 1986), 195–220.

2. In his review of Christine White's excellent study, Thomas Zeiler cites statistics that demonstrate that Russia remained a "minuscule export market for U.S. business" in the 1920s. He also

notes that White does not clarify the relationship between official governmental policy and private sector efforts to expand economic relations with the Soviet government. Thomas Zeiler, "Business Is Business," *Diplomatic History* 18 (Summer 1994): 419–23. For a study that demonstrates the extensive obstacles official governmental policy placed in the path of expanded commercial relations with the Soviet Union in the 1920s, see Joan Hoff Wilson, *Ideology and Economics: U.S. Relations with the Soviet Union, 1918–1933* (Columbia : Univ. of Missouri Press, 1974).

1. The Open Door, Wilsonianism, and the New Frontier in Siberia

1. This analysis is informed by the work of Carl Parrini and Martin Sklar who demonstrate that the corporate reorganization of the American economy in the late 1890s placed new demands on American foreign policy. Carl P. Parrini and Martin J. Sklar, "New Thinking About the Market, 1896–1904: Some American Economists on Investment and the Theory of Surplus Capital," *Journal of Economic History* 43 (Sept. 1983); 559–78; Martin J. Sklar, *The Corporate Reconstruction of American Capitalism, 1896–1916: The Market, the Law, and Politics* (Cambridge: Cambridge Univ. Press, 1988). For the original analysis of the phenomenon of surplus capital see Charles A. Conant, "The Economic Basis of Imperialism," *North American Review* 167 (Sept. 1898): 326–40.

2. For background on the American International Corporation, see Harry Scheiber, "World War 1 as Entrepreneurial Opportunity: Willard Straight and the American International Corporation," *Political Science Quarterly* 84 (Sept. 1969): 461–511. Henry D. Baker, "Prospects for Investment of American Capital in Russia," Petrograd, Feb. 14, 1916, U.S. Department of Commerce, Bureau of Foreign and Domestic Commerce, Record Group 151, file 620 (hereafter cited as RG 151, followed by file number). For a survey of America's developing economic interest in Russia after the outbreak of World War I, see Jeanette E. Tuve, "Changing Directions in Russian-American Relations, 1912–1917," *Slavic Review* 31 (Mar. 1972): 52–70. See also Christine A. White, *British and American Commercial Relations with Soviet Russia, 1918–1924* (Chapel Hill: Univ. of North Carolina Press, 1992), 4–34.

3. Charles H. Boynton, "Russia and Its Relationships to the United States" address at the National Exposition of Chemical Industry, Sept. 26, 1917, in *The American-Russian Chamber of Commerce, Service Bulletin,* Samuel N. Harper Papers, box 57.

4. Boynton, "Russia and Its Relationships to the U.S.," 4–5, 6.

5. "The Russian Opportunity," no author, *The American-Russian Chamber of Commerce,* ca. 1917.

6. Boynton, "Russia and Its Relationships to the U.S.," 5.

7. Cited in Edward H. Carr, *The Bolshevik Revolution, 1917–1923* (London: Macmillan, 1953), 3: 356–57.

8. Boynton, "Russia and Its Relationships to the U.S.," 2.

9. Boynton, "Russia and Its Relationships to the U.S.," 2–3. Linda Killen and N. Gordon Levin also emphasize that the American approach to the Russian question was predicated on the belief that the "March Revolution" represented the true democratic impulses of the Russian people while the Bolshevik Revolution was only a temporary phase. See Linda Killen, *The Russian Bureau: A Case Study in Wilsonian Diplomacy* (Lexington: Univ. Kentucky Press, 1983); N. Gordon Levin, *Woodrow Wilson and World Politics: America's Response to War and Revolution* (New York: Oxford Univ. Press, 1968).

10. Martin J. Sklar, "Woodrow Wilson and the Developmental Imperatives of Modern U.S. Liberalism," *The United Sates as a Developing Country: Studies in U.S. History in the Progressive Era and the 1920s* (Cambridge: Cambridge Univ. Press, 1992), 102–42.

11. I am indebted to Mary O. Furner, who suggested to me that Wilson's political economy was influenced by residual republican values.

12. Woodrow Wilson, "An Address to a Joint Session of Congress," Arthur S. Link, ed., *The Papers of Woodrow Wilson, January–April, 1917* (Princeton, N.J.: Princeton Univ. Press, 1983), 41:524.

13. Frederick Jackson Turner, "The Significance of the Frontier in American History," *Annual Report of the American Historical Association, 1893* (Washington, D.C.: 1894), 199–27.

14. "Russia and Far Eastern Problems," Nov. 10, 1921, an unsigned confidential memorandum drafted for American delegates to the Washington Naval Conference, in the Roland S. Morris Papers, box 7.

15. "Russia and Far Eastern Problems."

16. "Russia and Far Eastern Problems."

17. Woodrow Wilson, "Democracy and Efficiency," ca. Oct. 1, 1900, Arthur Link, ed., *The Papers of Woodrow Wilson, January–April, 1900–1902*, 12:8.

18. Ibid., 8.

19. Wilson concludes this essay by implying that America's new international obligations might stimulate the evolution of more rational administrative institutions in American society, ibid., 17–18.

20. Ibid., 19.

21. Donald W. Treadgold, *The Great Siberian Migration: Government and Peasant in Resettlement from Emancipation to the First World War* (Princeton, N.J.: Princeton Univ. Press, 1957), 6.

22. Ibid., 231–32.

23. Ibid., 171–76.

24. Stishov is cited in Paul Dotsenko, *The Struggle for Democracy in Siberia, 1917–1920* (Stanford: Hoover Institute Press,1983), 5.

25. Treadgold, *The Great Siberian Migration*, 158.

26. Donald W. Treadgold, "Russian Expansion in the Light of Turner's Study of the American Frontier," *Agricultural History* 26 (Oct. 1952): 150.

27. Treadgold, *The Great Siberian Migration*, 245.

28. Eugene Kayden and Alexis Antsiferov, *The Cooperative Movement in Russia During the War* (New Haven: Yale Univ. Press, 1929), 71, 169, 183.

29. Ibid., 206.

30. This overview of the Russian cooperative movement was drawn from the following sources: ibid.; Frederic E. Lee, "The Russian Cooperative Movement," U.S. Department of Commerce, *Bureau of Foreign and Domestic Commerce, Misc. Series*, no. 101 (Washington, D.C.: GPO, 1920); G. E. Corbaley to W. V. Couchman, Mar. 27, 1918, Cyrus H. McCormick Jr. Papers, McCormick Collections, series 2c, box 117, State Historical Society of Wisconsin, Madison.

31. Eugene Kayden, joint author of *The Cooperative Movement in Russia During the War,* and a specialist for the War Trade Board, stressed these cultural factors throughout his half of the study.

32. Kayden and Antsiferov, *The Cooperative Movement*, 159.

33. William C. Huntington to Rodney Dean, Mar. 17, 1919, RG 151, file 027.0.

34. For instance, the critical role the Union of Siberian Creamery Associations played in supplying the army can be adduced by the appointment of its officials, such as Joseph Okulitch and V. N. Baschkirov, to top governmental positions in the Ministry of Agriculture and the Central Committee for Food Supply. This biographical information appeared in "Agricultural Siberia and Industrial America," *The Russian Information Bureau in the U.S.,* Bulletin 38, ca. 1918, Samuel N. Harper Papers, box 54; Bertron to Cyrus McCormick Jr., Dec. 5, 1918, Cyrus H. McCormick Jr. Papers, box 118.

These American views regarding "nation-building" in Russia bring to mind Antonio Gramsci's insights into the fragility of the czarist state. Reflecting on the failure of bolshevism in the West after its success in Russia, Gramsci observed that "in Russia the State was everything, civil society was primordial and gelatinous; in the West, there was a proper relation between State and civil society, and when the State trembled a sturdy structure of civil society was at once revealed. The State was only an outer ditch, behind which there stood a powerful system of fortresses and earthworks: more or less numerous from one State to the next." Antonio Gramsci, *Selections from the Prison Notebooks* (New York: International Publishers, 1971), 238.

2. A Minister Plenipotentiary for Russia's Railroads: The Stevens Commission in Russia, June– December 1917

1. Lansing to Wilson, Mar. 19, 1917, U.S. Department of State, Personal and Confidential Letters from Secretary of State Lansing to President Wilson, 1915–1918 (Washington, D.C.: National Archives Microfilm, Microcopy 743, 1968), reel 1.

2. Ruth Amende Roosa, "Russian Industrialists During World War I: The Interaction of Economics and Politics," in Gregory Guroff and Fred Carstensen, eds., *Entrepreneurship in Imperial Russia and the Soviet Union* (Princeton, N.J.: Princeton Univ. Press, 1983), 159–87.

3. Baker to Lansing, Mar. 31, 1917, RG 59, U.S. Department of State, "Records Relating to the Internal Affairs of Russia and the Soviet Union, 1910–1929," 861.77/55 (Washington, D.C.: National Archives).

4. Lansing to Francis, Apr. 2, 1917, RG 59, 861.77/45a.

5. Francis to Lansing, Apr. 11, 1917; RG 59, 861,77/48; Lansing to Francis, Apr. 16, 1917, RG 59, 861.77/48.

6. Francis to Lansing, Apr. 25, 1917, RG 59, 861.51/137; McAddo to Francis, Apr. 28, 1917, RG 59, 861.51/138; Francis to McAddo, May 1, 1917, RG 59, 861.51/141; McAdoo to Francis, May 7, 1917, RG 59, 861.51/142; Francis to Lansing, Apr. 6, 1917, RG 59, 861.51/133; Francis to Lansing, Apr. 29, 1917, RG 59, 861.51/140.

7. McAdoo to Francis, May 17, 1917, RG 59, 861.51/148.

8. Lansing to Francis, May 3, 1917, RG 59, 861.77/64a.

9. *The National Cyclopedia of American Biography* (New York: White & Co., 1945): 32:326–27; David McCullough, *The Path Between the Seas: The Creation of the Panama Canal 1870-1914* (New York: Simon & Schuster, 1977), 459–89.

10. Root to Lansing, May 6, 1917, RG 59, 861.77/97½, U.S. Department of State, *Foreign Relations of the United States: The Lansing Papers, 1914–1920* (Washington, D.C.: GPO, 1940), 2:329.

11. Lansing to Wilson, May 7, 1917, RG 59, 861.77/97½, *The Lansing Papers*, 2:329–31.

12. Wilson to Lansing, May 7, 1917, RG 59, 861.77/98½, *The Lansing Papers*, 2:331.

13. Lansing to Francis, Apr. 14, 1917, RG 59, 763.72/4001a, U.S. Department of State, *Foreign Relations of the United States* (Washington, D.C.: GPO, 1932), Russia, 1918, 1:107 (hereafter cited as *FRUS*, followed by year, volume, and page number). Francis to Lansing, Apr. 19, 1917, 763.72/4002, *FRUS*, 1918, Russia, 1:107–8.

14. Francis to Lansing, Apr. 11, 1917, RG 59, 861.77/48.

15. Francis to Lansing, Apr. 21, 1917, RG 59, 861.00/327.

16. Francis to Lansing, Apr. 29, 1917, RG 59, 861.51/140.

17. The merits of Wilson's position became evident in the fall of 1918, when the United States entered into the long and contentious process of negotiating an inter-Allied agreement for administering the Trans-Siberian railway system in trust of the defunct Russian government. At the end of August 1918, the State Department explained to Roland Morris, the American ambassador to Japan, and chief author of the subsequent inter-Allied Railway Agreement of February 1919, that

It has been suggested that the members of the Stevens railroad mission be commissioned in the United States Army. This government is opposed to the incorporation with the American armed forces of this civilian commission that was sent to Siberia to serve the best interests of the Russian people. The members of these railroad units are the agents of the Russian people and are being paid and supported by their Ambassador here from funds belonging to them, and it is felt that further complications would not arise and best results would be had if Mr. Stevens for and in behalf of the Russian people were to have general direction of the Trans-Siberian and the Chinese Eastern Railways and their several branches. (Lansing to Morris, Aug. 30, 1918, RG 59, 861.77/451)

18. William Rosenberg, *Liberals in the Russian Revolution: The Constitutional Democratic Party, 1917–1921* (Princeton, N.J.: Princeton Univ. Press, 1974).

19. Lansing to Francis, May 15, 1917, RG 59, 861.77/78a.

20. Francis to Lansing, June 20, 1917, RG 59, 861.77/110.

21. "Report of George Gibbs on the Siberian Railway" (hereafter cited as Gibbs Report), enclosed in, Willard to Lansing, November 19, 1917, RG 59, 861.77/221.

22. Gibbs Report, 30, 35.

23. Stevens to Willard, July 30, 1917, RG 59, 861.77/136.

24. Stevens to Willard, Aug. 13, 1917, RG 59, 861.77/153.

25. Stevens to Willard, June 25, 1917 RG 59, 861.77/114; Willard to Stevens, July 14, 1917, RG 59, 861.77/125a; Willard to Stevens, July 20, 1917, RG 59, 861.77/126; Gibbs Report, 23.

26. Gibbs Report, 24–26; Willard to Stevens, July 20, 1917, RG 59, 861.77/126.

27. Gibbs Report, 29–30; Appendix F to Gibbs Report, General Report to the Minister Regarding Improvements Recommended on All Russian Railways, July 19, 1917, 7.

28. Appendix F to Gibbs Report, 2–6.

29. Appendix F to Gibbs Report, 6–7.

30. Appendix F to Gibbs Report, 7–20.

31. Gibbs Report, 13; Appendix F to Gibbs Report, 9–10.

32. Gibbs Report, 22, 35; Francis to Lansing, Aug. 6, 1917, RG 59, 861.00/462.

33. Gibbs Report, 22.

34. Francis to Lansing and Willard, Sept. 29, 1917, RG 59, 861.77/184.

35. Gibbs Report, 22.

36. Willard to Stevens, Aug. 27, 1917, RG 59, 861.77/150.

37. Stevens to Willard, Aug. 11, 1917, RG 59, 861.77/146.

38. Stevens to Willard, undated, received Sept. 17, 1917, RG 59, 861.77/166; Miller to Willard, Nov. 1, 1917, RG 59, 861.77/200½.

39. Francis to Lansing, Oct. 9, 1917, RG 59, 861.77/190.

40. Francis to Lansing and Willard, Sept. 28, 1917, RG 59, 861.77/183. The new Minister of Communications, A. V. Liverovskii, a member of the Social Revolutionary party, had apparently succeeded to the post after he had played an instrumental role in blocking the movement of Gen. L. G. Kornilov's forces during the latter's abortive coup in September. See Robert P. Browder and Alexander F. Kerensky, eds., *The Russian Revolution, 1917, Documents* (Stanford, Calif.: Stanford Univ. Press, 1961), 3:1578–79.

41. Francis to Lansing and Willard, Sept. 29, 1917, RG 59, 861.77/184.

42. Willard to Francis, Oct. 15, 1917, RG 59, 861.77/187.

43. Francis to Lansing and Willard, Oct. 23, 1917, RG 59, 861.77/200.

44. Stevens to Willard, Oct. 24, 1917, enclosed in Willard to Lansing, Dec. 11, 1917, RG 59, 861.77/239.

45. Francis to Lansing and Willard, Oct. 27, 1917, RG 59, 861.77/201.

46. Francis to Lansing, Oct. 29, 1917, RG 59, 861.77/206.

47. John Stevens, "Russia During the World War," address before the Engineers Club, Nov. 23, 1926, *Engineers and Engineering* 44 (Jan. 1927): 20, enclosed in Roland S. Morris Papers, box 7.

48. Tereschenko believed that the movement of traffic had increased threefold on the Trans-Siberian Railroad. Although Stevens thought this was an exaggeration, he was confident a "decided improvement" had been made on the line, Stevens to Willard, Oct. 24, 1917, RG 59, 861.77/239.

49. Stevens to Willard, Oct. 24, 1917, RG 59, 861.77/239.

50. Stevens to Willard, undated, Received Nov. 4, 1917, RG 59, 861.77/208; Willard to Stevens, Nov. 6, 1917, RG 59, 861.77/208.

51. Stevens to Willard, Oct. 24, 1917, RG 59, 861.77/239.

52. Stevens to Willard, Dec. 28, 1917, enclosed in Willard to Lansing, Jan. 19, 1918, RG 59, 861.77/278. Rex Wade believes that throughout 1917 the coalition members of the Provisional Government were unwilling to consider a separate peace in large part because this course might have opened the way to German political and economic domination of Russia. See Wade's, *The Russian Search for Peace, February–October, 1917* (Stanford, Calif: Stanford Univ. Press, 1969), 143.

53. Stevens to Willard, Oct. 24, 1917, RG 59, 861.77/239.

54. Stevens, "Russia During the World War," 20.

55. Stevens to Lansing, undated, received Nov. 26, 1917, RG 59, 861.77/229; Willard to Stevens, Nov. 27, 1917, RG 59, 861.77/231a; Willard to Stevens, Dec. 24, 1917, RG 59, 861.77/267a.

56. Stevens to Willard, Dec. 17, 1917, RG 59, 861.77/244; Willard to Stevens, Dec. 19, 1917, RG 59, 861.77/244.

57. F. M. Titus to C. M. Muchnic, Dec. 18, 1917, enclosed in John K. Caldwell to Lansing, Dec. 21, 1917, RG 59, 861.77/281.

58. Titus to Muchnic, Dec. 18, 1917, RG 59, 861.77/281.

59. Titus to Muchnic, Dec. 18, 1917, RG 59, 861.77/281.

60. Titus to Muchnic, Dec. 18, 1917, RG 59, 861.77/281.

61. Francis to Lansing and Willard, Jan. 3, 1918, RG 59, 861.77/264.

3. The Specter of a Divided World: The Sources and Conduct of American Economic Warfare against Germany, January–August 1918

1. Fritz Fischer examines in detail Germany's extensive global ambitions in his famous study, *Germany's Aims in the First World War* (New York: Norton, 1967).

2. William F. Sands to Lansing, Jan. 16, 1918, RG 59, 861.00/961.

3. Basil Miles, "German Propaganda in Russia," Jan. 4, 1918, RG 59, 861.00/939½.

4. Frank Polk to David Francis, Jan. 12, 1918, RG 59, 861.24/27.

5. W. V. Couchman to Alexander Legge, June 12, 1918, International Harvester Archives, Document no. 1373.

6. William Kent to Lansing, "German Financial Activity in Russia," Feb. 11, 1918, RG 59, 861.51/282.

7. Maddin Summers to Lansing, May 1, 1918, RG 59, 861.00/1820.

8. Diary excerpts Siberia, Feb. 25, 1918, Breckinridge Long Papers, box 186.

9. Diary excerpts Siberia.

10. Diary excerpts Siberia.

11. Diary excerpts Siberia, Feb. 26, 1918.

12. Breckinridge Long, "Memorandum of Conversation Had with Mr. John Sookine," Mar. 2, 1918, Long Papers, box 186.

13. Long to Wilson, Mar. 4, 1918, Wilson Papers, ser. 2.

14. House to Wilson, Mar. 3, 1918, House Papers, box 121; Betty M. Unterberger, *America's Siberian Expedition, 1918–1920: A Study of National Policy* (Durham, N.C.: Duke Univ. Press, 1956), 29-33.

15. Bullitt to Polk, Mar. 2, 1918, RG 59, 861.00/1290½. While Bullitt mistakenly believed the Bolshevik government represented a rudimentary "Russian democracy" that was compatible with Wilson's liberal-democratic world view, this misconception does not affect the crux of his argument.

16. Robert Lansing, "Memorandum on the Proposed Japanese Military Expedition into Siberia," Mar. 19, Apr. 10, 1918, Private Memoranda, Robert Lansing Papers, 1915–1922 and undated, box 2, (Washington D.C.: Library of Congress Microfilm, 1972), reel 1 (hereafter cited as Lansing Papers, followed box and reel number).

17. "Historical Report of the Operations and Business, Accompanied by a Statement of Accounts, of the so-called, 'Tovaro-Obmien,' or the Allied firm of 'Darcy, Marshall, and Stevens,'" Consul Frank C. Lee, Department of State, Russian Div., Feb. 10, 1920, RG 59, 811.20261 T/19, box 7461.

18. Lansing to Newton D. Baker, Jan. 30, 1918, RG 59, 861.24/18.

19. Lansing to Wilson, Feb. 12, 1918, Basil Miles, "Purchase of Supplies in Russia," Feb. 12, 1918, enclosed in, Baruch to Polk, Feb. 5, 1918, RG 59, 861.77/290½; Lansing to Francis, Feb. 14, 1918, RG 59, 861.24/30.

20. Post to Cyrus McCormick Jr., Feb. 3, 1918, Cyrus H. McCormick Jr. Papers, box 117.

21. George Lomonosov, "What Can America Do to Help Save Russia," speech before City Club of Chicago, Feb. 18, 1918; "Plead for Starving Russia: Commissioners Tell of Condition of People in New Republic," *The City Club Bulletin,* Feb. 25, 1918, 67–68, McCormick Papers, box 117.

22. "Plead for starving Russia," McCormick Papers, box 117.

23. "Plead for starving Russia," McCormick Papers, box 117.

24. "Memorandum of Conference with Russian Representatives," Feb. 19, 1918, McCormick Papers, box 117.

25. Lobogreikas were simple hand-rake reapers and the predominant mechanical harvester in Russia until 1910. They were considered ideal for Russian conditions because of their inexpensiveness, their low maintenance requirements, and the ease with which they could be repaired. See, Fred Carstensen, *American Enterprise in Foreign Markets: Studies of Singer and International Harvester in Imperial Russia* (Chapel Hill: Univ. of North Carolina Press, 1984), 120.

26. T. H. Anderson to International Harvester Corporation, "Contract with the Moscow Narodny Bank for Lubertzy Machines 1918," Feb. 21, 1918; McAllister to H. F. Perkins, Sept. 11, 1918, International Harvester Archives, Doc. no. 1373.

27. Miles to Polk, Feb. 23, 1918, RG 59, 861.77/299.

28. Confidential memorandum by Basil Miles, Mar. 4, 1918, McCormick Papers, box 117.

29. Memo by Basil Miles, Mar. 4, 1918.

30. Cyrus McCormick's notes from the meeting at Elihu Root's apartment, Mar. 9, 1918, McCormick Papers, box 115.

31. McCormick's notes.

32. Basil Miles, "Policy for Siberia," Mar. 26, 1918, RG 59, 861.00/1434½.

33. Miles, "Policy for Siberia"; Alonzo E. Taylor, "Memorandum of the necessity of a specialized survey of the internal conditions of Russia with reference to her economic and industrial relations to the Central Powers and the Neutral Countries of Europe." Feb. 16, 1918, in Taylor to Lansing, Feb. 19, 1918, RG 59, 661.119/79.

34. Long Diary, Mar. 29, 1918, box 186. Long's summary of a conference with Williams, Miles, and Lay is consistent with Miles's memo of Mar. 26, 1918.

35. Basil Miles, Memorandum for the Secretary of State: Senator Owen's letter concerning Russia, Jan. 29, 1918, RG 59, 861.00/1048½.

36. George F. Kennan, *Soviet-American Relations 1917-1920: The Decision to Intervene* (Princeton, N.J.: Princeton Univ. Press, 1958), 279–80.

37. Zemstvos were district and provincial institutions established by the czarist government in 1864 in an effort to encourage economic progress. Consisting of elected representatives, zemstvos constituted an important step toward self-government in the provinces. Joseph L. Wieczynski, *The Modern Encyclopedia of Russian and Soviet History* (Gulf Breeze, Fla.: Academic International Press, 1987), 45:234–35.

38. Basil Miles, "Policy for Siberia," Mar. 26, 1918, RG 59, 861.00/1434½.

39. Miles, "Policy for Siberia."

40. Lansing to Leffingwell, Feb. 25, 1918, RG 59, 861.51/287.

41. Lansing to Summers, Mar. 27, 1918, RG 59, 861.24/54a; Lansing to Francis, Apr. 19, 1918, RG 59, 861.00/1457.

42. Summers to Lansing, Apr. 16, 1918, RG 59, 861.00/1616.

43. Lansing to Francis, Apr. 22, 1918, RG 59, 861.00/1457.

44. Lansing to Summers, Apr. 26, 1918, RG 59, 861.00/1616.

45. Lansing to Francis, Apr. 26, 1918, RG 59, 861.24/69a.

46. Francis to Lansing, May 11, 1918, RG 59, 861.24/74.

47. Basil Miles, "Embargo on Germany (Safeguard Russian Supplies)," May 23, 1918, RG 59, 861.24/263.

48. Miles, "Embargo on Germany."

49. Peter Bukowski, "Report on activities directed towards restricting supplies to the enemy from Northern Russia," enclosure-extract in Francis to Lansing, Nov. 1, 1918, 763.72112/11086, *FRUS,* 1918, Russia, 3:161–62.

50. Peter Bukowski, Full text of his report enclosed in Lee, "Historical Report . . . of the Tovaro-Obmien."

51. Peter Bukowski in Lee, "Historical Report . . . of the Tovaro-Obmien." Soviet willingness to cooperate with the Allied military missions in this instance can also be explained by immediate strategic considerations. Richard Debo has shown that during the spring and early summer of 1918 Lenin wanted to avoid a clash between Germany and the Allies over control of these supplies because it would have placed his regime in immediate danger. Richard Debo, *Revolution and Survival: The Foreign Policy of Soviet Russia, 1917–1918* (Toronto: Univ. of Toronto Press, 1979), 262–99.

52. Francis to Lansing, May 31, 1918, RG 59, 861.00/1997.

53. Peter Bukowski in Lee, "Historical Report . . . of the Tovaro-Obmien."

54. Miles to Lansing, June 3, 1918, RG 59, 861.00/1887; Francis to Lansing, May 20, 1918; Lansing to Francis, June 13, 1918, RG 59, 861.00/1887.

55. Poole to Lansing, July 16, 1918, RG 59, 861.00/2353, 2354.

56. Poole to Lansing, July 16, 1918.

57. Unsigned (probably Darcy) to Huntington, June 27, 1918, document enclosed in Lee, "Historical Report . . . of the Tovaro-Obmien."

58. Poole to Lansing, July 16, 1918, RG 59, 861.00/2353, 2354; Poole to Lansing, July 19, 1918, RG 182, box 1566.

59. "Minutes of the meeting of the Tovaro-Obmien," Aug. 15, 1918, enclosed in Lee, "Historical Report . . . of the Tovaro-Obmien"; Whitehouse to Lansing, Nov. 13, 1918, resume of Huntington's letter to Francis dated Sept. 19, 1918, 861.24/105, *FRUS, 1918, Russia,* 3:166–68.

60. Poole to Lansing, Aug. 17, 1918, RG 59, 861.24/102; Poole to Lansing, May 8, 1919, RG 59, 861.24/151; see also file nos. 861.24/209–13.

61. Lee, "Historical Report . . . of the Tovaro-Obmien."

62. Lee, "Historical Report . . . of the Tovaro-Obmien," section 2, "Developments and Results," 14.

4. *Between Germany and Japan: Wilson, the Czecho-Slovaks, and the Decision to Intervene, May–July 1918*

1. Reinsch to Lansing, May 10, 1918, RG 59, 861.00/1773.

2. Reinsch to Lansing, Apr. 10, 1918, RG 59, 861.00/1571.

3. Cyrus H. McCormick Jr. to Edward M. House, June 10, 1918, McCormick Collections, box 116.

4. Woodrow Wilson, "The Relation of University Education to Commerce," address before The Chicago Commercial Club, Nov. 29, 1902, Link, ed., *The Papers of Woodrow Wilson, 1902–1903*, 14:230; William Diamond, *The Economic Thought of Woodrow Wilson* (Baltimore: Johns Hopkins Univ. Press, 1943), 54.

5. Redfield to Wilson, June 26, 1918, Wilson to Redfield, June 27, 1918, Wilson Papers, ser. 2.

6. Reinsch to Lansing, May 30, 1918, RG 59, 861.00/1900.

7. Reinsch to Lansing, May 16, 1918, Wilson to Lansing, May 20, 1918, Wilson Papers, ser. 2.

8. Wiseman to Drummond, May 30, 1918, Wiseman Papers, box 9.

9. William C. Huntington to Burwell C. Cutler, Irkutsk, Siberia, Apr. 1, 1918, enclosed in Huntington to Samuel N. Harper, Irkutsk, Siberia, Apr. 15, 1918, Samuel N. Harper Papers, box 5. The reliability of this report is enhanced when it is taken into account that German manufacturers had been competitive with International Harvester in the production of mowers on the European market since 1908. Carstensen, *American Enterprise in Foreign Markets*, 153.

10. Wright to Secretary of State, Apr. 6, 1918, RG 59, 861.00/1455.

11. Summers to Lansing, May 1, 1918, RG 59, 861.00/1790.

12. Poole to Secretary of State, July 13, 1918, RG 59, 861.00/2356.

13. Poole to Secretary of State, July 13, 1918.

14. Mirbach to Kuhlmann, June 25, 1918, in Z.A.B. Zeman, ed., *Germany and the Revolution in Russia, 1915–1918* (London: Oxford Univ. Press, 1958), 137–39.

15. Jules Jusserand to Lansing, May 28, 1918, enclosed in Bullitt to Wilson, June 4, 1918, Wilson Papers, ser. 2.

16. Jusserand to Lansing, May 28, 1918.

17. A. B. Coxe to Military Staff, no date, received June 6, 1918, RG 59, 861.00/1987½.

18. Rosenberg, *Liberals in the Russian Revolution*, 320.

19. J. Butler Wright memorandum, June 3, 1918, RG 59, 861.00/2166½.

20. J. Butler Wright memorandum, June 3, 1918.

21. J. Butler Wright memorandum, May 29, 1918, RG 59, 861.00/2079½.

22. J. Butler Wright memorandum, June 3, 1918, RG 59, 861.00/2166½.

23. J. Butler Wright memorandum, June 3, 1918.

24. Memorandum from the War Trade Board as to Aid for Russia, submitted by Thomas L. Chadbourne, Clarence M. Woolley, John Foster Dulles, June 5, 1918, enclosed in Chadbourne to Polk, June 7, 1918, RG 59, 861.00/2085½.

25. Memorandum from the War Trade Board . . . June 5, 1918.

26. Miles to Phillips, June 14, 1918, RG 59, 861.00/2085½.

27. Basil Miles, "Non-Military Measures in Russia," June 3, 1918, RG 59, 861.00/2083½.

28. Polk to Poole, June 5, 1918, RG 59, 861.00/1967a.

29. Poole to Lansing, June 12, 1918, RG 59, 861.00/2053.

30. Joseph Okulitch to Page, June 12, 1918, enclosed in Gunther to Lansing, June 15, 1918, RG 59, 861.00/2152.

31. Lansing to Wilson, June 19, 1918, 861.00/2053, Wilson to Lansing, June 19, 1918, 861.00/2148½, *The Lansing Papers*, 2:363–64.

32. Unterberger, *America's Siberian Intervention*, 54–57.

33. Ibid., 55–59; Richard Ullman, *Intervention and the War* (Princeton, N.J.: Princeton Univ. Press, 1961), 153–56. The British War Office had always questioned the utility of transporting the Czecho-Slovak troops to the western front. It believed their presence in Siberia would make intervention more palatable to the population.

34. Unterberger, *America's Siberian Intervention*, 55–56.

35. Reinsch to Lansing, June 13, 1918, RG 59, 861.00/2014.

36. Wilson to Lansing, June 17, 1918, 861.00/2145½, *The Lansing Papers*, 2:363.

37. Knight to Secretary of the Navy, June 21, 1918, RG 59, 861.00/2165½.

38. Wright to Miles, June 22, 1918, RG 59, 861.00/2165½.

39. Lansing to Wilson, June 23, 1918, 861.00/2164½, *The Lansing Papers*, 2:364.

40. Frazier (the diplomatic liaison officer, Supreme War Council) to Lansing, July 2, 1918, RG 59, 763.72Su/145. See also Unterberger, *America's Siberian Intervention*, 67–68.

41. "Memorandum on the Siberian Situation," initialed by Robert Lansing, July 4, 1918, RG 59, 861.00/2292½.

42. "Memorandum of a Conference at the White House in reference to the Siberian Situation," July 6, 1918, Private Memoranda, Lansing Papers, box 2, reel 1.

43. Wilson to House, July 8, 1918, Ray Stannard Baker, ed., *Woodrow Wilson Life and Letters* (New York: Doubleday, Doran, 1939), 8:266.

44. Reading to Foreign Office, July 3, 1918, William Wiseman Papers, box 9.

45. Reading to Foreign Office, July 3, 1918.

46. Reading to Foreign Office, July 9, 1918, Wiseman Papers, box 9.

47. Examples of émigré Russian liberal opinion that advocated an Allied military intervention to prevent a Russian capitulation to Germany appear in letters to Wilson from the American ambassadors to Rome and Bern, Nelson T. Page to Wilson, June 11, 1918; Pleasant Stovall to Wilson, June 11, 1918, Wilson Papers, ser. 2.

48. "Memorandum on the Siberian Situation," initialed by Robert Lansing, July 4, 1918, RG 59, 861.00/2292½.

49. "From the Diary of Josephus Daniels," July 6, 1918, in Link, ed., *The Papers of Woodrow Wilson*, 48:544.

50. Robert B. Teusler to Frank P. Keppel, Director, Foreign Operations, American Red Cross, Jan. 14, 1920, enclosed in Keppel to Secretary of State, Mar. 25, 1920, RG 59, 861.00/6683.

51. Reports on the evacuation of the Czecho-Slovak Military forces by Colonel B. O. Johnson, Chief Inspector of the Inter-Allied Technical Board, Apr. 7, 1920, enclosed in, Stevens to Colby, Apr. 12, 1920, RG 59, 861.77/1570.

52. Unterberger, *America's Siberian Intervention*, 70.

53. James Morley, *The Japanese Thrust into Siberia* (New York: Columbia Univ. Press, 1957), 277.

54. Aide-Mémoire from the Secretary of State to the Allied ambassadors, July 17, 1918, RG 59, 861.00/3054b.

55. Interview between Ambassador Morris and Mr. Vologodskii, Vladivostok, Sept. 21, 1918; Interview between Ambassador Morris and Mr. Vostrotin and Mr. Glukharov aboard the USS *Brooklyn*, Sept. 24, 1918, enclosed in Maj. David Barrows to General Graves, Sept. 21, 1918, Historical Files of the American Expeditionary Forces in Siberia, 1918–1920, file 21-21.3 (Washington D.C.: National Archives Microfilm Publication M917, 1973), reel 1.

56. Julius Lay, "Memorandum on Intervention in Siberia," July 22, 1918, given to Second Assistant Secretary William Phillips, RG 59, 861.00/6687.

57. Lay, "Memorandum on Intervention in Siberia."

58. Julius Lay, "Memorandum on the German Policy in Russia," July 19, 1918, Long Papers, box 187.

59. Julius Lay, "Memorandum on an Economic Mission to Russia," July 23, 1918, Long Papers, box 187.

60. Paul Reinsch, *An American Diplomat In China* (Garden City N.Y.: Doubleday, Page & Co., 1922), 356.

61. Jenkins to Lansing, Sept. 6, 1918, RG 59, 861.77/464.

5. The Genesis of the Russian Bureau: The Sources and Conduct of the American Economic Assistance Program, July–September 1918

1. Polk to American Embassy Tokyo, July 17, 1918, RG 59, 861.00/2275.

2. Ullman, *Intervention and the War*, 226, 261; "The British Embassy to the Department of State," Memorandum, Aug. 12, 1918, RG 59, 861.00/2501.

3. Richard Ullman's *Intervention and the War*, demonstrates that Wilson's appraisal of Britain's motives was quite accurate.

4. Balfour to Lord Reading, July 25, 1918, RG 59, 861.00/2568.

5. Arno Kolz, "British Economic Interests in Siberia During the Russian Civil War, 1918–1920," *Journal of Modern History* 48 (Sept. 1976): 483–91.

6. Miles to Vance McCormick, Oct. 4, 1918, RG 182, box 1551; *The Moscow Narodny Bank: Its History and Achievements, 1912–1917,* (London: N.p., n.d.), 20.

7. Kolz, "British Economic Interests in Siberia," 486; Ullman, *Intervention and the War,* 273–79.

8. Kolz, "British Economic Interests in Siberia," 486.

9. Memorandum of the Counselor for the Department of State (Polk) of a conversation with the British Chargé (Barclay) in regard to telegram from Mr. Balfour to Lord Reading, dated July 25, [1918], on the subject of the Proposed Mission to Siberia, RG 59, 861.00/ 2567.

10. Memorandum of the Counselor for the Department of State . . . July 25.

11. Polk to Wilson, Aug. 5, 1918, RG 59, 861.00/2567.

12. Phillips to Lansing, Aug. 22, 1918, RG 59, 861.00/2659.

13. Lansing to Wilson, Aug. 22, 1918, RG 59, 861.00/2659.

14. Wilson to Lansing, Aug. 23, 1918, RG 59, 861.00/2660.

15. Wilson to Lansing, Aug. 23, 1918.

16. Long Diary, Sept. 8 (written Sept. 15), 1918, Long Papers, box 186.

17. Long Diary, Sept. 8.

18. Lansing to Wilson, Sept. 9, 1918, Wilson Papers, ser. 2.

19. Long Diary, Sept. 8, 1918. The term "separate organization" was apparently used by Wilson, because Long placed quotation marks around it in his diary entry.

20. Long Diary, Sept. 8, 1918.

21. Long Diary, Sept. 8, 1918.

22. Long Diary, Sept. 8, 1918.

23. Gordon Auchincloss Diary, Sept. 14, 1918, Gordon Auchincloss Papers, box 2.

24. Lansing to Wilson, June 29, 1918, RG 59, 861.00/2219½ b.

25. Auchincloss to Polk, June 29, 1918, Frank L. Polk Papers, box 1.

26. Caldwell to Lansing, Sept. 14, 1918, RG 182, box 1584.

27. August Heid to International Harvester Company, July 31, 1918, International Harvester Archives, Doc. no. 1350.

28. Caldwell to Lansing, June 24, 1918, RG 59, 611.61171/5-6.

29. Isaac J. Sherman to B. S. Cutler, Sept. 11, 1918, RG 182, box 1572.

30. Caldwell to Lansing, Sept. 24, 1918, RG 182, box 1553.

31. Alvey A. Adee to War Trade Board, Sept. 16, 1918, RG 182, box 1572.

32. Lansing Diary, Sept. 19 and 24, 1918, Lansing Papers, reel 2.

33. Diary of Edward M. House, Sept. 24, 1918, ser. 2:14.

34. Gordon Auchincloss Memorandum, undated, House Papers, box 7.

35. *The National Cyclopedia of American Biography* (New York: White & Co., 1949), 35:242–43.

36. H. B. Van Sinderen Memorandum for McCormick, Sept. 23, 1918, House Papers, box 182.

37. "Plan 1 Russ Amb," Sept. 1918, Long Papers, box 187.

38. H. B. Van Sinderen, Memorandum of conversation with Serge Ughet, Sept. 26, 1918, RG 182, box 1585.

39. Eugene M. Kayden, "Report on Economic Assistance to Siberia," Oct. 2, 1918, RG 182, box 1551.

40. Polk to Morris (for Heid from the War Trade Board), Oct. 10, 1918, RG 59, 861.50/29.

41. Polk to Morris, Oct. 10. 1918; E. C. Porter to Clarence W. Woolley, Oct. 8, 1918, H. B. Van Sinderen to E.C. Porter, Oct. 16, 1918, RG 182, box 1560.

42. War Trade Board to Heid, Oct. 10, 1918, RG 59, 861.50/29.

43. War Trade Board to Heid, Oct. 10, 1918.

44. War Trade Board to Heid, Oct. 10, 1918.

45. Killen, *The Russian Bureau,* 53–54.

46. Morris to State Department, Nov. 14, 1918, RG 59, 861.77/549½.

47. B. S. Cutler to Redfield, Aug. 26, 1918, U.S. Department of Commerce, RG 40, 77295; Redfield to Cutler, Aug. 27, 1918, RG 40, 77295.

48. Unsigned, undated memorandum attached to Caldwell to Lansing, Sept. 24, 1918, RG 182, box 1553.

49. Heid to War Trade Board, undated, received Oct. 25, 1918, RG 59, 861.77/526.

50. Cutler to McCormick, Oct. 19, 1918, McCormick to Cutler, Oct. 23, 1918, RG 151, box 2966.

51. Cutler to Preston, July 26, 1918, RG 59, 661.119/226.

52. War Trade Board to Heid, Oct, 22, 1918, RG 59, 611.616/12a. Arthur Bullard confirmed this assessment in his *The Russian Pendulum: Autocracy, Democracy, Bolshevism* (New York: Macmillan, 1919), 188–91.

53. Rueben R. MacDermid to Caldwell, Sept. 18, 1918, enclosed in Caldwell to the State Department, Sept. 24, 1918, RG 182, box 1553. On the credibility of MacDermid see, Caldwell to Lansing, June 27, 1918, RG 59, 661.119/194.

54. Morley, *The Japanese Thrust into Siberia,* 215–16.

55. Ibid., 294–96.

6. *A Stillborn Program: The Russian Bureau, October–December 1918*

1. For Linda Killen's treatment of the difficulties encountered by the Russian Bureau from October through December 1918, see *The Russian Bureau,* 48–77.

2. Lansing to Wilson, Sept. 21, 1918, "Memorandum for the Secretary of the Treasury," Aug. 28, 1918, Wilson Papers, ser. 4.

3. Knight to Secretary of the Navy, July 21, 1918, RG 59, 861.00/2913.

4. Memorandum initialed by Breckinridge Long, July 23, 1918, Long Papers, box 187.

5. William B. Owen to Vance McCormick, Sept. 16, 1918, Record Group 39, United States Department of Treasury, Country File: Russia, folder 47. (Hereafter cited as RG 39, followed by Russia and either a file or folder number).

6. Owen to McCormick, Sept. 16, 1918.

7. Owen to McCormick, Sept. 16, 1918; Long to Leffingwell, July 25, 1918, RG 39, Russia, folder 110; Polk to Strauss, Aug. 9, 1918, RG 59, 861.00/2913.

8. Leffingwell to Phillips, Aug. 16, 1918, RG 59, 861.00/2542.

9. "Memorandum for the Secretary of the Treasury," Aug. 28, 1918, Wilson Papers, ser. 4; Bakhmetev to Phillips, Aug. 21, 1918, RG 59, 86100/2443.

10. William Anderson to International Banking Corporation, Aug. 26, 1918, RG 182, box 1566.

11. Francis to Lansing, Sept. 14, 1918, RG 59, 861.51/357.

12. Francis to Lansing, Sept. 24, 1918, RG 59, 861.51/359.

13. Paraphrase of telegram from Ambassador Francis, Oct. 1, 1918, RG 59, 861.51/361.

14. Crosby to McAdoo, Sept. 26, 1918, RG 39, Russia, folder 110.

15. Crosby to McAdoo, Sept. 26, 1918; Crosby to Leffingwell, Sept. 17, 1918, RG 59, 861.00/2719.

16. Lansing to Barclay, Oct. 5, 1918, RG 59, 861.51/392a. The objections stated in this memo probably originated in the Treasury Department.

17. Lansing to Barclay, Oct. 5, 1918.

18. Extract of War Trade Board minutes, Oct. 4, 1918, RG 182, box 1551.

19. Morley, *The Japanese Thrust into Siberia*, 216.

20. Barclay to Lansing, Oct. 16, 1918, RG 59, 861.51/392.

21. Department of State to British Embassy, Oct. 21, 1918, RG 59, 861.51/392.

22. Cravath to McAdoo, Oct. 26, 1918, RG 59, 861.51/380.

23. Albert Rathbone to Oscar T. Crosby, Nov. 2, 1918, RG 59, 861.51/382; War Trade Board to Owen, Nov. 2, 1918, RG 39, Russia, folder 110. For background on these ruble notes, which had been printed in the United States and which the Russian Embassy in Washington wanted to use as an emergency currency, see Caldwell to Lansing, Oct. 23, 1918, RG 59, 861.51/379; Bakhmetev to Polk, Oct. 25, 1918, RG 59, 861.51/396; Lansing to Baker, Oct. 30, 1918, RG 59, 861.51/384.

24. This summary was cabled to War Trade Board representative Owen as an instruction. Owen was en route to Archangel for the purpose of examining monetary conditions there and to gain Britain's acceptance of the United States's position. War Trade Board to Owen, Nov. 2, 1918, RG 39, Russia, folder 110.

25. Memo by Vladimir Novitskii, Oct. 22, 1918, enclosed in, Miles to Van Sinderen, Nov. 1, 1918, RG 182, box 1586.

26. Heid to War Trade Board, Nov. 11, 1918, RG 182, box 1566.

27. Heid to War Trade Board, Oct. 21, 1918, RG 182, box 1566.

28. Heid to War Trade Board, Nov. 11, 1918, RG 182, box 1566.

29. Unterberger, *America's Siberian Intervention*, 102.

30. Ibid., 96.

31. Ibid., 109. Betty M. Unterberger has noted that Britain encouraged Japan to cooperate with the United States in the management of the railroad in order to engage America more deeply in the military aspects of the intervention. Betty M. Unterberger, *The United States, Revolutionary Russia, and the Rise of Czechoslovakia* (Chapel Hill: Univ. of North Carolina Press, 1989), 299.

32. Basil Miles, "Control of Siberian Railways," Oct. 28, 1918, Wilson Papers, ser. 2.

33. Vance McCormick to Lansing, Nov. 8, 1918, RG 59, 861.00/3214½.

34. Morris to Lansing, Nov. 8, 1918, RG 59, 861.77/544.

35. Morris to Lansing, Oct. 6, 1918, RG 59, 861.515/42.

36. Paraphrase of cable from John Sukin to Russian Embassy, Oct. 21, 1918, RG 182, box 1566.

37. Morris to Lansing, Oct. 6, 1918, RG 59, 861.515/42.

38. Heid to War Trade Board, Oct. 17, 1918, RG 182, box 1566.

39. Van Sinderen to Strauss, Oct. 27, 1918, Rathbone to Lansing, Oct. 30, 1918, RG 39, Russia, folder 57.

40. Owen to War Trade Board, Nov. 16, 1918, RG 182, box 1566.

41. "Memorandum for Captain Van Sinderen," L. K. Thorne, Nov. 27, 1918, RG 182, box 1566.

42. "Memorandum for Major Dulles," L. K. Thorne, Dec. 10, 1918, RG 182, box 1566.

43. Dulles to Thorne, Dec. 10, 1918, RG 182, box 1566.

44. The Russian Embassy Proposal for a Temporary Ruble Plan, Aug. 28, 1918, Wilson Papers, ser. 4.

45. "Memorandum on Trade Certificates," L. K. Thorne, Dec. 14, 1918, RG 182, box 1566.

46. "Memorandum for Captain Van Sinderen," L. K. Thorne, Dec. 16, 1918, RG 182, box 1566.

47. The clauses in the Versailles Treaty that repealed the Brest-Litovsk Treaty are reprinted in John W. Wheeler-Bennett, *The Forgotten Peace: Brest-Litovsk, March 1918* (New York: Morrow & Co., 1939), 451–53.

48. E. A. Brittenham to International Harvester Company, Jan. 11, 1919, International Harvester Archives, file 1241.

49. Brittenham to International Harvester, Jan. 11, 1919.

7. An Insoluble Dilemma: Economic Assistance and the Kolchak Government

1. Barclay to Lansing, Oct. 3, 1918, RG 59, 861.77/515.

2. Morris to Lansing, Nov. 8, 1918, RG 59, 861.77/544.

3. Morley, *The Japanese Thrust into Siberia*, 205.

4. Ibid., 204–7.

5. Morris to Lansing, Nov. 8, 1918, RG 59, 861.77/544.

6. Morris to Lansing, Nov. 30, 1918, RG 59, 861.77/563.

7. Stevens's threat to withdraw badly needed lubricating oils unless he received complete control over the railroad can be traced through the following cables, Stevens to Lansing, Sept. 13, 1918, RG 59, 861.77/478; Stevens to Lansing, Sept. 28, 1918, RG 59, 861.77/502; Stevens to Lansing, Nov. 15, 1918, RG 59, 861.77/549; Heid to Lansing, Dec. 9, 1918, enclosed in, Woolley to Polk, Jan. 15, 1919, RG 59, 861.77/620.

8. Stevens to MacGowan, June 17, 1922, RG 59, 861.77/3387.

9. Reinsch to Lansing, Feb. 18, 1919, RG 59, 861.77/684.

10. Polk to American Mission at Paris, Jan. 14, 1919, RG 59, 861.77/612.

11. American Mission to Polk, Jan. 21, 1919, RG 59, 861.77/634.

12. Polk to American Mission at Paris, Jan. 24, 1919, RG 59, 861.77/634.

13. "Assails President for Use of Big Fund," *New York Times*, Jan. 14, 1919, 4.

14. American Mission to Polk, Jan. 31, 1919, RG 59, 861.77/655.

15. American Mission to Polk, Jan. 31, 1919.

16. Polk to American Mission, Feb. 4, 1919, RG 59, 861.77/655.

17. Wilson to Lansing, Jan. 10, 1919, Wilson Papers, ser. 5B.

18. Levin, *Woodrow Wilson and World Politics*, 206–18. See also, John M. Thompson, *Russia, Bolshevism and the Versailles Peace* (Princeton, N.J.: Princeton Univ. Press, 1966), 82–130.

19. Polk to American Mission, Feb. 4, 1919.

20. Polk to American Mission, Feb. 4, 1919.

21. McCormick to Lansing, Dec. 24, 1918, RG 59, 661.119/304i.

22. Extract from a report of the commander-in-chief of the Asiatic Station at Vladivostok [Admiral Knight], dated Dec. 29, 1919, in Josephus Daniels to Secretary of State (undated, early March 1919), RG 59, 661.119/338.

23. Woolley to American Embassy at Paris (for McCormick), Feb. 24, 1919, RG 39, Russia, file 212.20a.

24. Miles to Stanert, Feb. 21, 1919, RG 182, box 1571.

25. Stevens to Secretary of State, Mar. 15, 1919, RG 39, Russia, file 212.20a; Smith to Polk, Mar. 17, 1919, RG 59, 861.77/750.

26. Minutes of Inter-Allied Railway Committee, Mar. 18, 1919, enclosed in Smith to Colby, Nov. 12, 1920, RG 59, 861.77/1882.

27. "Outline of the Activities of the Inter-Allied Railway Committee for the Supervision of the Siberian and Chinese Eastern Railway's, 1919–1922," unsigned, Oct. 1922, 31, RG 59, 861.77/3387.

28. Minutes of the Inter–Allied Railway Committee, Apr. 7–8, 1919, enclosed in Smith to Colby, Nov. 12, 1920, RG 59, 861.77/1882.

29. Polk to Stevens, Mar. 14, 1919, RG 59, 861.77/761a.

30. Polk to American Mission, Mar. 21, 1919, RG 59, 861.51/526b.

31. Phillips to American Mission, Mar. 28, 1919, RG 59, 861.77/759.

32. Phillips to American Mission, Mar. 28, 1919.

33. Polk to Morris, May 6, 1919, RG 59, 861.77/827.

34. Dorothy Q. Reed to Samuel N. Harper, May 27, 1919, Samuel N. Harper Papers, box 6.

35. Morris to Polk, Apr. 12, 1919, RG 59, 861.00/4266; Morris to Polk, Apr. 19, 1919, 861.00/4332; Polk to American Mission, Apr. 24, 1919, RG 59, 861.00/4543a.

36. American Mission to Polk, Apr. 16, 1919, RG 59, 861.51/549; American Mission to Polk, Apr. 21, 1919, RG 59, 861.51/551.

37. American Mission to Polk, Apr. 16, 1919, RG 59, 861.51/549.

38. Polk to American Mission, Apr. 26, 1919, RG 59, 861.51/549.

39. American Mission to Polk, May 5, 1919, RG 59, 861.77/831.

40. U.S. Congress, House, Sundry Civil Appropriation Bill, H.R. 6176, 66th Cong., 1st Sess., June 20, 1919, 58, pt. 2: 1069–2142.

41. Polk to American Mission, May 9, 1919, RG 59, 861.77/831.

42. American Mission to Polk, May 16, 1919, RG 59, 861.77/851.

43. American Mission to Polk, May 5, 1919, RG 59, 861.77/831.

44. "Memorandum of conversation with Mr. Alexander Kerensky at Paris," May 4, 1919, RG 59, 861.00/598; see also Thompson, *Russia, Bolshevism and the Versailles Peace,* 291–92.

45. Polk to American Mission, May 6, 1919, RG 59, 861.00/4435.

46. Polk to Morris, May 15, 1919, RG 59, 861.00/4536b.

47. Notes of a meeting held at President Wilson's house in the Place des Etats-Unis, Paris, on Friday, May 23, 1919, 180.03401/26, *FRUS, 1919,* Russia, 354–55.

48. American Mission to Polk, May 26, 1919, RG 59, 861.51/587.

49. American Mission to Polk, June 25, 1919, RG 59, 861.01/71.

50. Wilson to Lansing, May 28, 1919, Wilson Papers, ser. 5B; Phillips to American Mission, Mar. 27, 1919, Wilson Papers, ser. 5B. Subsequently, the War Department extended an $8 million credit to the Omsk regime, only $1 million more than it had given the Czechs. See D. C. Poole's memoranda to Phillips regarding U.S. matériel aid to Russia on Nov. 8 and 11, 1919, RG 59, 861.77/2010, 861.00/5879. In June, the Omsk regime also entered into negotiations with a consortium of Allied banks, including the Equitable Trust Company and the National City Bank, in order to purchase munitions on the basis of a 10 percent initial cash payment. Polk to American Mission, June 27, 1919, 861.01/71; Harris to Polk, July 9, 1919, RG 59, 861.24/155. These negotiations were initially given full support by the Wilson administration, but the American banks backed out in the early fall when they lost confidence in the Omsk regime. British sources indicate that Ambassador Morris's negative views of the Omsk government were responsible for the decision by the American banks to break off the loan negotiations. See O'Reilly to Lord Curzon, Sept. 27, 1919, no. 798 [136302/11/57], published in Rohan Butler and E. L. Woodward, eds. *Documents on British Foreign Policy, 1919–1939,* ser. 1:3, 1919 (London: His Majesty's Stationary Office, 1949), 573–74 (hereafter cited as *DBFP*).

51. Diary of Vance C. McCormick (microfilm), June 23, 1919, MS group 478, HM 74, Vance C. McCormick Papers; American Mission to Polk, June 25, 1919, RG 59, 861.01/71.

52. Diary of Vance C. McCormick, June 23, 1919; Hoover to Wilson, June 21, 1919, RG 59, 861.00/786.

53. Smith to Lansing, May 31, 1919, RG 59, 861.77/875½.

54. Smith to Lansing, Aug. 20, 1919, RG 59, 861.77/1031.

55. Polk to Morris, July 11, 1919, RG 59, 861.77/978a.

56. Wilson to the President of the Senate, July 22, 1919, *FRUS,* 1919, Russia, 391–94.

57. Morris to Polk, July 22, 1919, RG 59, 861.00/4905.

58. Morris to Polk, July 27, 1919, RG 59, 861.00/4931.

59. Emerson to Stevens, May 11, 1919, Stevens to Chairman of Inter-Allied Railway Committee, May 12, 1919, Record Group 43, "Records of the Advisory Commission of Railway Experts to Russia, the Russian Railway Service Corps and the inter-Allied Railway Committee, 1917–1922," Vladivostok (U.S. National Archives Microfilm, located at the Hoover Institute Library, Stanford, California), reel 28 (hereafter cited as RG 43, U.S. Commission of Railway Experts to Russia, followed by the reel number).

60. Emerson to Stevens, May 11, 1919, Stevens to Chairman of Inter-Allied Railway Committee, May 12, 1919, RG 43, reel 28.

61. Johnson to Stevens, Jan. 3, 1920, RG 43, U.S. Commission of Railway Experts to Russia, reel 36.

62. A. G. Peterson to Tower, Sept. 22, 1919, RG 43, U.S. Commission of Railway Experts to Russia, reel 28.

63. Johnson to Stevens, Dec. 23, 1919, RG 43, U.S. Commission of Railway Experts to Russia, reel 28.

64. Charles H. Smith, "Four Years of Mistakes in Siberia," *Asia* 22 (June 1922): 482.

65. Smith to State Department, May 5, 1919, RG 59, 861.51/588.

66. Smith to State Department, May 5, 1919. It is interesting to note that in 1992 most of the $670 million loaned to the Russian Republic from the World Bank was used to purchase transportation and agricultural equipment. See Louis Uchitelle, "New Man Old Burden: Moscow Owes $86 Billion," *New York Times,* Dec. 16, 1992. N. Gordon Levin has described the unsuccessful attempt to establish the Hoover-Nansen Relief Commission for Soviet Russia during the spring of 1919 as a precursor to the Marshall Plan. Levin, *Woodrow Wilson and World Politics,* 191, 203, 218. For a discussion of the failed Hoover-Nansen proposal see, Thompson, *Russia, Bolshevism, and the Versailles Peace,* 247–67. Hoover's later famine relief program for Soviet Russia during 1921–23 can also be viewed in this light. See Benjamin Weissman, *Herbert Hoover and Famine Relief to Soviet Russia,* 1921–1923 (Stanford, Calif.: Hoover Institute Press, 1974).

67. State Department to Heid, Mar. 6, 1919, RG 59, 661.119/342b.

68. Heid to War Trade Board, Mar. 22, 1919, RG 59, 661.119/353.

69. Heid to War Trade Board, Apr. 15, 1919, RG 59, 661.119/388.

70. Polk to Heid, June 27, 1919, RG 59, 811.24/406a; Lansing to Harris, Aug. 25, 1919, RG 59, 861.00/5127a. For copies of the initial contracts see, "United States of America and Union of Siberian Co-operative Unions Inc., Purchase, Storage, and Traffic Division, U.S. Army, Contract for Sale of General Merchandise," June 20, 1919, Morris Papers, box 9.

71. War Trade Board to Heid, Apr. 3, 1919, RG 59, 661.119/363.

72. Heid to State Department, Sept. 20, 1919, RG 59, 861.00/5248.

73. Harris to State Department, May 28, 1919, RG 59, 861.51/590.

74. Smith, "Four Years of Mistakes in Siberia," 482.

75. Undated, Unsigned memorandum, Morris Papers, box 9.

76. Jenkins to State Department, Aug. 2, 1919, RG 59, 861.77/984; Stevens to State Department, Aug. 4, 1919, RG 59, 861.77/988; "Outline of the Activities of the Inter-Allied Railway Committee for the Supervision of the Siberian and Chinese Eastern Railways, 1919–1922," Oct. 1922, RG 59, 861.77/3387.

77. Smith to State Department, Aug. 1, 1919, RG 59, 861.77/978.

78. Smith, "Four Years of Mistakes in Siberia," 482.

79. Stevens to Emerson, July 17, 1919, RG 43, U.S. Commission of Railway Experts to Russia, reel 28.

80. Emerson to Johnson, Aug. 2, 1919, RG 43, U.S. Commission of Railway Experts to Russia, reel 28.

81. Smith to Lansing, Aug. 6, 1919, RG 59, 861.77/997.

82. Morris to State Department, Aug. 4, 1919, RG 59, 861.00/4990.

83. Memorandum on meeting between Finance Ministry and Allied Representatives, July 30, 1919, Roland S. Morris Papers, box 9; Morris to State Department, Aug. 4, 1919, RG 59, 861.51/646.

84. Morris to Lansing, Aug. 16, 1919, RG 59, 861.01/116.

85. Morris to Lansing, Aug. 4, 1919, RG 59, 861.00/4990.

86. Morris to Lansing, Aug. 11, 1919, RG 59, 861.01/106.

87. Emerson to Stevens, Sept. 14,18, 1919, RG 43, U.S. Commission of Railway Experts to Russia, reel 28.

88. Johnson to Stevens, Jan. 3, 1920, RG 43, U.S. Commission of Railway Experts to Russia, reel 36.

89. O'Reilly to Gregory, Aug. 25, 1919, no. 404 [140080/11/57], *DBFP*, ser. 1: 3, 1919, 529.

90. Basil Miles Memorandum, "Russia and the Peace Conference," Sept. 9, 1919, RG 59, 861.00/5461.

91. Basil Miles Memorandum for the Secretary of State, Sept. 29, 1919, RG 59, 861.00/5288.

92. Robert Lansing, "The Suggested Recognition of the Kolchak Government," Oct. 9, 1919, Lansing Papers, Private Memoranda, box 2, reel 1.

93. Lansing to Morris, Nov. 19, 1919, RG 59, 861.00/5665.

94. Lansing to Wilson, Dec. 3, 1919, RG 59, 861.00/5829a, enclosed in Lansing to Wilson, Dec. 4, 1919, RG 59, 861.00/5845a.

95. Lansing to Wilson, Dec. 3, 1919; Carl P. Parrini, *Heir to Empire: United States Economic Diplomacy, 1916–1923* (Pittsburgh: Univ. of Pittsburgh Press, 1969), 49.

96. Lansing to Wilson, Dec. 3, 1919. In a memorandum to William Phillips on Nov. 7, 1919, Poole explained that some force would be needed to "oust" the Bolsheviks when their social basis of support had eroded following an improvement in social and economic conditions. He therefore placed military assistance under the category of a "police measure." Enclosed in Poole to Phillips, Nov. 11, 1919, RG 59, 861.00/5879.

97. Norman G. O. Periera, "The Partisan Movement in Western Siberia, 1918–1920," *Jahrbucher fur Geschichte Osteuropas* 38 (1990): 87–97.

8. *A Critical Juncture: The Chinese Eastern Railway in Far Eastern Rivalries, 1920–22*

1. Memorandum by Thomas W. Lamont of his conversation with John Stevens May 2, 1920, RG 59, 861.77/1574.

2. Stevens to Lansing, Dec. 12, 1919, RG 59, 861.77/1247.

3. Notes on Economic Conditions in Foreign Countries, Manchuria, Department of State, *Foreign Trade Adviser's Office, Economic Intelligence Section Weekly Report*, no. 16, Nov. 22, 1919, RG 151, file 151.2.

4. Stevens to Lansing, Jan. 6, 1920, RG 59, 861.77/1281.

5. Stevens to Lansing, Dec. 12, 1919, RG 59, 861.77/1247.

6. "Outline of the Activities of the Inter-Allied Railway Committee for the Supervision of the Siberian and Chinese Eastern Railways, 1919–1922," unsigned, Oct. 1922, RG 59, 861.77/3387. In early May, the Technical Board announced it would no longer accept Siberian rubles as payment for

transportation charges on the Chinese Eastern Railway. Stevens to the Administration of the Chinese Eastern Railway, May 3, 1920, enclosed in, Stevens to Vyvodtzev, May 24, 1920, RG 43, U.S. Commission of Railway Experts to Russia, reel 2.

7. Stevens to Colby, July 21, 1920, RG 59, 861.77/1629.

8. E. H. Carr, *The Bolshevik Revolution, 1917–1923* (London: Macmillan, 1953), 3:504–6.

9. Davis to Colby, Apr. 28, 1920, RG 59, 861.77/1493; Colby to Bell, May 17, 1920, RG 59, 861.77/1533c.

10. Tenney to Colby, Apr. 15, 1920, RG 59, 893.51/2773.

11. Memorandum from Bakhmetev to Polk, May 7, 1920, RG 59, 861.77/1513.

12. Colby to Bell, May 17, 1920, RG 59, 861.77/1533c.

13. Davis to Colby, May 22, 1920, RG 59, 861.77/1534.

14. Colby to Davis, May 27, 1920, RG 59, 861.77/1534.

15. Colby to Tenney, Apr. 21, 1920, RG 59, 893.51/2775.

16. Colby to Davis, May 27, 1920.

17. Memorandum by John V. A. MacMurray, June 15, 1920, RG 59, 861.77/1569; Colby to Bell, June 19, 1920, RG 59, 861.77/1568; Davis to Davis, June 30, 1920, RG 59, 861.77/1583.

18. Geddes to Curzon, June 15, 1920, no. 444 [F 1179/19/10], *DBFP,* ser. 1:14, Apr. 1920–Feb. 1922, 42.

19. Colby to Davis, June 19, 1920, RG 59, 861.77/1568.

20. Stevens to Colby, May 19, 1920, RG 59, 861.77/1527; Smith to Colby, May 22, 1920, RG 59, 861.77/1535; Davis to Davis, June 30, 1920, RG 59, 861.77/1583.

21. Bell to Colby, June 23, 1920, RG 59, 861.77/1583.

22. Davis to Davis, June 30, 1920, RG 59, 861.77/1583.

23. Davis to Colby, July 8, 1920, RG 59, 861.77/1600.

24. Memorandum by Ashton-Gwatkin on Japan and the Open Door, July 7, 1920 [F 2142/2142/10], *DBFP,* ser. 1:14, Apr. 1920–Feb. 1922, 57–66.

25. Curzon to Sir B. Alston, Oct. 24, 1921, no. 1013 [F 3924/2635/10], *DBFP,* ser. 1:14: Apr. 1920–Feb. 1922, 451–52.

26. Stevens to Colby, July 19, 1920, RG 59, 861.77/1614.

27. Lamont to Davis, Oct. 18, 1920, RG 59, 861.77/1773.

28. Bell to Colby, Nov. 5, 1920, RG 59, 861.77/1804.

29. Davis to Davis, Dec. 28, 1920, RG 59, 861.77/1902.

30. "Memorandum by the Department of State," Jan. 13, 1921, RG 59, 861.77/2082b.

31. Poole to Colby, Jan. 14, 1921, RG 59, 861.77/2390.

32. Portion of a conversation between Secretary Colby, the British ambassador and Mr. Norman H. Davis, Feb. 24, 1921, RG 59, 861.77/2015.

33. Hughes to Crane, Apr. 13, 1921, RG 59, 861.77/2033; Hughes to Geddes, Apr. 25, 1921, RG 59, 861.77/2054a; Hughes to Wright, Apr. 27, 1921, RG 59, 861.77/1962.

34. Chilton to Hughes, May 14, 1921, RG 59, 861.77/2077.

35. Memorandum by John MacMurray to Hughes, May 18, 1921, RG 59, 861.77/2427.

36. E. W. Edwards, *British Diplomacy and Finance in China, 1895–1914* (New York: Oxford Univ. Press, 1987), 184–86.

37. Memorandum by John MacMurray to Hughes, May 18, 1921, RG 59, 861.77/2427; MacMurray to Hughes, May 25, 1921, RG 59, 861.77/2426.

38. This information is derived from daily letters Benjamin Johnson, the acting Technical Board president in Stevens's absence, received regarding social and political matters from Paul T. Pastall, acting special transportation inspector. See Pastall to Johnson, Nov. 6, 9, 10, 1920, RG 43, U.S. Commission of Railway Experts to Russia, reel 19. See also, the biographical sketch of the Russian and Chinese directors of the Chinese Eastern Railroad enclosed in, Crane to Hughes, Mar. 18, 1921, RG 59, 861.77/2053.

39. Johnson to Stevens, Feb. 19, Apr. 25, 1921, RG 43, U.S. Commission of Railway Experts to Russia, reel 16.

40. Johnson to Stevens, Mar. 18, 1921, RG 43, U.S. Commission of Railway Experts to Russia, reel 16.

41. Minutes of the Technical Board, May 6, 1921, RG 59, 861.77/3387.

42. Johnson to Stevens, May 16, 1921, RG 43, U.S. Commission of Railway Experts to Russia, reel 16.

43. Johnson to Crane, Apr. 28, 1921, enclosed in Crane to Hughes, May 28, 1921, RG 59, 861.77/2164.

44. "The Chinese Eastern Railway," *Peking and Tientsin Times,* July 11, 1921, enclosure 6F, in Ruddock to Hughes, July 16, 1921, RG 59, 861.77/2209.

45. "Col. J. F. Stevens to Fight New C.E. Bonds," *The Peking Leader,* July 10, 1921, enclosure 6E, in Ruddock to Hughes, July 16, 1921.

46. Memorandum of interview between A. B. Ruddock and Dr. Yen, July 13, 1921, enclosure 4, in Ruddock to Hughes, July 16, 1921; Stevens to Hughes, July 6, 1921, RG 59, 861.77/2143.

47. Ruddock to Hughes, July 16, 1921. This dispatch summarizes the contents of the seven enclosed documents, RG 59, 861.77/2209.

48. Ruddock to Stevens, July 8, 1921, enclosure 1, in Ruddock to Hughes, July 16, 1921.

49. Interview between A. B. Ruddock and W. W. Yen, Aug. 3, 1921, enclosure 1, in Ruddock to Hughes, Aug. 6, 1921, RG 59, 861.77/2232.

50. Edwards, *British Diplomacy and Finance in China,* 94–95.

51. Addis to Morgan Grenfell and Company, June 29, 1921, enclosed in Morgan Grenfell to J.P. Morgan and Company, June 30, 1921, RG 59, 861.77/2184.

52. Hughes to Bell, Aug. 2, 1921, RG 59, 861.77/2167.

53. J. P. Morgan and Company to Hughes, Aug. 2, 1921, RG 59, 861.77/2184.

54. J. Paul Jameson Memorandum on J. P. Morgan and Company note to State Department, Aug. 2, 1921, RG 59, 861.77/2184.

55. Hughes to J. P. Morgan and Company, Aug. 8, 1921, RG 59, 861.77/2184.

56. Stevens to Hughes, Aug. 11, 1921, RG 59, 861.77/2199, 2200.

57. Stevens to Hughes, Aug. 9, 1921, RG 59, 861.77/2196.

58. J. P. Morgan and Company to Hughes, Aug. 23, 1921, RG 59, 861.77/2214.

59. For a very good survey of the Washington Naval Conference see, Thomas H. Buckley, *The United States and the Washington Conference,* 1921–1922 (Knoxville: Univ. of Tennessee Press, 1970).

60. Warren to Hughes, Oct. 29, 1921, RG 59, 861.77/2301.

61. John F. Stevens, "Memorandum in Connection with a Suggested Plan for the International Control of the Chinese Eastern Railway submitted at the request of the Department of State," Dec. 9, 1921, Charles Evans Hughes Papers, box 161, reel 124.

62. D. C. Poole to Hughes, Dec. 3, 1921, RG 59, 861.77/2465.

63. Hughes to Schurman, Dec. 24, 1921, RG 59, 861.77/2364a.

64. Schurman to Hughes, Jan. 1, 1922, RG 59, 861.77/2370.

65. Hughes to Schurman, Jan. 10, 1922, RG 59, 861.77/2377.

66. Hughes to Schurman, Jan. 19, 1922, RG 59, 861.77/2390.

67. Schurman to Hughes, Feb. 2, 1922, RG 59, 861.77/2404.

68. Fletcher to Warren, Feb. 16, 1922, RG 59, 861.77/2425a.

69. "Report of the Technical Sub-Committee on the Chinese Eastern Railway," enclosed in Charles Evans Hughes Papers, box 161, reel 124.

70. "Observations Made by Dr. Hawkling Yen, Chinese Representative of the Sub-Committee on the Chinese Eastern Railway," Hughes Papers, box 161, reel 124.

71. Westel W. Willoughby, *China at the Conference: A Report* (Baltimore: Johns Hopkins Univ. Press, 1922), 230–32; U.S., Congress, Senate, Conference on the Limitation of Armament, S. Doc., 126, 67th Cong., 2nd Sess., 10: 1922, 750–53.

72. Hughes to Schurman, Feb. 3, 1922, RG 59, 861.77/2408a.

73. Schurman to Hughes, Feb. 22, 1922, RG 59, 861.77/2431.

74. Stevens to Hughes, Jan. 31, 1922, Hughes to Root, Jan. 31, 1922, RG 59, 861.77/2588.

75. Stevens to Hughes, May 25, 1922, RG 59, 861.77/2552.

76. Schurman to Hughes, Mar. 25, 1922, RG 59, 861.77/2489; Schurman to Hughes, Mar. 28, 1922, RG 59, 861.77/2494.

77. Johnson to Hughes, Mar. 13, 1922, RG 59, 861.77/2457.

78. This ratio refers to the difference between the prewar gold standard value of the ruble and the depreciated value of the ruble following its devaluation after the outbreak of war in August 1914.

79. Technical Board Minutes, July 15, 1921, RG 59, 861.77/3387.

80. Technical Board Minutes, Sept. 6, 1921, RG 59, 861.77/3387.

81. Technical Board Minutes, Aug. 19, 1921, RG 59, 861.77/3387; Inter-Allied Railway Committee Minutes, Oct. 13, 1921, RG 43, U.S. Commission of Railway Experts to Russia, reel 5.

82. Technical Board Minutes, Sept. 6, 1921, RG 59, 861.77/3387.

83. Beckett to Stevens, June 12, 1922, RG 43, U.S. Commission of Railway Experts to Russia, reel 26; Technical Board Minutes, June 19, 29, 1922, RG 59, 861.77/3387.

84. Stevens to Hughes, May 3, 1922, RG 59, 861.77/2519.

85. Stevens to Hughes, July 8, 1922, RG 59, 861.77/2603; Stevens to D. B. MacGowan, "Enclosed Memo of Changchun Conference," July, 10, 1922, RG 59, 861.77/3387.

86. For a discussion of the 1920 Transportation Act see, K. Austin Kerr, *American Railroad Politics, 1914-1920: Rates, Wages, Efficiency* (Pittsburgh: Univ. of Pittsburgh Press, 1968), 222–27.

87. Inter-Allied Railway Committee Minutes, Feb. 24, 1922, RG 59, 861.77/3387.

88. Stevens to Hughes, Jan. 6, 1920, RG 59, 861.77/1283.

89. Poole to Hughes, Dec. 3, 1921, RG 59, 861.77/2465.

90. Warren to Hughes, Jan. 17, 1922, RG 59, 861.77/2382; Warren to Hughes, Dec. 6, 1921, RG 59, 861.77/2342.

91. Johnson to Stevens, Mar. 3, 1922, RG 59, 861.77/2439.

92. Stevens to Johnson, Mar. 14, 1922, RG 59, 861.77/2460; D. C. Poole to Hughes, Mar. 9, 1922, RG 59, 861.77/2543.

93. Johnson to Stevens, Mar. 17, 1922, RG 59, 861.77/2470.

94. Stevens to Hughes, May 8, 1922, RG 59, 861.77/2526.

95. Hanson to Hughes, Sept. 20, 1922, RG 151, file 520.

96. E. G. Pauly to T. R. Taylor, Nov. 9, 1922, RG 151, file 520.

Conclusion

1. Martin Walker, "Russia and the West: What Is to Be Done Now" *World Policy Journal* 11: 1 (Spring 1994): 1–10. For a good explanation of the European Payments Union see Philip A. S. Taylor, *A New Dictionary of Economics* (London: Routledge & Kegan Paul, 1969), 99–101. Also see, Fred Block, *The Origins of International Economic Disorder: A Study of United States International Monetary Policy from World War II to the Present* (Berkeley: Univ. of California Press, 1977), 100–102.

2. Dean Acheson, "A Democrat Looks at His Party," in his *Private Thoughts on Public Affairs* (New York: Harcourt, Brace & World, 1955), 156–57. For Woodrow Wilson's views see his, *The State: Elements of Historical and Practical Politics* (Boston: Heath, 1918). Thomas Knock's *To End All Wars: Woodrow Wilson and the Quest for a New World Order* (New York: Oxford Univ. Press, 1992) demonstrates

that Wilson's progressivism, both in the national and international arenas, was influenced by the broad social democratic reform currents of the time.

3. Walter LaFeber has noted that the Marshall Plan "marked the last phase in the Administration's use of economic tactics as the primary means of tying together the western world," in his *America, Russia and the Cold War, 1945–1992*, 7th ed. (New York: McGraw-Hill, 1993), 62.

4. Charles S. Maier, "American Visions and British Interests: Hogan's Marshall Plan," *Reviews in American History* 18 (Mar. 1990): 107. Maier and Michael Hogan also note that American officials were divided over the question of currency convertibility in the late 1940s. Keynesian-influenced officials in the European Cooperating Committee preferred to be flexible about currency convertibility and payments deficits in the short and medium term because they could use Marshall Plan aid to reduce the external pressure on European currencies. In contrast, Treasury Department officials and IMF representatives insisted on rapid convertibility, even if it resulted in deflation. Charles Maier, "The Two Post-War Eras and the Conditions for Stability in Twentieth-Century Europe," in his *In Search of Stability: Explorations in Historical Political Economy* (Cambridge: Cambridge Univ. Press, 1987), 153–84; Michael J. Hogan, *The Marshall Plan: America, Britain, and the Reconstruction of Western Europe, 1947–1952* (New York: Cambridge Univ. Press, 1987).

5. Richard M. Freeland, *The Truman Doctrine and the Origins of McCarthyism: Foreign Policy, Domestic Politics, and Internal Security: 1946–1948* (New York: Schocken, 1971).

Bibliography

Archival Materials

Historical Files of the American Expeditionary Forces in Siberia, 1918–1920. RG 395. Microfilm Publication M917. National Archives, Washington, D.C.

International Harvester Archives, Navistar Corporation, Chicago, Illinois.

Records of the Advisory Commission of Railway Experts to Russia, the Russian Railway Service Corps and the Inter-Allied Railway Committee, 1917–1922. RG 43. Microfilm made by the U.S. National Archives. Deposited at the Hoover Institute Library. Stanford, California.

U.S. Department of Commerce. General Records of the Department of Commerce, 1918–1933. RG 40. National Archives, Washington, D.C.

——. Records of the Bureau of Foreign and Domestic Commerce, 1918–1933. RG 151. National Archives, Washington, D.C.

——. General Records of the Department of State. RG 59. National Archives, Washington D.C.

——. Records of the U.S. Department of State Relating to United States Commercial Relations with Russia/Soviet Union, 1910–1929. RG 59. National Archives. Washington, D.C.

——. Records Relating to the Internal Affairs of Russia and the Soviet Union, 1910-1929. RG 59. National Archives. Washington, D.C.

U.S. Department of Treasury. Country File: Russia. RG 39. National Archives, Washington, D.C.

U.S. War Trade Board. Records of the Russian Bureau. RG 182. National Archives, Suitland, Maryland.

Manuscript Collections

Gordon Auchincloss Papers. Yale University Library, New Haven, Connecticut.

Tasker Bliss Papers. Library of Congress, Washington, D.C.

Richard Crane Papers. Georgetown University, Washington, D.C.

Samuel N. Harper Papers. University of Chicago Library, Chicago.

Edward M. House Papers. Yale University Library, New Haven, Connecticut.

Charles Evans Hughes Papers. Library of Congress Microfilm, Washington, D.C.

Robert Lansing Papers. Library of Congress, Washington, D.C.

Breckinridge Long Papers. Library of Congress, Washington, D.C.

Cyrus H. McCormick Jr. Papers. Wisconsin State Historical Society, Madison, Wisconsin.

Vance C. McCormick Diary. Yale University Library, New Haven, Connecticut.

Roland S. Morris Papers. Library of Congress, Washington, D.C.

Frank L. Polk Papers. Yale University, New Haven, Connecticut.

Woodrow Wilson Papers. Presidential Papers Microfilm, Library of Congress, Washington, D.C.

William Wiseman Papers. Yale University Library, New Haven, Connecticut.

Published Documents

Documents on British Foreign Policy, 1919–1939. Series 1. E. L. Woodward and Rohan Butler, eds. London: H. M. Stationery Office, 1949.

U.S. Department of State. Papers Relating to the Foreign Relations of the United States (FRUS). 1917–23. Washington, D.C.: GPO, 1931–40.

Select Published Sources

Acheson, Dean. Private Thoughts on Public Affairs. New York: Harcourt, Brace & World, 1955.

Baker, Ray Stannard, ed. Woodrow Wilson Life and Letters. 9 Vols. New York: Doubleday, Doran, 1939.

Bell, Sidney. Righteous Conquest: Woodrow Wilson and the Evolution of the New Diplomacy. Port Washington, N.Y.: Kennikat Press, 1972.

Block, Fred. The Origins of International Economic Disorder: A Study of United States International Monetary Policy from World War II to the Present. Berkeley: Univ. of California Press, 1977.

Bradley, John. Allied Intervention in Russia. New York: Basic Books, 1968.

Browder, Robert P., and Alexander Kerensky, eds. The Russian Revolution, 1917, Documents. Stanford, Calif.: Stanford University Press, 1961.

Buckley, Thomas H. *The United States and the Washington Conference, 1921–1922.* Knoxville: University of Tennesse Press, 1970.

Bullard, Arthur. *The Russian Pendulum: Autocracy, Democracy, Bolshevism.* New York: Macmillan, 1919.

Calhoun, Frederick. *Power and Principle: Armed Intervention in Wilsonian Foreign Policy.* Kent, Ohio: Kent State Univ. Press, 1986.

Carr, Edward H. *The Bolshevik Revolution, 1917–1923,* 3 Vols. London: Macmillan, 1953.

Carstensen, Fred, and Gregory Guroff, eds. *Entrepreneurship in Imperial Russia and the Soviet Union.* Princeton, N.J., Princeton University Press, 1983.

Carstensen, Fred V. *American Enterprise in Foreign Markets: Studies of Singer and International Harvester in Imperial Russia.* Chapel Hill: Univ. of North Carolina Press, 1984.

Conant, Charles A. "The Economic Basis of Imperialism." *North American Review* 167 (Sept. 1898): 326–40.

Curry, Roy Watson. *Woodrow Wilson and Far Eastern Policy, 1913–1921.* New York: Bookman, 1957.

Davis, Clarence B. *Partners and Rivals: Britain's Imperial Diplomacy Concerning the United States and Japan in China, 1915–1922.* New York: Garland, 1987.

Dayer, Roberta A. *Bankers and Diplomats in China, 1917–1925: The Anglo-American Relationship.* London: Frank Cass, 1981.

Debo, Richard K. *Revolution and Survival: The Foreign Policy of Soviet Russia, 1917–1918.* Toronto: Univ. of Toronto Press, 1979.

——. *Survival and Consolidation: The Foreign Policy of Soviet Russia, 1918–1921.* Montreal: McGill-Queen's Univ. Press, 1992.

Diamond, William. *The Economic Thought of Woodrow Wilson.* Baltimore: Johns Hopkins Univ. Press, 1943.

Dotsenko, Paul. *The Struggle for Democracy in Siberia, 1917–1920: Eyewitness Account of a Contemporary.* Stanford, Calif.: Hoover Institute Press, 1983.

Edwards, Ernest W. *British Diplomacy and Finance in China, 1895–1914.* New York: Oxford Univ. Press, 1987.

Fischer, Fritz. *Germany's Aims in the First World War.* New York: Norton, 1967.

Foglesong, David S. *America's Secret War Against Bolshevism: U.S. Intervention in the Russian Civil War, 1917–1920.* Chapel Hill: Univ. of North Carolina Press, 1995.

Fowler, W. B. *British-American Relations, 1917–1918: The Role of Sir William Wiseman.* Princeton, N.J.: Princeton Univ. Press, 1969.

Freeland, Richard M. *The Truman Doctrine and the Origins of McCarthyism: Foreign Policy, Domestic Politics, and Internal Security, 1946–1948.* New York: Schocken, 1971.

Gardner, Lloyd C. *Safe for Democracy: The Anglo-American Response to Revolution, 1913–1923.* New York: Oxford Univ. Press, 1984.

———. *A Covenant With Power: America and the World from Wilson to Reagan.* New York: Oxford Univ. Press, 1984.

———, ed. *Redefining the Past: Essays in Diplomatic History in Honor of William Appleman Williams.* Corvallis: Oregon State Univ. Press, 1986.

Gramsci, Antonio. *Selections from the Prison Notebooks.* New York: International Publishers, 1971.

Graves, William S. *America's Siberian Adventure, 1918–1920.* New York: Peter Smith, 1941.

Hoff-Wilson, Joan. *Ideology and Economics: U.S. Relations with the Soviet Union, 1918–1933.* Columbia: Univ. of Missouri Press, 1974.

Hogan, Michael J. *The Marshall Plan: America, Britain, and the Reconstruction of Western Europe, 1947–1952.* New York: Cambridge Univ. Press, 1987.

Hoyt, Edwin P. *The Army Without a Country.* New York: Macmillan, 1967.

Ingram, Alton Earl. "The Root Mission to Russia, 1917." Ph.D. diss.: Louisiana State Univ., 1970.

Kaufman, Burton I. *Efficiency and Expansion: Foreign Trade Organization in the Wilson Administration, 1913–1921.* Westport, Conn.: Greenwood Press, 1974.

Kautsky, Karl. "Ultra-Imperialism." *New Left Review* 59 (Jan.–Feb. 1970): 39–46.

Kayden Eugene, and Alexis Antsiferov. *The Cooperative Movement in Russia During the War.* New Haven: Yale Univ. Press, 1929.

Kennan, George. *Siberia and the Exile System.* 2d ed., abridged. Chicago: Univ. of Chicago Press, 1958.

Kennan, George F. *Russia and the West Under Lenin and Stalin.* Boston: Little, Brown, 1961.

———. *Soviet-American Relations 1917–1920,* Vol. 1, *Russia Leaves the War.* Princeton, N.J.: Princeton Univ. Press, 1956.

———. *Soviet-American Relations 1917–1920,* Vol. 2, *The Decision to Intervene.* Princeton, N.J.: Princeton Univ. Press, 1958.

Kerr, K. Austin. *American Railroad Politics, 1914–1920: Rates, Wages, Efficiency.* Pittsburgh: Univ. of Pittsburgh Press, 1968.

Kettle, Michael. *Russia and the Allies, 1917–1920,* Vol. 1, *The Allies and the Russian Collapse, March 1917–March 1918.* Minneapolis: Univ. of Minnesota Press, 1981.

———. *Russia and the Allies, 1917–1920,* Vol. 2, *The Road to Intervention, March–November, 1918.* London: Routledge, 1988.

Killen, Linda. *The Russian Bureau: A Case Study in Wilsonian Diplomacy.* Lexington: Univ. Press of Kentucky, 1983.

Knock, Thomas. *To End All Wars: Woodrow Wilson and the Quest for a New World Order.* New York: Oxford Univ. Press, 1992.

Kolz, Arno W. F. "British Economic Interests in Siberia During the Russian Civil War, 1918–1920." *Journal of Modern History* 48 (Sept. 1976): 483–91.

LaFeber, Walter. *America, Russia, and the Cold War, 1945–1992.* 7th ed. New York: McGraw-Hill, 1993.

Lasch, Christopher. "American Intervention in Siberia: A Reinterpretation." *Political Science Quarterly* 77 (June 1962): 205–33.

Lee, Frederic E. *The Russian Cooperative Movement.* U.S. Department of Commerce. Bureau of Foreign and Domestic Commerce, Miscellaneous series 101. Washington, D.C., 1920.

Levin, N. Gordon. *Woodrow Wilson and World Politics: America's Response to War and Revolution.* New York: Oxford Univ. Press, 1968.

Lincoln, W. Bruce. *The Conquest of a Continent: Siberia and the Russians.* New York: Random House, 1994.

———. *Red Victory: A History of the Russian Civil War.* New York: Simon & Schuster, 1989.

Link, Arthur, ed. *Woodrow Wilson and a Revolutionary World, 1913–1921.* Chapel Hill: Univ. of North Carolina Press, 1982.

———. *The Papers of Woodrow Wilson.* 35 vols., Princeton N.J.: Princeton Univ. Press, 1966–.

Livermore, Seward W. *Politics Is Adjourned: Woodrow Wilson and the War Congress, 1916–1918.* Middleton: Wesleyan Univ. Press, 1966.

Luckett, Richard. *The White Generals: An Account of the White Movement and the Russian Civil War.* New York: Viking, 1971.

McCormick, Thomas J. *America's Half-Century: United States Foreign Policy in the Cold War.* Baltimore: Johns Hopkins Univ. Press, 1989.

McCullough, David. *The Path Between the Seas: The Creation of the Panama Canal, 1870–1914.* New York: Simon & Schuster, 1977.

McFadden, David W. *Alternative Paths: Soviets and Americans, 1917–1920.* New York: Oxford Univ. Press, 1993.

MacMurray, John. *Treaties and Agreements with and Concerning China, 1894–1919,* Vol. 2, *Republican Period, 1912–1919.* New York: Oxford Univ. Press, 1921.

Maddox, Robert J. *The Unknown War with Russia: Wilson's Siberian Intervention.* San Rafael, Calif.: Presidio Press, 1977.

Maier, Charles S. *In Search of Stability: Explorations in Historical Political Economy.* New York: Cambridge Univ. Press, 1987.

———. "American Visions and British Interests: Hogan's Marshall Plan." *Reviews in American History* 18 (March 1990): 102–11.

Matsuda, Takeshi. "Woodrow Wilson's Dollar Diplomacy in the Far East: The New Chinese Consortium 1917–1921." Ph.D. diss., University of Wisconsin, 1979.

Mawdsley, Evan. *The Russian Civil War*. Boston: Allen & Unwin, 1987.

Mayer, Arno J. *Political Origins of the New Diplomacy, 1917–1918*. New York: Vintage, 1970.

———. *Politics and Diplomacy of Peacemaking: Containment and Counterrevolution at Versailles, 1918–1919*. New York: Vintage, 1967.

Morley, James William. *The Japanese Thrust into Siberia*. New York: Columbia Univ. Press, 1957.

Nish, Ian. *Alliance in Decline: A Study in Anglo-Japanese Relations, 1908–1923*. London: Athlone Press, 1972.

Norton, Henry K. *The Far Eastern Republic*. New York: J. Day, 1927.

Notter, Harley. *The Origins of the Foreign Policy of Woodrow Wilson*. Baltimore: Johns Hopkins Univ. Press, 1937.

Palmer, Frederick. *Newton D. Baker: America at War*. New York: Dodd, Meade, 1931.

Parrini, Carl. *Heir to Empire: United States Economic Diplomacy, 1916–1923*. Pittsburgh: Univ. of Pittsburgh Press, 1969.

Parrini, Carl P., and Martin J. Sklar. "New Thinking About the Market, 1896–1904: Some American Economists on Investment and the Theory of Surplus Capital." *Journal of Economic History* 43 (Sept. 1983): 559–78.

Pereira, N. G. O. "The Idea of Siberian Regionalism in Late Imperial and Revolutionary Russia." *Russian History* 20 (1993): 163–78.

———. "The Partisan Movement in Western Siberia, 1918–1920." *Jahrbucher fur Geschichte Osteuropas* 38 (1990): 87–97.

———. "Regional Consciousness in Siberia Before and after October 1917." *Canadian Slavonic Papers* 30 (Mar. 1987): 113–33.

———. "White Power during the Civil War in Siberia (1918–1920): Dilemmas of Kolchak's 'War Anti-Communism.'" *Canadian Slavonic Papers* 29 (Mar. 1987): 45–62.

———. *White Siberia: The Politics of Civil War*. Montreal: McGill-Queen's Univ. Press, 1996.

Polner, Tikhon I. *Russian Local Government during the War and the Union of Zemstvos*. New Haven: Yale Univ. Press, 1930.

Reinsch, Paul S. *An American Diplomat in China*. Garden City, N.Y.: Doubleday, Page, 1922.

Rhodes, Benjamin D. *The Anglo-American Winter War with Russia, 1918–1919: A Diplomatic and Military Tragicomedy*. New York: Greenwood Press, 1988.

Rosenberg, William G. *Liberals in the Russian Revolution: The Constitutional Democratic Party, 1917–1921*. Princeton, N.J.: Princeton Univ. Press, 1974.

Salzman, Catherine. "Consumer Cooperative Societies in Russia, Goals Vs. Gains, 1900–1918." *Cahiers du Monde Russe et Sovietique* 23 (July–Dec. 1982): 351–69.

Scheiber, Harry N. "World War I as Entrepreneurial Opportunity: Willard Straight and the American International Corporation." *Political Science Quarterly* 84 (Sept. 1969): 486–511.

Siegel, Katherine A. S. *Loans and Legitimacy: The Evolution of Soviet-American Relations, 1919–1933.* Lexington: Univ. Press of Kentucky, 1996.

Sklar, Martin J. *The Corporate Reconstruction of American Capitalism, 1896–1904: The Market, the Law, and Politics.* New York: Cambridge Univ. Press, 1988.

———. *The United States as a Developing Country: Studies in U.S. History in the Progressive Era and the 1920s.* New York: Cambridge Univ. Press, 1992.

Smith, C. F. *Vladivostok Under Red and White Rule.* Seattle: Univ. of Washington Press, 1975.

Smith, Charles. "Four Years of Mistakes in Siberia." *Asia* 22 (June 1922): 479–83.

Snow, R. E. *The Bolsheviks in Siberia, 1917–1918.* Princeton, N.J.: Princeton Univ. Press, 1977.

Sokolsky, George E. *The Story of the Chinese Eastern Railway.* Shanghai: 1929.

St. John, Jacqueline. "John F. Stevens: American Assistance to Russian and Siberian Railroads." Ph.D. diss., University of Oklahoma, 1969.

Stevens, John F. "Russia during the World War." *Engineers and Engineering* 44 (Jan. 1927): 17–23.

Tang, Peter S. H. *Russian and Soviet Policy in Manchuria and Outer Mongolia, 1911–1931.* Durham, N.C.: Duke Univ. Press, 1959.

Thompson, John M. *Russia, Bolshevism, and the Versailles Peace.* Princeton, N.J.: Princeton Univ. Press, 1966.

Treadgold, Donald W. *The Great Siberian Migration: Government and Peasant in Resettlement from Emancipation to the First World War.* Princeton, N.J.: Princeton Univ. Press, 1957.

———. "Russian Expansion in the Light of Turner's Study of the American Frontier." *Agricultural History* 26 (Oct. 1952): 147–52.

Turner, Frederick Jackson. "The Significance of the Frontier in American History." *American Historical Association, Annual Report* (Washington, D.C., 1893).

Tuve, Jeanette E. "Changing Directions in Russian-American Relations, 1912–1917." *Slavic Review* 31 (Mar. 1972): 52–72.

Ullman, Richard H. *Anglo-Soviet Relations, 1917–1921,* Vol. 1, *Intervention and the War.* Princeton, N.J.: Princeton Univ. Press, 1961.

———. *Anglo-Soviet Relations, 1917–1921,* Vol. 2, *Britain and the Russian Civil War, November 1918–February 1920.* Princeton, N.J.: Princeton Univ. Press, 1968.

Unterberger, Betty M. *America's Siberian Intervention, 1918–1920: A Study of National Policy*. Durham, N.C.: Duke Univ. Press, 1956.

————. "Woodrow Wilson and the Russian Revolution," in Arthur S. Link, ed., *Woodrow Wilson and a Revolutionary World, 1913–1921*. Chapel Hill: Univ. of North Carolina Press, 1982. 49–104.

————. *The United States, Revolutionary Russia, and the Rise of Czechoslovakia*. Chapel Hill: Univ. of North Carolina Press, 1989.

Wade, Rex A. *The Russian Search for Peace, February-October 1917*. Stanford, Calif.: Stanford Univ. Press, 1969.

Walker, Martin. "Russia and the West: What Is to Be Done Now?" *World Policy Journal* 11 (Spring 1994): 1–10.

Weissman, Benjamin. *Herbert Hoover and Famine Relief to Soviet Russia, 1921–1923*. Stanford, Calif.: Hoover Inst. Press, 1974.

Wheeler-Bennett, John W. *The Forgotten Peace: Brest-Litovsk, March 1918*. New York: Morrow, 1939.

White, Christine. *British and American Commercial Relations with Soviet Russia, 1918–1924*. Chapel Hill: Univ. of North Carolina Press, 1992.

White, John A. *The Siberian Intervention*. Princeton, N.J.: Princeton Univ. Press, 1950.

Williams, William A. *American-Russian Relations, 1781–1947*. New York: Octagon Books, 1971.

————. *The Tragedy of American Diplomacy*. New York: Dell, 1972.

Willoughby, Westel W. *China at the Conference: A Report*. Baltimore: Johns Hopkins Univ. Press, 1922.

Wilson, Woodrow. *The State: Elements of Historical and Practical Politics*. Boston: Heath, 1918

Woodward, David R. "The British Government and Japanese Intervention in Russia During World War I." *Journal of Modern History* 46 (Dec. 1974): 663–85.

Young, Carl W. *The International Relations of Manchuria*. Chicago: Univ. of Chicago Press, 1929.

Zeiler, Thomas. "Business Is Business." *Diplomatic History* 18 (Summer 1994): 419–23.

Zeman, Z. A. B., ed. *Germany and the Revolution in Russia, 1915–1918*. New York: Oxford Univ. Press, 1958.

Index

Anderson, William, 111–12
Archangel, 29, 113, 115, 135–36
Armistice, 105, 118, 123, 136, 153
Army surplus sales, 137–38, 143, 153
Ashton-Gwatkin, Frank, 170–71
Auchincloss, Gordon, 46, 89–92, 94–95
Aziatskaia Rossiia, 21–22

Baker, Henry D., 13
Baker, Newton D., 76, 121
Bakhmetev, Boris, 32, 45, 96–97, 108
Balance of power, 7
Balfour, Arthur, 86
Bankruptcy commission, for Chinese
    Eastern Railway, 168–70
Banks, 105; Allied, 113–14; as backing for
    inter-Allied economic commission, 109,
    111; Russian, 111–12; U.S., 13, 122–23,
    217n. 50
Barter, 93; and need for currency, 104–5;
    between rail lines, 190–91; regulation of,
    99–100; of U.S. manufactured goods,
    62–63, 90
Baruch, Bernard, 90–91
Bean crops, and rail rates, 186–90
Beckett, Brig. Gen. W. T. C., 186
Bell, Edward, 167
Benson, Adm. William, 76
Berkenheim, Alexander, 72
Berton, Samuel, 108
Bolshevik Revolution, 19, 38, 204n. 9
Bolsheviks, 34, 56–57, 70, 78; currency of,
    107, 123; and Czechs, 66, 73; Germany
    seen as alternative to, 64, 66–68, 83; and
    Kolchak government, 6, 145, 154–55;
    Kolchak government seen as alternative
    to, 140, 157; and peasant cooperative
    societies, 49–50; Russian opposition to,
    54, 68–69, 72, 81; U.S. opinion of, 4–5,
    38–39, 41, 209n. 15, 219n. 96; victory of, 6,
    196; *vs.* bolshevism, 162; Wilson's
    handling of, 57, 135–36
Bolshevism, 2, 205n. 34; *vs.* Bolsheviks, 162;
    Wilson's plan to undermine, 134–35
Bond issue, on Chinese Eastern Railway,
    176–78
Boynton, Charles H., 14–15
Brest-Litovsk Treaty (1918), 43, 56, 67, 107

Britain, 27, 174; and China, 170–71, 178–79;
    on control of Chinese Eastern Railway,
    166–70, 172, 183–84; and Czecho-Slovaks,
    73–74, 212n. 33; in economic rivalries, 1–2,
    103, 109, 113–18; on funding for Inter-
    Allied Railway Committee, 138–39,
    146–47; and Japan, 46, 129–30, 178–79,
    180–81; and military intervention in
    Siberia, 44–46, 66, 79, 215n. 31; mistrust
    of, 109, 116; and Railroad Commission,
    29, 35; and Siberia, 76–77, 86–88, 103, 119–
    20, 137, 195; supporting Kolchak
    government, 6, 130, 144; supporting
    reactionary forces, 144, 159–60. *See also*
    Allies; Imperialists/Great Powers
British and American Commercial Relations
    with Soviet Russia, 1918–1924 (White), 10
British Imperial Conference, 181
Brittenham, E. A., 125–27
Buchanan, George (British ambassador), 29
Bukowski, Lt. Peter I., 56–57, 210n. 51
Bullitt, William, 46–47, 78, 209n. 15
Bunting, M. H., 189, 192

Caldwell, John K., 92, 94, 102–3, 190
Capitalism, 200–201, 203n. 1; development
    of U.S., 11–13; and Dollar Diplomacy,
    196; state, 179–80
Carr, Wilbur J., 53, 54
Central Union of Consumers' Societies,
    22–23, 58–59,
Chadbourne, Thomas L., 70
Chaikovskii, Nikolai V., 136
Chang Tso-lin, Gen., 177, 182, 190
Chih-t'an, Chang, 178
China: agreements at Far East conference,
    181–82; and Britain, 170–71, 174, 181;
    and Chinese Eastern Railway, 165–67,
    172, 174–78, 183–84, 186, 189–91;
    communist victory in, 201; economy of,
    12–13, 118–19, 164; and funding for Inter-
    Allied Railway Committee, 143, 147; and
    Japan, 178, 181; resistance to Technical
    Board's power, 173, 180, 182, 184–86. *See*
    also Manchuria
China Banking Consortium, 163; and
    Chinese Eastern Railway, 7, 166–71,
    178–80

economic plans, 42–43, 48, 113; on Russia's railroads, 30, 32, 35–36, 40

Freight cars, 27, 31–32, 35, 149, 191

Geddes, Sir Auchland, 169, 173

Germany, 71–72, 83; ambitions in Russia, 41–45, 66–68, 84; and Bolsheviks, 41, 56, 70, 72; buying rubles, 43, 105–8, 110, 123; in currency issues, 124–25; domination of Ukraine, 51, 53; economic influence in Russia, 14, 44, 49–50, 61–62, 65–66, 78–79; economic warfare against, 48, 52–53, 55–56, 59–60, 66, 68; *Mitteleuropa* economic system of, 38; purchasing agents of, 43, 51, 56, 59, 65–66, 84; spring offensive of, 56, 71–72; U.S. declaration of war against, 16, 25–26; U.S. fear of influence of, 1–2, 41–42, 51–52, 63–64, 71, 82–83; and U.S. fears of Japanese intervention, 45–47, 61–62, 64, 69. *See also* Imperialists/Great Powers

Gibbs, George, 30, 34, 35

Global economy: Russia's importance to, 161, 176; U.S. in, 3, 200, 203n. 1

Good, James W., 133

Gotō, Foreign Minister, 80, 103, 121

Government. *See* State; specific countries

Grain, 37–38, 65–66, 118

Gramsci, Antonio, 205n. 34

Graves, Gen. William S., 120–21

Greene, Sir William C., 130–31

Greiner, John G., 30, 35

Grew, Joseph E., 74

Hanson, G. C., 192–93

Harding administration, 6, 180–81

Harriman, E. H., 6–7

Harris, Ernest, 141, 154

Heid, August, 93, 101; on economic conditions, 118–19, 122–23, 153–54; in Russian Bureau of War Trade Board, 98, 100

Hogan, Michael, 223n. 4

Hong Kong and Shanghai Banking Corporation, The, 87, 122, 179

Hoover, Herbert, 15, 83, 146

Horn, Henry, 37

House, Edward, 45–46, 94

Hsiao-lien, Sung, 178

Hughes, Charles Evans, 15, 174, 181, 185

Hughes, Evan, 180–81, 184–85

Huntington, William C., 23–24, 65, 107

Hurley, 90–91

Imperialists/Great Powers, 7; Japan as autocratic, 46; rivalry among, 12, 159–60, 164, 174, 203n. 1; rivalry over Russia, 1–3, 5, 29, 104–18; and Wilson's vision, 4, 200. *See also* Allies; specific countries

Industrial mission, to Russia, 71

Industry, developing Russia's, 14–15

Inter-Allied banking organization, 115, 152

Inter-Allied board, to oversee economic intervention, 87, 89

Inter-Allied Council on War Purchases and Finance, 114

Inter-Allied currency plans, 114–17, 125

Inter-Allied economic commission, 109, 146

Inter-Allied Purchasing Committee, 191

Inter-Allied purchasing company, 48. *See also* Tovaro-Obmien (purchasing company)

Inter-Allied Railway Agreement, 159, 206n. 17; end of, 164, 189

Inter-Allied Railway Committee, 128–29, 131–33, 184, 189; and Chinese Eastern Railway, 166–68, 185; and currencies in Chinese Eastern Railway zone, 165, 176; funding for, 137–38, 141–42, 146–47, 158; monetary plan of, 151–55. *See also* Technical Board

Inter-Allied trading company, for distribution of supplies, 115

International Banking Corporation (IBC), 111

International conservancy, for Chinese Eastern Railway, 183–84

International economy. *See* Global economy

International Harvester, 49–51, 54, 65, 126, 196, 211n. 9

International law, Wilson's vision for, 4

International Monetary Fund (IMF), 7; alternative to plans of, 197–99

International relations, Wilson's vision for, 4

International trusteeship, proposed for Chinese Eastern Railway, 166–68, 173

Liberal worldview, influence of, 96–97
Liberal-internationalist system, 4, 121
Lindley, Francis O., 113
Link, Arthur S., 10
Liu, C. S., 178
Liverovskii, A. V., 35–36, 207n. 40
Locke, John, Natural Law of, 17
Locomotives, 55; poor condition of Far Eastern republic's, 191, 193; replacement of Russian with American, 33–35; Russian need for, 27, 31–32
Lomonosov, George, 32, 49–50
Long, Breckinridge, 44; on military intervention in Siberia, 45, 47; on monetary crisis, 105, 107–8; in Siberian policy debate, 89–91

McAddo, William Gibbs, 27
McCormick, Cyrus, 50, 52–53, 62
McCormick, Vance C., 87, 125; on commercial assistance, 70, 90–91, 95, 101, 115, 120–21, 158–59; on recognition of Kolchak government, 145–46; and Russian Bureau, 133, 137, 144
MacDermid, Reuben R., 102–3
McFadden, David, 10
MacGowan, David B., 189
McKinstry, A. E., 50
MacMurray, John V. A., 173
Maier, Charles, 199, 223n. 4
Manchuria, 6, 164; British vs. Japanese interests in, 170–71, 174; Japanese control of, 146, 168, 177, 189
March, Gen. Peyton C., 76
March Revolution, 149; U.S. response to, 13–17, 25–26, 204n. 9
Market: China as, 12–13; Russia as, 14–15, 161, 163–64, 203n. 2
Market economy, helping to develop, 197–98
Marshall, Arthur G., 48
Marshall, Thomas R., 136
Marshall Plan, 7, 152, 199, 223n. 3; successes of, 197, 199
Masaryk, Thomas, 72
Matsuda Bank, 112
Mayer, Carl, 189
Metals/ores: Germany's desire for, 55, 57, 65; in trade, 48, 53

Mikhailov, I. A., 154, 156
Miles, Basil, 74, 160; and cooperative societies, 48–49, 51–54, 71, 87; on Germany, 42, 56, 71; on Japan, 47, 120; on Siberian policies, 71, 89–90, 140–41
Military: demanding priority use of railroads, 149–51, 156; Russian, 34, 37–38
Military assistance, 48; to anti-Communist governments, 201; for Kolchak government, 158; offered to Provisional Government, 25–27, 145
Military interference, on railroads, 140–41, 171–72
Military mission, U.S., 54
Military supplies, 48, 158; evacuated from Petrograd, 56–57; shipping, 99, 131
Military Transportation Board, 131–32, 149–51
Miliukov, Pavel, 26, 68, 84
Miller, Henry, 30, 35–36
Ministry of Communication. See Ministry of Ways of Communication
Ministry of Ways of Communication, Russian, 30, 32–34, 36–37, 150–51
Mirbach, Baron Wilhelm von, 42, 66–68
Mitteleuropa economic system, 38, 42
Monarchists, Russian, 66–67
Morality: of military intervention in Siberia, 46–47, 72–73, 75; and Wilsonianism, 16, 18; of Wilsonianism, 201
Morgan, J. P., 179–80
Morris, Roland, 81, 100, 101, 121–22; and Inter-Allied Railway Committee, 131–33, 206n. 17; on Japan and Trans-Siberian Railroad, 120, 129–30, 140–41; and Kolchak government, 130–31, 144–45, 147–48, 155–59, 217n. 50
Moscow Committee, 55
Moscow District Supply Committee, 49–50
Moscow–Donets Basin lines, 33
Moscow-Omsk line, 37–38
Moscow-Petrograd line, 33
Multinational corporations, and sovereignty, 198
Mumm, Baron Philip, 68
Municipalities, 54, 124–25, 157
Murmansk, 113

Washburn, Stanley, 26
Washington Conference: effects of, 188–89; on Far East policies, 180–86; U.S. trying to demonstrate goodwill at, 190, 191
Washington Naval Conference, 17, 181
Western front, 54, 56, 64; Czecho-Slovak Corps going to, 73, 212n. 33
White, Christine, 10, 203n. 2
White, John A., 10
Willard, Daniel, 26, 31, 35–36, 40; and Stevens, 37–39
Williams, E. T., 53
Williams, William A., 10
Wilson, Woodrow, 5, 125, 160, 205n. 19, 223n. 2; and Bolsheviks, 41, 49, 57; and British commercial proposals, 88–89; and Commerce Department, 93–94; and commercial assistance, 15, 19, 62–63, 90–92, 100–104; concept of self-government, 4, 18–19; on Czecho-Slovaks, 73–75, 119–20; and debt of Russian Embassy, 140, 142; declining political fortunes, 128–29; on economic assistance, 103, 109, 125; economic assistance plan of, 199; formation of Russian policies of, 76–78, 80; and Kolchak government, 6, 141, 144–46, 160; and military assistance, 25–27; and military intervention in Siberia, 44–47, 61–62, 64–66, 72, 76, 89; objectives of Russian policies of, 25–27, 83–84; paralysis of, 61; politics around Russian policies of, 133–36, 147, 158–59, 195–96; and Russian

governments, 2, 16–17, 81; Russian policies of, 49, 54; and Russian reconstruction, 7, 161–62; and status of Railroad Commission, 28–30
Wilsonianism: ethics of, 201; studies of, 9–10
Wiseman, William, 64
Woodrow Wilson and a Revolutionary World (Link), 10
Woodrow Wilson and World Politics (Levin), 10
Woolley, Clarence M., 70, 144
Workers, railroad: difficulty of paying, 133, 155; lack of middle management, 30–31; patronage, 175, 186; urged to increase productivity, 3; U.S. in Russia, 54, 69; U.S. training Russian, 31, 35–36, 38–40
World Bank, 7
World War I, 1, 13, 29, 33; Russian withdrawal from, 34, 41–42
World War II, 3, 7–8. *See also* Marshall Plan
Wright, J. Butler, 65, 68–71, 74

Yen, 164
Yen, W. W., 178–79, 183–85
YMCA, 69; efforts combined with economic mission, 112
Yun-p'eng, Gen. Chin, 178
Yurenev, Kadet P. P., 34

Zakupsbyt. *See* Union of Cooperative Unions
Zeiler, Thomas, 203n. 2
Zemstvos, 54, 157, 160–61, 210n. 37